INDOMITABLE

A Legacy of Love, Courage and Perseverance

Joseph Albert Lumsdaine

ISBN: 978-0-578-82340-9

The events and conversations in this book have been set down to the best of the author's ability. Every effort has been made to trace or contact all copyright holders. The author will be pleased to make good any omissions or rectify any mistakes brought to his attention at the earliest opportunity.

Managing editor: Silver Lumsdaine
Copy editor/designer: Mark Goldstein
Cover design: Dickie Chapin
Cover illustration: James Churchill

First edition

For my mother and father, Ho Miao Ying and Clifford Vere Lumsdaine,

and their legacy of courage, love, and commitment.

To Mark & Tracy,
May this story of
Mark's grandparents
enrich your lives.
Your uncle,
Albert

"Don't forget, your family is counting on you."

– Ho Miao Ying

Dear Family,

I hope you will find this book to be both interesting and informative about our family's history.

The copious endnotes contain citations to individual interviews, pictures and documents that will be made available digitally only to those family members who request them. I do not intend to make them public as they sometimes contain personal information which some may think inappropriate to make available to the public at large.

The book is now only available to family members. It is my intention to make it available for sale to the general public after allowing for a brief comment period. So, if there is anything about you in the book, and its endnotes, that you would rather not have the public see or know, please let me know in writing before March 8, 2021.

Please feel free to call me at (562) 397-0741, or write to me at joelumsdaine@gmail.com

Your Uncle,

Joe / Albert

February 5, 2021

Contents

Preface

The concept of this book had been on my mind and had been suggested by several family members since at least 2012, but the actual commencement of the process began in earnest with the systematic interviewing of my siblings in 2016.

I conducted the first interview over the telephone with my eldest sister, YaoTim, employing open-ended questions such as "What do you recall happening?" More detailed questions were asked to clarify dates, times, places, people, etc. My handwritten notes from each session were typed up and sent for review and edits. Upon return of each edited interview, I asked specifically whether it could be made available to others.

The same general methodology was employed with each of my siblings, whom I interviewed individually. Every living sibling was interviewed: YaoTim, Ed, George, Philip, Milly, and Dolly. My wife, Dianne (Niethamer) Lumsdaine, interviewed me. Interviews were usually conducted by phone, but sometimes they were in person.

For my deceased brothers, Chuck and Robert, I used a different methodology. For Chuck, I relied on a recorded interview done by Ed's daughter, Anne (Lumsdaine) Ross, that Dolly transcribed. I also interviewed Chuck's son, Cory Lumsdaine; Robert's wife, Joyce (Pang) Lumsdaine; George's wife, Elaine (Tsui) Lumsdaine; Milly's husband, Marcel Ratermann; Philip's wife, Linda (Dees) Lumsdaine; and Dianne.

Edited and returned interviews are noted in the endnotes as Appendix V. These interviews tell a story about my parents, but they also provide stories about the storyteller. As such, these interviews can be used as a resource for the next generation to learn more about their own parents.

I also used original public and family documents (Appendix I), previous family compilations such as YaoTim's 1995 *The Grandparent Book* (Appendix II), emails and other communications (Appendix III), Geoffrey Lumsdaine's 1997 *Transition to the Colony: An Australian Family* (Appendix IV), and family photos (Appendix VI). These appendices may be made available with the digital copy of the book to family members with permission from me, or my heirs, successors, or assigns.

I have endeavored to get every person's story as it related to Clifford and Miao Ying Lumsdaine because I believe that everyone's story matters. To the extent I found variances because of individuals' perceptions or recollections, I narrated that which I believed most likely. Ultimately, I do not claim to be free from "writer's bias." As has been said with biblical scripture itself, not everything herein is historically accurate, but hopefully all of it is ultimately truthful in telling the story of my incredible parents, Clifford and Miao Ying Lumsdaine.

Joseph Albert Lumsdaine
December 2020
Downey, Calif.

Acknowledgments

This book was inspired by my sister YaoTim, who started compiling the Lumsdaine family history as *The Grandparent Book* while our Dad was still alive. My spouse, Dianne, provided the unfailing encouragement and support I needed to persist with this project these past four years as well as the recollection of past events when my own memory faltered.

I am grateful to my sister Milly, whose kind encouragement helped me through the occasional dispiritedness brought on by obstacles. This project would not have been possible without the active cooperation and collaboration of my other siblings – Ed, George, Philip, and Dolly – as well as Joyce (Pang) Lumsdaine, the spouse of my deceased brother Robert; my niece Anne (Lumsdaine) Ross, who interviewed my brother Chuck in 2000 before he passed in 2004; my nephew Cory Lumsdaine, who provided stories his dad, Chuck, told him; and my other siblings' spouses, particularly those who provided separate interviews, such as Elaine (Tsui) Lumsdaine, Marcel Ratermann, and Linda (Dees) Lumsdaine.

I thank my children, Jodi, Jenny, Paul, and Casey, who provided valuable input. I am especially grateful to Paul for designing the book's family trees and the interactive timeline of world events and family history.

I am indebted to my writer-editor niece Silver Lumsdaine, who provided the editorial expertise needed by a career lawyer like me, whose previous writings were trial and appellate briefs, contracts, and estate plans. Her compassionate coaching in rewriting my parents' story was indispensable.

Of course, none of this would have come into being without the invisible spirits of my Mom and Dad, who accompanied me throughout the research and writing of this book.

To everyone named above, and to anyone I've inadvertently forgotten, a heartfelt *Thank You.*

CLIFFORD VERE LUMSDAINE
FAMILY TREE

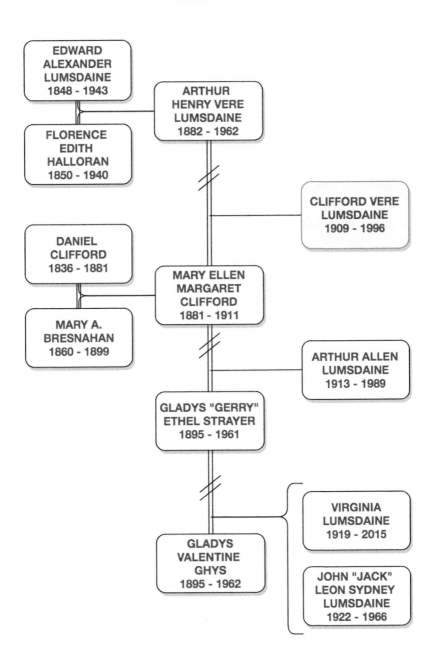

EDWARD ALEXANDER LUMSDAINE
1848 - 1943

FLORENCE EDITH HALLORAN
1850 - 1940

ARTHUR HENRY VERE LUMSDAINE
1882 - 1962

CLIFFORD VERE LUMSDAINE
1909 - 1996

DANIEL CLIFFORD
1836 - 1881

MARY A. BRESNAHAN
1860 - 1899

MARY ELLEN MARGARET CLIFFORD
1881 - 1911

ARTHUR ALLEN LUMSDAINE
1913 - 1989

GLADYS "GERRY" ETHEL STRAYER
1895 - 1961

VIRGINIA LUMSDAINE
1919 - 2015

GLADYS VALENTINE GHYS
1895 - 1962

JOHN "JACK" LEON SYDNEY LUMSDAINE
1922 - 1966

HO MIAO YING
FAMILY TREE

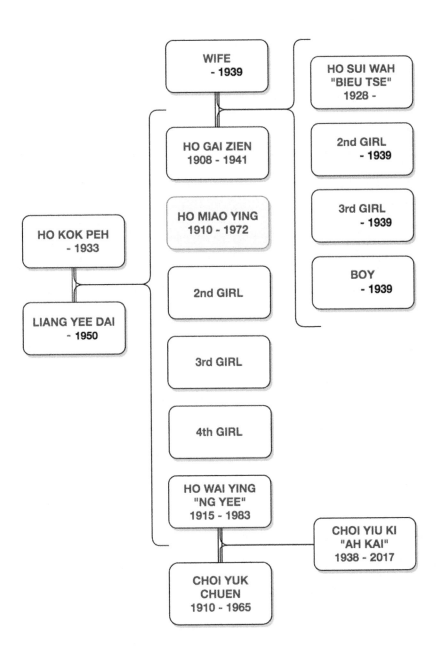

HO MIAO YING + CLIFFORD VERE LUMSDAINE
FAMILY TREE

CLIFFORD VERE LUMSDAINE
1909 - 1996

HO MIAO YING
1910 - 1972

CHARLES "CHARLIE" "CHUCK" JAMES LUMSDAINE
1933 - 2004

ANNE LUMSDAINE
1935 - 1936

YAOTIM "MARIA" LUMSDAINE
1936 -

EDWARD LUMSDAINE
1937 -

MAY LUMSDAINE
1938 - 1939

GEORGE LUMSDAINE
1940 -

ROBERT ALLEN LUMSDAINE
1942 - 2008

PHILIP LUMSDAINE
1943 -

MILDRED "MILLY" MARGARET LUMSDAINE
1946 -

DOLLY LUMSDAINE
1948 -

JOSEPH ALBERT LUMSDAINE
1950 -

INDOMITABLE

1

SEATTLE AND SHUNDE: WORLDS APART

THE SEATTLE START

Clifford Vere Lumsdaine was born at Seattle General Hospital in Seattle, Washington, in November 1909. His father, Arthur Henry Vere Lumsdaine, was 27 years old,[1] and his mother, Mary Ellen Margaret (Clifford) Lumsdaine, was 28.[2] Clifford, who was given his mother's family name, was their first and only child together. Weighing only 4 pounds at birth,

Clifford, age 1

Clifford spent 10 days in the hospital before coming home with his parents to Densmore Avenue in Seattle.[3]

The three of them lived in Seattle until Clifford was about 6 months old. In May 1910, Mary Ellen took Clifford with her to visit some of her relatives in Farmington, Iowa, where she was born. They then visited other relatives in Des Moines, Iowa, and Beatrice, Nebraska.[4] Clifford was baptized Catholic and given the baptismal name of Joseph while in Iowa.[5] Mary Ellen and Clifford returned to Seattle in September 1910, and the family lived happily together as Clifford celebrated his first Christmas, as well as his first and second birthdays, with his loving parents by his side.

Tragedy struck just a month after Clifford's second birthday. He suffered, in the words of his father, "the greatest loss and most terrible calamity of

1

baby's life" – the death of his beloved mother.[6] On December 6, 1911, Mary Ellen fell into a diabetic coma, from which she never recovered. She died just

four days later.[7] Years later, Clifford recalled that his mother had "died before I really got to know her."[8]

Fourteen months after Mary Ellen's death, Arthur Henry married Gladys "Gerry" Strayer, a schoolteacher, in February 1913, in Seattle.[9] Clifford was 3 years old. Gerry was much more than just a stepmother to Clifford; from his earliest recollections, she was the only person that he knew and loved as his mother. Clifford would miss her love and kindness greatly whenever they were separated.[10]

In November 1913, Gerry gave birth to Clifford's biological half-brother, Arthur Allen Lums-

Arthur Henry, Clifford, and Mary Ellen Lumsdaine, Dec. 5, 1911

daine.[11] Shortly afterward, in 1914, Arthur Henry received a job opportunity and moved his young family to Juneau, Alaska. Clifford and Arthur Allen spent the next four years growing up in Juneau before the family moved back to Seattle in 1918.[12] The brothers would become lifelong friends, despite spending many years apart in the coming years.

Arthur Henry did not stay long in Seattle. Whether because of marital difficulties or merely because he wanted to introduce 8-year-old Clifford to his many relatives in Australia, [13] he and Clifford sailed to Australia on the RMS Niagara in October 1918.[14]

Their trip unfortunately coincided with the global 1918 flu pandemic – commonly known as the Spanish Flu in the U.S. – which infected approximately one-third of the world's population and killed an estimated 50 million people before it ended in 1920.[15] As a result, Arthur Henry and Clifford spent almost 10 months at sea, under quarantine and going from port to port – Hawaii, New Zealand, Fiji, then New Zealand again – before being allowed to dock in Sydney, Australia in August 1919.[16] During this lengthy time at sea, Arthur Henry became involved with a young woman, Gladys Valentine Ghys.[17] Together, they conceived Clifford's half-sister, Virginia Lumsdaine.[18]

From Sydney, Arthur Henry quickly returned to Seattle with the then-pregnant Gladys, leaving young Clifford with his grandparents in a Sydney suburb.[19] Incredibly, back in Seattle, Arthur Henry convinced his wife, Gerry, to care for Gladys and her newborn daughter.[20]

In 1920, Arthur Henry returned to Australia with Gladys and Virginia. As "a kind of a pacifier" to Gerry, Arthur Henry later sent for her and Arthur Allen to join him, Gladys, Clifford, and Virginia in Australia.[21] Gerry and Arthur Allen reunited with Clifford, and the three of them lived happily

Clifford, left, and his half-brother, Arthur Allen Lumsdaine, in Juneau, Alaska, c. 1916

Clifford swimming with his Aunt Kate "Allie" Lumsdaine in Sydney, Australia

The RMS Niagara in 1918

together in Manly, a suburb across the harbor from Sydney. Meanwhile, Arthur Henry presumably lived elsewhere with Gladys and baby Virginia. This brief reunion ended when Arthur Henry sent Gerry and Arthur Allen back to Seattle, causing young Clifford tremendous grief from the separation. Years later, Clifford recalled that he "cried like the dickens" when Gerry and Arthur Allen left Australia.[22]

Clifford spent seven formative years, from August 1919 until June 1926, in the suburbs outside Sydney.[23] For much of that time, he lived with his elderly paternal grandparents, Edward Alexander Lumsdaine, a retired Crown Solicitor, and Florence Edith (Halloran) Lumsdaine.[24] Clifford was very fond of his grandparents, whom he also greatly admired. They were well-educated, deeply religious people, and they made sure that Clifford enrolled in school, prayed daily, and regularly attended Sunday school. Clifford excelled in school and advanced extra grades because of his academic standing.[25] His grandfather eventually helped 15-year-old Clifford obtain a job as a junior clerk at a Sydney law office.[26]

4

Clifford's health improved greatly during his time in Australia. He was admittedly "rickety" when he arrived there at age 9, but was "quite healthy" by age 16 when he returned to the U.S. Clifford recalled his years in Australia with his grandparents, aunts, uncles, and cousins, as "pretty happy."[27] He was especially fond of his Aunt Allie, as well as his three uncles and numerous cousins, who lived in and around Sydney.

It is unclear where Arthur Henry was during Clifford's time in Australia. He may have traveled overseas on business, as he had done most of his life, or he may have remained in Australia with Gladys and Virginia. Regardless, he apparently was not a major part of Clifford's life during those years and left Australia for Shanghai, China, with Gladys and Virginia – but without Clifford – sometime before 1923. While in Shanghai, Arthur Henry and Gladys had another child, Jack Lumsdaine, in January 1923.[28]

In June 1926, Arthur Henry sent a telegram to Clifford asking if he wanted to join them in Shanghai or return to be with Gerry in Seattle. Clifford chose to return to the U.S. to be reunited with his beloved stepmother and half-brother. Gerry and Arthur Allen drove up from Seattle to Vancouver, British Columbia, where Clifford's ship, the RMS Niagara, docked, to pick him up and bring him home.[29] Clifford went to school and joined the Boy Scouts with Arthur

Clifford (standing) and brother Arthur Allen (in car) c. 1926, Seattle, Washington

Clifford Vere Lumsdaine in the late 1920s

Allen, but unfortunately, this happy reunion wouldn't last.

In early 1927, Arthur Henry, Gladys, and their children, Virginia and Jack, moved from Shanghai to San Francisco. The year before, Arthur Henry had divorced Gerry and married Gladys. Arthur Henry then traveled to New York but sent Gladys to Seattle to fetch Clifford and bring him to San Francisco to live with them.[30]

While he was in San Francisco, Clifford finished high school and worked part-time as a pharmaceutical stockroom clerk. Later in 1927, after he turned 18, Clifford signed on to work as a crew messman on a ship called the *SS Oregonian*, which was bound for New York through the newly completed Panama Canal.[31] When the ship reached New York after a month of travel, Clifford found that Arthur Henry had already left without a word as to his destination. Disappointed, Clifford stayed on the ship for its return trip to San Francisco, where he again hoped to catch up with his father and his family.[32]

When the ship docked in San Francisco in January 1928, Clifford was admitted to the Public Health Service Hospital in the Presidio, where he was treated for tonsillitis and other ailments for several months. By the time he was released, his father, Gladys, Virginia, and Jack had left San Francisco for Shanghai.[33] For the next year and a half, Clifford worked at the Embarcadero, San Francisco's eastern waterfront, as a messenger and clerk for the ferry boat division of the Southern Pacific Railroad.[34] He also joined the California National Guard, where he was combat-trained in the artillery division, and attended evening classes to learn Spanish and shorthand.

The Shanghai Maru, *c. 1929*

In November 1929, Clifford once again received a telegram from his father asking if Clifford wanted to join him in Shanghai, at his import-export business. Now 20 years old, Clifford said yes. He resigned from his longest-held job up to that point in his life and boarded the Shanghai Maru, bound for China. There, a chance meeting would radically change the course of his life.[35]

THE SHUNDE START

In 1910, China was convulsing with constant conflicts and rapid changes to ancient traditions. The country had been closed to outsiders for more than three millennia, but in the 20th century, it acquiesced to a rapidly growing influx of Westerners bringing new ideas, industries, businesses, and clothing. Thousands of years of imperial rule gave way to Western encroachment as well as territorial wars among local warlords, nationalists, communists, and Japanese armed forces.

It was into this transforming society that Ho Miao Ying[36] was born in July 1910,

Ho Miao Ying at about age 16

7

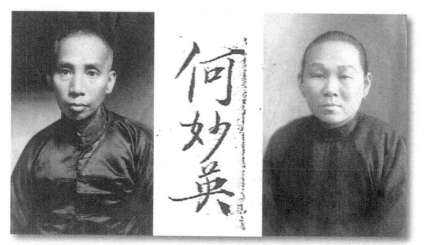

*Miao Ying's father, Ho Kok Peh, left; and mother, Liang Yee Dai "Pau Pau,"
right. In the center, "Ho Miao Ying" in Chinese, in Miao Ying's handwriting*

in a small, rural village in the Shunde District of Foshan City, China. The
specific village is unknown, but the Shunde District is on the fertile Pearl River
delta, about 30 miles south of Guangzhou (formerly known as Canton).[37]

Although there is no written record of Miao Ying's birth, the date was
determined by converting her birth date on the Chinese calendar to the date on
the Western calendar.[38] Traditionally for the Chinese, the last name or surname
is patrilineal and listed first, so her maiden name is written in Chinese as Ho
Miao Ying, with the first character on top being the surname of her father,
Ho Kok Peh.[39]

Little is known about Miao Ying's father except that according to his
daughter, he was a talented artist and poet. He sometimes was paid commis-
sions by influential people, but he only worked when he felt like it or when
he needed money.[40] The date and location of his birth, his parents' names,
and his level of education are not known. It is known, however, that Ho
Kok Peh died of a heart attack in 1933,[41] likely when he was in his mid-50s.[42]

Miao Ying's mother, Liang Yee Dai – affectionately referred to in the
family as "Pau Pau" – Cantonese for "Grandma" – survived her husband
by about 17 years. She was around 72 years old when she died in 1950.[43]
Although there is no record of where and when she was born, it is likely that
both she and Ho Kok Peh came from the Shunde District, where Miao Ying

was born. The maternal and paternal sides of the family probably go back many generations from the same general area around Shunde.[44]

Miao Ying was the oldest daughter. She had an older brother named Ho Gai Zien, and a younger sister, Ho Wai Ying, who was called Ng Yee, which means "fifth aunt" in Cantonese. Given her nickname, it seems likely that Ho Kok Peh and Liang Yee Dai had three other daughters, who died in childbirth or shortly thereafter, between Miao Ying and Ng Yee;[45] infant mortality was common in China at that time.[46]

Due to the lack official documents from the early 1900s in China, and because neither Pau Pau nor Miao Ying spoke much about it, there is little information about Miao Ying's early childhood or education, except that she completed the equivalent of second grade. Chinese girls – and especially girls coming from small towns or villages and not born of nobility – generally were not given any formal education at that time. Education was actually considered to be morally corrupting to young girls, rendering them unsuitable for marriage.[47]

When she was 11 or 12 years old, Miao Ying started working in a silk-worm factory. (As an adult, she would remark that she could tolerate putting her hands in extremely hot water due to her years spent in the factory remov-

Shunde District, China, and the Pearl River delta area

9

ing the silk from the silkworm cocoons.)[48] Miao Ying worked in the factory until about age 17, when her family moved from the Shunde District countryside to the bustling mega-city of Shanghai around 1927.[49]

Shunde to Shanghai is almost 1,000 miles, a considerable distance to travel in the early 1900s in China. Miao Ying's father, an artist and poet, would have had more opportunities to make money in a prosperous metropolis like Shanghai than in a rural area like the Shunde District. As in many other parts of the world, artists and poets in China mostly made their living by finding wealthy or influential families to commission their art or poetry.[50] Ho Kok Peh's half-brother lived in Shanghai and was reputed to be very wealthy, which meant that there would be ready referrals for patrons from among his wealthy friends and colleagues.[51]

Not much is known about what Miao Ying did or how she was employed during her first few years after arriving in Shanghai in 1927. But she certainly could not have known that a chance meeting there would alter the course of her life in unimaginable ways.[52]

2

AN UNLIKELY MATCH

"The Bund" in 1930s Shanghai, with commercial buildings including the famous Cathay Hotel to the left and the busy port on the Huangpu River to the right

CITY OF OPPORTUNITIES

In the 1930s, Shanghai was undergoing rapid, unique, and dramatic changes that were unparalleled in world history up to that time. Against a backdrop of worldwide economic depression and surging nationalism, Shanghai was an iconoclastic symbol of economic prosperity, cultural diversity, and internationalism.[53]

The economic and population boom in Shanghai in the early 1900s grew the city from a simple port town into an industrial and financial power-

11

house by the 1930s. Although a significant portion of Shanghai's population growth came from foreigners seeking economic opportunity, much of the growth came from the migration of rural Chinese seeking work.[54] Within this context, it makes sense that Miao Ying migrated with her family from rural China to Shanghai. It also makes sense that Clifford would follow his entrepreneurial father, just two months after the October 29, 1929, U.S. stock market crash, to work at his father's import-export business in Shanghai's booming International Settlement.

The central commercial area of Shanghai that formed part of the International Settlement

The International Settlement was a nine-square-mile area that technically was under Chinese sovereignty but politically and practically was controlled by foreign powers, including Great Britain, France, and the United States, after China lost the First Opium War in 1842. The ensuing treaty forced China to, among other concessions, surrender control of the commercial and residential areas adjacent to the Huangpu River in Shanghai. The International Settlement prospered with the European and American population influx, financial investment, and political control but not without resentment from the Chinese in Shanghai and elsewhere.[55]

In the 1930s, most Chinese tolerated Westerners in their country as a necessary evil. All non-Chinese, or foreigners, were considered Westerners because the Chinese viewed their countries as west of China, with nothing to the east but the ocean. Westerners were particularly disliked in the

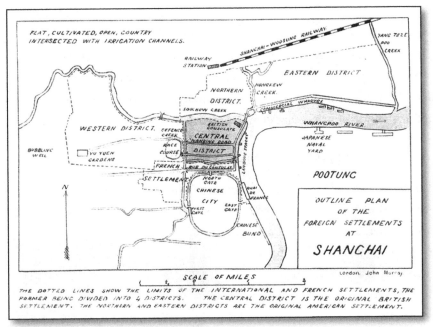

The International Settlement occupied a large part of Shanghai, with different areas controlled by foreign governments including the U.S., U.K., and France.

foreign-occupied International Settlement. Despite losses in two Opium Wars, China generally still thought of itself as superior in culture and civility, if not in military or economic might. It generally viewed Westerners as arrogant, uncouth, and even barbaric. Europeans and Americans were called *gweilo* or *fan gwei*, derogatory terms that translate popularly from Cantonese to "ghost man" and "foreign devil," respectively. [56]

Most Chinese, especially those living in or near the International Settlement, resented the foreigners. They felt disrespected by the Westerners who took over part of their city for their own use. Emblematic of this resentment was the urban legend about the "Public Garden" in the International Settlement. It was supposed to be the first park in China that was open to the public in 1886. But for almost 40 years, from 1890 until 1928, neither the Chinese people nor their dogs could enter. This gave rise to the popular myth – one held by Miao Ying – that the sign on the Public Garden gate read "No dogs or Chinese allowed," [57] thereby showing that these *gweilo* equated the Chinese people with dogs.

Just as most Chinese thought Westerners inferior, Westerners in China – especially those in the International Settlement – likewise viewed the Chinese primarily as an inferior race, one to be used or exploited as necessary. Books and articles of the period that were widely read by Westerners described the Chinese people in patronizing and condescending terms, noting their deviousness, lack of intelligence, corruption, and immorality.[58]

CLIFFORD: A WORLD TRAVELER AT 20

Clifford arrived in Shanghai just before Christmas 1929. He was barely 20 years old but already had traveled extensively, lived in numerous different environments, and worked at a variety of jobs. His breadth of life experience and associated maturity made him well-suited for assisting his father with his business.

Clifford c. 1930

Arthur Henry renamed the business "Lumsdaine Oriental Co." from "AHV Lumsdaine" to reflect the company's new status as a joint venture between him and his son. He also gave Clifford the power of attorney to act on his behalf as Arthur Henry continued to travel significantly overseas.[59]

Clifford would live and work in the International Settlement for the next 22 years. He stayed in Arthur Henry's home with his father's second family – Gladys, 11-year-old Virginia, and 7-year-old Jack – until 1931, when Arthur Henry, at Gladys' request, suggested that Clifford move out to be with young men his own age. Apparently, there was tension in the house because Gladys did not appreciate her adult stepson residing there.[60] Clifford, then 21, moved first to the YMCA and then to a less expensive place within the International Settlement.[61] Arthur Henry kept in touch with Clifford by occasionally meeting him for a round of golf at the course across the street from the YMCA.[62]

In 1930, Clifford joined the American Company Shanghai Volunteer Corps, an unpaid, volunteer military formed to protect the International Settlement, originally from imperial forces and later from "warlords" and others who might challenge the Westerners' self-rule of the settlement.[63] The Shanghai Volunteer Corps mobilized in January 1932 to stabilize the

Miao Ying c. 1930

settlement and assist refugees during the "First Shanghai Incident," a period of civil unrest and armed conflict between Japanese forces and anti-Japanese demonstrators in the International Settlement.[64] Clifford was not involved in the conflict because he became ill with pneumonia and moved back into his father's family home to recover while Arthur Henry was traveling in Canada and England.[65]

Shortly after recovering, in August 1932, Clifford was introduced to a pretty Chinese woman by the name of Ho Miao Ying.[66]

MIAO YING: A WOMAN AHEAD OF HER TIME

A picture of Miao Ying from 1930 shows a modern Shanghai woman of that era, in hairstyle, makeup, and dress. Where she worked and lived in August 1932 is unknown. She could have lived in the International Settlement, as many Chinese did then,[67] or in the adjacent Chinese sections of Shanghai. It is likely that she still lived with her parents, as was traditional for an unmarried woman. However, Miao Ying appears to have been quite unconventional and rebellious for a Chinese woman of that time.

Traditionally, Chinese women followed three centuries-old Confucian principles: A woman obeys her father until married, obeys her husband until his death, and obeys her son after that.[68] During the early 1930s, Miao Ying rebelled against tradition by wearing white tennis shoes, going to movies, and riding on the back of her boyfriend's motorcycle – all of which were forbidden by her father.[69] Wearing the color white, whether clothing or tennis shoes, was not only contrary to her father's expressed wishes but also considered taboo except for funerals because white represents death.[70] As for hugging a man's back while riding a motorcycle, tradition forbade women from showing any interest in a man, even one intended for marriage. Chinese women were to be passive, demure, and not speak unless spoken to. A Chinese woman showing interest in a man or selecting a companion was totally anathema to traditional Chinese mores and culture.[71]

Miao Ying's boyfriend, who owned a motorcycle shop, was quite serious about their relationship. The two of them had plans for marriage. However, the man's mother disapproved on the grounds that Miao Ying was "too skinny and would not bear sons."[72] (Miao Ying would repeat this story many times in subsequent years, followed by the observation that she had clearly proven the man's mother wrong.)

THE FIRST DATE

The Cathay Hotel (now the Fairmont Peace Hotel) was located in The Bund, a historic waterfront area in Shanghai. The hotel was famous for the Old Jazz Bar adjacent to its main foyer. Clifford and Miao Ying first met there in August 1932 but not on a date with each other. They were there because of a mutual friend by the name of Harry Ho.

Clifford knew Harry because Harry had spent time in the U.S., spoke English and Cantonese, and worked at a department store.[73] Harry brought a blind date for Clifford, but he also brought Miao Ying, a good friend of his.

When Clifford saw Miao Ying in the foyer, he lost all interest in the young lady who was to be his blind date. Clifford told Harry that he was interested in being Miao Ying's date. He was instantly attracted to her because, as he later remarked, "She was very pretty."[74] The attraction was mutual, as Miao Ying agreed to be Clifford's date for the evening.

From then forward, Clifford requested that Harry set up further dates with Miao Ying. Harry was their chaperone and translator since Clifford was not fluent in Cantonese, despite having taken formal lessons some time earlier,[75] and Miao Ying did not know any English. Clifford would have Harry ask Miao Ying where she wanted to go for dinner, but the translation always turned out to be a place that Harry preferred. Very quickly, Miao Ying figured out what was happening and decided that she and Clifford needed to be able to talk without Harry as their translator.[76]

CATHAY HOTEL
THE BUND
SHANGHAI

"THE CATHAY"—the most modern Hotel in China

Cable:—"CATHOTEL, SHANGHAI"

The Cathay Hotel, where Clifford and Miao Ying met, opened in 1929 as "the most beautiful hotel in the Far East."

After a few dates, Miao Ying told Clifford he had to learn to speak Cantonese better if they were to continue dating without Harry as a translator. She saw no need to learn English while living in China[77] and expressed that it would be more advantageous for him to speak Chinese better as he obviously intended to stay in Shanghai.[78] Resolved, Clifford learned to read and write some Chinese as well as speak fluent Cantonese, and the couple soon enjoyed dates *sans* chaperone.

Miao Ying's assertiveness in dispatching their chaperone and telling Clifford he needed to master Chinese were emblematic of her character. Once, when she and Clifford encountered her motorcycle-riding Chinese ex-boyfriend, the man threatened Clifford with a gun. Miao Ying stepped in between them and sent the ex-boyfriend on his way.[79]

Unbeknownst to both of them, Clifford's tenacity in mastering a language as difficult as Chinese and Miao Ying's courage in the face of danger would serve them well in the turbulent years to come.

*The Old Jazz Band still performs at the Fairmont
Peace Hotel (formerly the Cathay Hotel) in Shanghai,
just as it has since the 1930s.*

ONE MARRIAGE, TWO WEDDINGS

After that first date at the Old Jazz Bar, Miao Ying and Clifford's court-
ship progressed quickly. In April 1933, eight months after they met, they
defied tradition, customs, taboos, and their own families and got married.[80]
Miao Ying and Clifford entered into a civil "wedding contract" witnessed
by a government official, and that was followed by a Buddhist ceremony at
which a monk celebrated their marriage.[81]

Both Clifford's and Miao Ying's fathers objected to the marriage. Arthur
Henry so disapproved of his son marrying a Chinese woman that he stopped
talking to Clifford upon learning of his intention to marry Miao Ying.[82] Ho
Kok Peh and Liang Yee Dai were so incensed by the intended union of their
daughter to a *gweilo* that they disowned her completely.[83] Their reactions
were not surprising given the widespread and deeply negative views that
Chinese and Westerners had of each other in 1930s China – even in metro-
politan Shanghai[84] – and especially of mixed marriages between them.

Other family members, friends, and their respective communities also
undoubtedly disapproved of Clifford and Miao Ying's marriage. Such a
marriage was commonly referred to as miscegenation – a term for interracial
marriage or intimate relations.[85] Interracial marriage was socially taboo in

18

the United States and China at the time.[86] Many sociologists considered it "unnatural" and believed it caused "congenital degeneracy."[87] It was also illegal under anti-miscegenation laws in many parts of the world, including much of the U.S.[88] Those who crossed this deep-seated racial and cultural divide often were shunned by their communities, denied promotions, or terminated from employment; they even risked losing their citizenship.[89] The bias against mixed marriages was so prevalent that they were extremely rare, even in Shanghai.[90]

Years later, as World War II loomed, and Japan occupied much of China, including Shanghai, Clifford and Miao Ying would learn that the U.S. government did not recognize their Chinese wedding contract or their Buddhist wedding ceremony. As a result, the U.S. would not grant citizenship to the couple's four children. As U.S. citizens, the children would have more rights in Shanghai's International Settlement, which was not yet subject to the Japanese occupied forces.[91] However, for the children to gain

The American Consular Service declared Clifford and Miao Ying "officially" married on September 27, 1940, although they had already been married for seven years.

*"Official wedding" photo of Ho Miao Ying and Clifford Vere Lumsdaine,
Shanghai, China, Sept. 27, 1940*

citizenship, Miao Ying and Clifford would have to be married again, this time at the U.S. Consulate in Shanghai with an approved Christian minister and a certificate issued by the Consul of the United States.[92]

Thus, for the sake of her children, on September 27, 1940, Miao Ying endured the embarrassment and humiliation of a second wedding – just 47 days after giving birth to her son George. At the consulate, she donned a Western-style wedding gown, stood for a ceremony performed by a Baptist minister, Rev. Charles Boyton, and sat for her official wedding picture. She and Clifford dressed up just for this event; there was no reception and no celebration afterward. Miao Ying tolerated this perfunctory duty in exchange for an official Certificate of Marriage from the U.S. Consular Service, which made her children U.S. citizens, but she always considered her official U.S. wedding as nothing more than a "fake marriage" ceremony, her real one having taken place seven years and four children earlier.[93]

Miao Ying with 6-month-old Charlie (Chuck), 1934

3

A YOUNG BIRACIAL FAMILY BEGINS

THE SHANGHAI START

Charles James Lumsdaine was born to Clifford and Miao Ying in November 1933, at Shanghai General Hospital. ("Charlie" was the name originally on his birth certificate; he would take the nickname "Chuck" when he moved to the US.[94])

Miao Ying was 23, and Clifford would celebrate his 24th birthday three days later. Miao Ying's hospital experience was so aversive that she gave birth to all of her subsequent children at home, usually with assistance of a midwife. The joy of Charlie's birth was tempered by the recent death of her father, Ho Kok Peh, from a heart attack.[95] After Miao Ying's father died, her mother, Pau Pau, came to live with them.

In the 21st century United States, having a biracial, Chinese-American baby is neither unusual nor noteworthy.[96] However, in early 1930s China, a biracial baby was a rarity. Such children were seen as part of a "half-caste" and were stigmatized as symbols of "moral degradation" and "racial impurity" in both Western and Chinese communities.[97] Racial intermixing was considered by many to be "hybrid degeneracy" that would lead to children born with physical deformities and a propensity toward violence and crime.[98]

The societal challenges for the parents of a biracial child would have been significant. Clifford and Miao Ying had been ostracized by their parents, and likely by their extended families, even before having Charlie.[99] They presumably received little family support for either the pregnancy or the birth of their child, let alone any family celebrations.

Their problems were not only societal but also financial. Lumsdaine Oriental Co., the primary business that Clifford owned with his father, closed permanently in June 1933, just five months before Charlie's birth.[100] By the time Charlie was born, Clifford's father, Arthur Henry, had fled China to escape the Lumsdaine Oriental Co.'s creditors, leaving his wife, Gladys, and their children Virginia and Jack, who were about 14 and 10, respectively, to fend for themselves. He allegedly gave Gladys the choice of fleeing China with him, but she refused. After Arthur Henry left, Clifford stopped by their home to check in on them, but his appearance was not welcome. Gladys met him at the door and told him never to visit them again. Consequently, the two families lost touch and Clifford never again met with Gladys, Virginia, or Jack.[101]

As Arthur Henry's business partner, Clifford was left to deal with the mess of business debts and angry creditors that Arthur Henry had abandoned. Some creditors threatened Clifford with imprisonment; others threatened his life. At first, Clifford, then 24, made several short trips to the countryside with his family to avoid debtors' prison. After the threats on his life, he fled Shanghai with his young family and Miao Ying's mother, Pau Pau, for the island of Hong Kong in 1935. The British ruled Hong Kong and Kowloon, the nearby peninsula, so Clifford's creditors wouldn't pursue him there.

THE HONG KONG YEARS, PART 1

Clifford and Miao Ying's next four children were born at home. The growing family lived in an apartment on Tai Po Road, near the Sham Shui Po District in Kowloon, Hong Kong,[102] from 1935 to 1939.[103] Clifford obtained a good job as a secretary for Paramount Studios, the U.S. film company, which had offices and a studio in Hong Kong.[104]

In May 1935, Anne became the first of Clifford and Miao Ying's children to be born in Hong Kong,[105] but heartbreak soon followed. Two months after her first birthday, Anne died, possibly due to disease contracted from

Charlie, YaoTim, Miao Ying, and Edward, early 1938

the wet nurse employed by Miao Ying after she became pregnant with her third child.[106]

Three days after Anne's death in July 1936, Clifford and Miao Ying welcomed their second daughter. Pau Pau, the baby's maternal grandmother, named her YaoTim – the Cantonese word for "sweetness" – to soften the bitterness and pain of Anne's death.[107]

Less than 15 months after YaoTim's birth, Miao Ying gave birth to Edward Lumsdaine in September 1937.[108] Now 27, Miao Ying had three infants and toddlers to care for, so she enlisted the help of two older women living in the apartment building. The two women cared for and developed an especially close bond with YaoTim and became more like family than hired help. In later years, YaoTim recalled that one of her earliest memories was the painful parting from these two devoted caretakers at age 3, when the family left Hong Kong.[109]

Clifford and Miao Ying's fifth child, May Lumsdaine, was born in May 1938 but died of unknown causes when she was only 7 months old. Infant mortality was still not uncommon.[110] May would be their last child born in

Hong Kong; the Lumsdaine family moved back to the International Settlement of Shanghai in late 1938 or early 1939.

Clifford and Miao Ying had several possible reasons to return to Shanghai. Clifford's job at Paramount Studios in Hong Kong may have ended in 1938,[111] and he may have had a job prospect back in Shanghai.[112] Miao Ying's family, including her only sister, were still in Shanghai. Lastly, the International Settlement in Shanghai may have seemed safer due to Hong Kong's proximity to southern China and Japanese incursions there in late 1938 and early 1939.[113]

Recent events had left Clifford and Miao Ying concerned for their family's safety. By early 1939, Japanese atrocities in China, including the "Rape of Nanking," were well known, especially among the Chinese.[114] Japanese Imperial forces already occupied much of China, including Shanghai, but the International Settlement was largely left alone because Japan was not yet at war with the countries controlling that territory. Many expected the Japanese to occupy British-controlled Hong Kong next, but the International Settlement in Shanghai seemed out of harm's way.[115]

THE HOUSE AT BUBBLING WELL ROAD

The Lumsdaine family moved into a unit on Bubbling Well Road in the International Settlement in 1939.[116] A year later, in August 1940, Clifford and Miao Ying's third son, George, was born at home, joining Charlie, 6; YaoTim, 4; Edward, 2; and their cousin Bieu Tse, 11, who had come to live with the family a year earlier.[117] Some part of the family would reside at the Bubbling Well Road house for the next 16 years, until the last of them left Shanghai in 1955.

After George, five more babies were born to Clifford and Miao Ying in that house, which became full of both memories and children. Even the youngest child, Joseph Albert, who

George at 6 months, early 1941

(A) View of metal gateway exiting to Bubbling Well Road; (B) view of lane and former neighbors Mr. and Mrs. Chin in doorway; (C) the unit on Bubbling Well Rd. where the family lived from 1939 to 1955; (D) view from rooftop terrace. Photos (A, B, D) by Robert Lumsdaine, 1985; photo (C) by YaoTim Allen, 1987.

At left, the communal sink in Unit 1, 1168 Bubbling Well Road, Shanghai. Above, the communal stove. Photos by YaoTim Allen and Bob Allen, 1987.

spent the least amount of time there, has vivid recollections of his first five years of life in that house. His older siblings became adults, or at least precocious teens, there. It became a place as rich in family history as it was in family legends.

The home at Bubbling Well Road – now called Nanjing Road – was only two miles from the Cathay Hotel where Clifford and Miao Ying first met in 1932.[118] In the 1940s and 1950s, it was part of a larger, enclosed residential compound.[119] The many, mostly two-story residential units sat behind commercial businesses and stores lining the bustling Bubbling Well Road, in the heart of the International Settlement. One entered the residential compound through a metal gate that opened to the main commercial street.

Inside the enclosed compound was a series of lanes or alleyways leading to doorway entrances and large windows of the individual units. The lanes or alleyways separating the buildings created open areas resembling the inner courtyards of traditional Chinese homes, allowing sunlight, ventilation, and shelter from commotion of the busy street. The lanes were closed to the commercial street traffic, making them ideal for residents to sit and socialize with each other and for neighborhood children to run and play.

The terraced buildings adjoined each other – a Western urban adaptation made to resemble English townhomes. The rooftop terraces were used for drying clothes on poles extending from the terrace wall. The Lumsdaine children played on these terraces, where their mother and grandmother dried clothes and dehydrated fruits, vegetables, and other foods.

Each building usually housed several families, as was typical of the era. The Lumsdaine family lived on the second floor of of their unit from 1939 until 1941.[120] From 1941 to 1955, the family occupied at least two rooms on

Below: Clockwise from top left, Robert, Mr. Ching, former landlords Mr. and Mrs. Lee, 1985. At right, Robert in 2005 at the former site of the Bubbling Well Road house.

29

the first floor in addition to a loft above the hallway that was reachable by ladder.[121] The next five babies, beginning with Robert in 1942 and ending with Joseph Albert in 1950, were born in the first-floor room on the right side of the hallway.

All tenants entered through a door that led into the communal kitchen. YaoTim, the oldest daughter, recalled:

> *"Five families lived in that building, and one corner of the kitchen was for each tenant to cook where different tenants had their own utensils and pots. There was also one big communal tub that was used for bathing, for washing dishes, for butchering poultry and fish, and sometimes for washing clothes."* [122]

Straight back from the kitchen was a stairway. After the stairway was a room on the left where grandmother Pau Pau slept, often with one of her grandchildren, usually Edward or Philip. The rest of the family slept in another room to the right.

The landlords lived in the building with their tenants, as was common at the time.[123] In the 1980s, several of the Lumsdaine children, including YaoTim, Ed, George, and Robert, revisited their childhood home and talked with the former landlord and some of the former neighbors. On a separate visit in 1985, Robert met with former neighbors Mr. and Mrs. Chin and former landlords Mr. and Mrs. Lee, who were 99 and 91 years old, respectively, at the time.

The Lumsdaine family home is only a memory now, as the housing and commercial area around their building on Bubbling Well Road was replaced by modern high-rises, large corporate offices, and numerous retail stores, including two icons of corporate America, McDonald's and Starbucks.[124]

4

WAR AND SEPARATION

Japanese troops march through Shanghai after capturing the city in 1937.

THE BATTLE ZONE EXPANDS

After the Japanese captured Shanghai in November 1937, they occupied the city and terrorized the Chinese in the city and the surrounding countryside, but not the Chinese or the Westerners living in the International Settlement.

Japanese troops guarded the bridges and other entries and exits between the Settlement and the rest of Shanghai, but they largely left alone the people who lived there, as well as their businesses, governing entities, and police force. That's because until late 1941, Japan was not at war with Great Britain, the U.S., France, or other nations whose citizens lived in and controlled the International Settlement.

However, by 1940, Great Britain had withdrawn its infantry battalions that had been stationed in Shanghai and warned British citizens that the country could not defend them if Japan invaded the Settlement. The U.S. government followed suit. All that remained was a small contingent of volunteer troops and two under-manned ships on the Huangpu River in Shanghai to deter a Japanese incursion.[125]

On December 7, 1941, Japan attacked the U.S. Pacific Fleet at Pearl Harbor. The next day, the U.S. and Great Britain declared war on Japan.[126] In response, Japanese tanks, trucks, and troops invaded the International Settlement where Clifford was working to support Miao Ying and their four children, the youngest of whom was only a toddler.

Japan was now officially at war with the U.S., Great Britain, and their allies[127] and would no longer overlook the 8,000 British nationals, 2,000 Americans, and thousands of citizens of other nations, including Russia,[128] in the International Settlement.

Clifford and Miao Ying were plunged into shock and fear by the Japanese armed forces' invasion into

Japanese tanks roll on the Bund of the International Settlement on Dec. 8, 1941, after the U.S. declared war on Japan.

their previously safe haven. It had only been four years since the infamous Rape of Nanking, when Japanese troops massacred up to 300,000 Chinese residents of Nanking and the surrounding area. The especially brutal treatment of Chinese women and children by the Japanese invaders was still painfully fresh in the psyche of most Shanghai residents[129] as they beheld

Japanese soldiers march as they take control of city streets in the International Settlement in Shanghai, Dec. 8, 1941

the terrifying sight of Japanese soldiers with bayonets and swords stationed on most street corners and in front of residential gates such as the one on Bubbling Well Road. In effect, all Allied citizens in the International Settlement were now Japanese prisoners of war.

Less than a year later, in November 1942, Allied civilians were rounded up and placed in concentration camps.[130] It was during the interim that Miao Ying gave birth to Robert, in June 1942.[131] Robert would be too young to remember his parents' constant fear and occasional terror during the Imperial Japanese forces' occupation of the International Settlement, which lasted until the war ended in August 1945.

After the Japanese takeover, Allied civilians were required to purchase and wear red armbands with a capital letter designating their nationality. Americans wore an "A," Britons a "B," citizens of the Netherlands an "N." These Allied foreigners could not conduct businesses as usual.[132] Many were suspected of supporting, aiding, or abetting the Allied powers in the war against Japan. Talk circulated of arrests, brutal interrogations, and death for those accused of supporting the Allies. While the adults suffered constant

*Armband worn by a British national
during Japanese occupation of the
International Settlement*

anxiety and worry about having property confiscated, being interrogated, or even arrested and tortured, children in the settlement at first continued with their routines and carefree play.[133] Soon, however, the children noticed the changes – formidable-looking Japanese soldiers, many of whom did not speak their language, armed with swords or rifles with bayonets. The older Lumsdaine children, Charlie, then 8; YaoTim, 5; and Edward, 4, would each experience the terrorizing effects of the Japanese occupation.[134]

THROUGH A CHILD'S EYES

The three oldest Lumsdaine children all had disturbing encounters with the horrors of war and with the Japanese soldiers. During the war years in Shanghai, Charlie, YaoTim, and Edward had wartime experiences that caused Clifford and Miao Ying unimaginable anxiety and sleepless nights.[135]

Charlie (Chuck)

One event terrified Charlie and unnerved his parents: a close encounter with a stray .50-caliber bullet. As Charlie entered the house, it whizzed past him, splintering the thick wooden entry door to Unit 1.[136] The bullet likely came from an attacking airplane shooting at the anti-aircraft gun mounted atop the Uptown Theater, which was located diagonally across the street from the family home.

On another occasion, Charlie accompanied Miao Ying to the Swiss Consulate, located on an upper floor of a tall commercial building guarded by Japanese soldiers. After leaving the consulate, Miao Ying realized that she had left something behind and asked Charlie, who was 10 or 11 at the time, to return and retrieve it. In the building's stairwell, Charlie encountered a Japanese soldier "with the tallest bayonet you've probably ever seen in your life." He stopped Charlie for questioning; Chuck (Charlie took the nickname upon coming to the U.S. in 1951) later recalled that at the time, he thought, "Boy, I'm dead, I'm just dead, you know." Tense moments passed before the soldier patted Charlie on the head and let him go. Upon returning to his mother, Charlie related what had happened, evoking in her both angst and regret.[137]

The family home was not immune from the Japanese occupiers' tyranny and terror. Charlie and Edward often played on the neighborhood rooftop terraces, pretending to use a BB gun to shoot at the Japanese aircraft

Diagram of the house at 1168 Bubbling Well Road and neighborhood, sketched by Philip Lumsdaine, with the family's residence in Unit 1 at right center.

35

A Japanese Special Naval Landing Force infantryman guards a building his unit had just seized in Shanghai's International Settlement on Dec. 8, 1941.

that frequently flew overhead. Once, after playing this game, Charlie saw a Japanese officer with a long sword and several soldiers with rifles with bayonets approaching their house. Thinking that the Japanese had found out they were shooting at their airplanes, Charlie was "scared to death" that the soldiers were going into his house to "shoot my mom." Much to his relief, he later found out that the soldiers were there only to tag furniture, denoting it was now the property of the Japanese Imperial Army, which could confiscate it any time they wished.[138]

Charlie's childhood was marked and marred by many more experiences during the Japanese occupation, including air-raid sirens, blackouts, and an escape from school as it was being bombed by Japanese aircraft. He also remembered the specter of neighborhood retaliation after the assassination of a Japanese sentry outside the gate to Unit 1. One experience that especially stood out was when he was confronted by two Japanese soldiers with large knives and their two German Shepherd attack dogs while playing in a closed park.[139] Chuck also recalled the difficulty of the pervasive daily hardships endured by the whole family – the constant lack of food, Clifford's inability to earn money to support his wife and children,[140] and the lack of adequate medical care and nutrition. These hardships and deprivations persisted throughout the Japanese forces' occupation of the International Settlement from 1941 to 1945.[141] The fact that not one of their six children perished in this "City of Terror"[142] was a testament to Clifford and Miao Ying's ingenuity and perseverance, as well as the strength of their love of family and each other.

YaoTim

YaoTim recalled that during the occupation, she saw severely injured and dead people, including babies and children, as she walked on the streets of Shanghai. She has spent a lifetime trying to forget those images.[143]

Other memories, unpleasant but less gruesome, remain quite vivid. Both YaoTim and Ed recalled night-time forays to steal food from street vendors.[144] Charlie would plan out their foraging runs during the daytime, calculating the number of steps it would take to reach various food stalls. At night, during the brief period of complete darkness when the lights were out after the air-raid sirens sounded but before people started lighting candles, the three of them would grab whatever they could and then run. Miao Ying knew about their forays, but she did not stop them because food was always scarce during the war, and the children were always hungry.[145] The nighttime forays came to an end when YaoTim attempted to grab food from a vendor Edward had already visited. The vendor grabbed YaoTim's hand, but YaoTim bit the woman's hand and escaped. The children never stole from the food vendors again.[146]

Another night, Charlie was sent out to buy hot water, and YaoTim, as usual, begged to go along.[147] She was 5 or 6 years old at the time. On this occasion, the air-raid sirens sounded, and the lights went out. In the ensuing darkness, YaoTim was terrified. Her big brother dragged her along, but when they saw that the gate to 1168 Bubbling Well Road was locked, YaoTim started crying hysterically. Suddenly, Miao Ying and Clifford appeared, and Miao Ying said, "AhTim[148], no need to cry; your brother will take care of you." Miao Ying soothingly talked to Charlie, and Clifford held YaoTim's hand to keep them calm until the sirens sounded again, and the gate opened to let them in.[149]

The constant anxiety and outright fear of death and destruction was part of daily life during the war. Once, YaoTim was hospitalized for a month with an intestinal disorder.[150] The hospital was seven miles from home, but Miao

Ying or Charlie walked that distance to visit her daily. However, one day, neither of them visited, probably because of blockades or bombings. That day terrified YaoTim; she imagined the worst and assumed that no one came to visit because everyone in the family had been killed.[151]

Less frightening but more painful was when a cut on YaoTim's foot got infected, necessitating a visit to the doctor. The young YaoTim was in great pain after the doctor treated her foot. As there was no money to pay for a bus or streetcar, Miao Ying and YaoTim had to walk the long distance to get home as YaoTim cried in pain. Miao Ying spoke softly to YaoTim and told her to lean on her to relieve some of the burden on YaoTim's painful foot. Miao Ying told YaoTim silly stories as they walked, hoping to distract her daughter from the pain. They stopped many times so YaoTim could rest. Despite the medical treatment, YaoTim's foot refused to heal, so she once again had to be hospitalized. As before, Miao Ying visited YaoTim almost daily, walking the seven miles and always being upbeat on these visits.[152] For YaoTim, these visits showed her mother's ability to be gentle with her children, despite the inward and outward toughness she otherwise needed to help her family survive the dangers and hardships of life in wartime Shanghai.

Edward

Edward was only 4 years old in 1941 when Japanese soldiers marched into the International Settlement. He grew up quickly during the war years, both because he spent much time with his older brother Charlie and because he was given a lot of independence early, in part because Miao Ying was busy with her three younger children.

Edward recalled a frightening encounter with the Japanese. As he walked with Charlie down Bubbling Well Road, they saw three soldiers walking toward them on the sidewalk. Edward saw his older brother move over to the curb and attempted to also get out of the way. However, he stumbled, fell, and hit the leg of one of the soldiers. Later, he recalled:

> *"Terrified and trembling, I got up and bowed quickly, expecting some terrible punishment. [Fortunately], the soldier simply kicked me aside, like a dog, and kept on walking."* [153]

In play, Charlie and Edward would arrange benches and boards on the rooftop terrace into make-believe American warplanes. They made up English words, played mock aerial dogfights and made imaginary bombing runs, sometimes involving George.[154] Miao Ying likely was aware of their shenanigans but did not stop her sons from supporting their American "half-brothers." A darker side of this childhood role-playing related to perhaps the most gruesome sight Edward witnessed during the war: an American pilot being dragged behind a truck along Bubbling Well Road.[155]

PRISONER OF WAR

Japanese forces sustained a summer of losses in the Pacific theater of World War II in 1942, including defeats at the battles of Midway and Guadalcanal.[156] It was after that summer that Japanese forces tightened their grip on the International Settlement and began rounding up civilians who were citizens of countries they considered enemies of Japan – namely, the Allied countries. From November 1942 to July 1943, about 7,800 Allied men, women, and children were rounded up and sent to various camps, sometimes after suffering a forced march through the streets of Shanghai to humiliate them in front of the Chinese.[157] Initially, 350 men, mostly British and U.S. citizens, were hauled off to a prison camp run by the Imperial Japanese Army. These prisoners were designated "prominent citizens,"[158] but fortunately, Clifford was not among them.

However, his luck ran out three months later. In February 1943, Japanese soldiers removed Clifford from his home and took him to a "Civilian Assembly Center." In reality, these were simply walled, well-guarded prisons for Allied civilians.

The exact circumstances of how Clifford was taken and sent to his first concentration camp are unknown; Miao Ying and Clifford never talked about it with the children. Clifford was first taken to Pootung (also called "Pudong") Camp, where mostly single men were held captive during the early months of 1943.[159] When he was taken away, Miao Ying, who had five young children at home and was pregnant with a sixth, told Charlie, her eldest son, that she did not expect to ever see Clifford again.[160]

Pootung Camp, located across the Huangpu River from the Bund, was a condemned industrial area of six abandoned warehouses with numerous broken windows. The buildings were vermin-infested and grimy from coal dust "which had impregnated every corner of the building."[161] Pootung Camp was notorious for its filth, overcrowding, lack of food, rampant thefts, and unchecked violence among the prisoners.[162]

Clifford was incarcerated at Pootung Camp for seven months, from February to September 1943.[163] The official entry record for him at Pootung stated that he was a "merchant" for "Hong Kong & Shanghai Lace Co."[164] Little other official information exists about how Clifford fared or what he did at this infamous camp. Initially, visits by family were allowed, and Miao Ying took advantage of this by visiting Clifford frequently. She would take Charlie with her, but the visits were strained for a number of reasons. First, they were always blindfolded as they were taken across the Huangpu River by boat to the meeting place in the prison. Although the blindfolds

The Japanese Imperial Army turned this condemned Shanghai warehouse complex into a "civilian assembly center" – in reality, a prison camp for citizens of the Allied countries fighting against Japan. Clifford spent seven months during 1943 at "Pootung Camp," which was notorious for its filth.

were removed at the meeting place, Miao Ying and Charlie could stand no closer than 5 feet from Clifford, and a prison guard stood between them. Other than seeing that Clifford was alive, there was little talk or interaction between the family members during these visits at Pootung.[165]

Clifford never specifically told his children about how he was treated at Pootung Camp or the other two camps to which he was later transferred. The only information he revealed was that others were beaten and tortured, but he was not beaten or tortured and was mostly left alone.[166] Still, reports from other Japanese internees during that time are horrifying.

"There was a culture of violence and a constant threat of aggression from the guards," according to one account.[167] Almost a third of the prisoners, including civilian internees, died in captivity from starvation, disease, or other causes. One contributing factor was that the Japanese captors were conditioned to view war prisoners as having dishonored themselves, and thus, they did not deserve dignity.[168] Japanese guards routinely abused and tortured prisoners. Constant food shortages meant that, "universal at camps, men were quickly reduced to living skeletons."[169] This took a toll on Clifford. As his two eldest children would later recall, he was not the same person after his wartime incarceration as he was before it.[170]

In September 1943, Clifford was transferred from Pootung Camp to Yu Yuen Road Camp, located in a former public high school at 404 Yu Yuen Road in Shanghai.[171] The school's gymnasium had been converted into a men's dormitory. Curtains divided up the classrooms into ad hoc rooms for married couples, families with children, and single women.[172] Nine hundred and seventy-two internees were held at Yu Yuen,[173] and Clifford would spend the next 19 months there.[174] The book *Captives of Empire*, by Greg Leck, includes a photo of Clifford working at the camp's soya dairy.[175] He reportedly rose at 4:30 a.m. every day to make soymilk in time for the other internees to have it for breakfast.[176]

Miao Ying and Clifford had, through daring and ingenuity, surreptitiously arranged for Clifford and his family to see each other on Sundays. He would sit at the same spot outside a camp building and face the gate. She would walk by with the children so he could see them, and they could see their daddy,

41

The book Captives of Empire: The Japanese Internment of Allied Civilians in China (1941-1945) *by Greg Leck includes this photo of the soya dairy work crew at Yu Yuen Camp; Clifford, standing at far right, spent 19 months there.*

through the sliver of space between the iron gate's hinges and the concrete wall surrounding the compound. The meetings were clandestine, and no talking was allowed. Japanese soldiers patrolled the street, so it was imperative that the family walk by quietly and not draw the soldiers' attention, or Clifford could be punished. One occasion nearly ended with tragic results.

Miao Ying had coached each child to make no noise and only look at their father. She had previously taken Charlie and Edward using this strategy, with successful results. But this time, 7-year-old YaoTim was so excited upon seeing her father that she yelled out "Daddy! Daddy!" As Miao Ying grabbed YaoTim hard by the hand, her face turned ashen as a Japanese soldier wielding a long sword took notice and approached them.[177] Miao Ying was terrified because it was common knowledge that civilians could be beaten or killed at the slightest provocation.[178] Fortunately, the soldier only patted YaoTim on the head and smiled.

After this close call, YaoTim never got the opportunity to see Clifford again until his release from the concentration camp after the war, although Miao Ying bravely continued to bring some of the other children for these Sunday "visits."[179]

Miao Ying and Clifford's attempts to ensure that the children got to see their captive father extended to an encounter while Miao Ying was hospitalized after an appendectomy. With the help of the International Red Cross, they arranged for the Japanese to take Clifford to the hospital to visit his wife

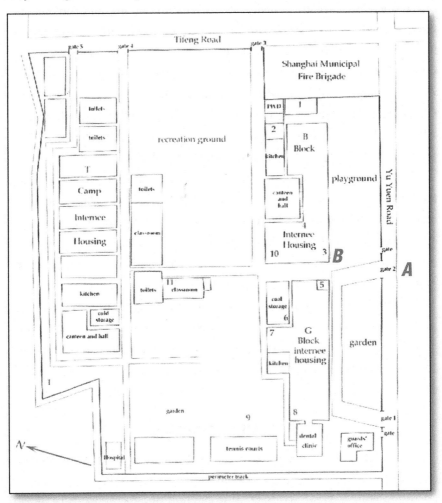

Diagram of Yu Yuen Road Camp showing where Miao Ying (A) and Clifford (B) would position themselves on Sundays

and for Pau Pau to take all the kids to stand in the hallway outside the ward where Miao Ying was recovering. While the children could not go inside the ward because two Japanese soldiers stood guard nearby, they were able to see their dad sitting by their mom's bedside at the hospital as they talked and smiled at each other.[180]

As the fortunes of war turned increasingly against Japan in 1945, the Japanese guards became stricter and more brutal. Food was scarce. "The feeding of the internees during the last six months of the war [March to August 1945] was reduced to starvation level...."[181] As Allied bombing raids on Shanghai increased, the Japanese occupiers moved the civilian internees at some Shanghai camps to the location of former troop barracks that stored ammunition. This may have been strategic on the part of the Japanese in hopes that Allied bombers would spare these ammunition depots. A darker reason, as Chuck later speculated, may have been that Allied bombings would create Allied civilian casualties.[182] Regardless of the reason, Clifford was moved from Yu Yuen Camp to Yangshupu Camp in April 1945.[183]

"Internees in the Yangshupu Camp endured constant bombing raids until the Japanese in Shanghai surrendered."[184] They were fed a starvation diet of about 300 calories a day, far less than the amount of calories the average adult requires to survive.[185] Clifford likely suffered greatly from both starvation and constant bombings near Yangshupu Camp, as has been reported by others.[186] However, he never mentioned this directly to any of his children.

Thankfully, Clifford was only at Yangshupu Camp for four months. On August 6 and August 9, 1945, the U.S. detonated two atomic bombs over the Japanese cities of Hiroshima and Nagasaki. Six days later, on August 15, 1945, Japan surrendered. Clifford had been imprisoned for 30 months by the time he and the other prisoners of war were released on August 26, 1945.[187]

STRUGGLING TO SURVIVE

While Clifford's situation was extraordinarily difficult, Miao Ying's was nearly impossible. She was two months pregnant when Clifford was taken prisoner in February 1943, plus she had the five other children to care for: Charlie, 9; YaoTim, 6; Edward, 5; George, 2; and Robert, 8 months.

She doubted that she would ever see her husband, the sole support for the family, again.[188] At age 32, with only a second-grade education, Miao Ying's task of keeping her family alive must have seemed almost insurmountable.

Money was tight for the couple, even before Clifford was imprisoned. When the Japanese took over the International Settlement in December 1941, Allied civilians there generally were unable to conduct business as usual, and most were unable to find work.[189] Clifford likely had little, if any, import or export business in the year before his imprisonment, so how he managed to support his large family during that time is both a mystery and a miracle.

In addition to his wife, children, and mother-in-law Pau Pau, the household had also included Miao Ying's niece, Ho Sui Wah, whom the family called Bieu Tse.[190] Bieu Tse joined the family in 1939 under tragic circumstances.

In 1937, China's second war with Japan had begun. Two years later, Bieu Tse's father, Ho Gai Zien – Miao Ying's older brother – arranged for his entire family to move from Hong Kong to Shanghai around the same time that Clifford and Miao Ying also were moving from Hong Kong to Shanghai.

Bieu Tse, around 11 years old at the time,[191] traveled with the Lumsdaine family to help care for

Miao Ying during Clifford's incarceration

the three small children, 5-year-old Charlie, 3-year-old YaoTim, and 2-year-old Edward.[192] Her mother and three siblings were traveling to Shanghai separately, but their boat was torpedoed by a Japanese submarine, killing all four of them. Ho Gai Zien, who was traveling separately from his wife and children, was captured by Japanese forces that suspected he was a spy and tortured him nearly to death. He managed to reach the Lumsdaine family

*Bieu Tse with her aunt and uncle, Miao Ying and
Clifford; and her cousin Charlie, May 1934*

home but died shortly thereafter, leaving Bieu Tse orphaned and in Miao
Ying and Clifford's care.[193]

Miao Ying wasn't completely alone with a house full of children; she
did have her mother, Pau Pau, to lean on for help. Pau Pau had come to
live with the family after her husband died, and she was treated with great
respect by Miao Ying and Clifford, in accordance with the well-established
Chinese custom of deference to elders.[194] On rare occasions when there
was disagreement about disciplining the children – for example, if Pau Pau
thought Miao Ying was too harsh – Pau Pau's word was the final say. (In
this and other respects, Clifford's conduct toward his mother-in-law was
more Chinese than Western. Pau Pau, in turn, treated him with great affection and admiration.)

Pau Pau was a talented homemaker. She was resourceful and creative in food preparation, drying and preserving fruits and vegetables, such figs or sweet potatoes, for snacks. She could cook a tasty meal with whatever was at hand. She also was a skilled seamstress, knitting sweaters then taking them apart in early spring and reusing the yarn to knit new sweaters for the kids the following winter. She would also use old rags, tracing a child's feet for a pattern, and make "winter shoes" with multiple layers of cloth for warmth.[195]

Pau Pau's skills, her help with the children, and her adult companionship were great assets to Miao Ying during Clifford's incarceration. Pau Pau would do the wash for the entire household and help with baby Philip while Miao Ying did all the procuring of food and cooking, as well as decision-making, trying to be both mother and father for the family.[196] While Pau Pau's help was invaluable, Miao Ying still dealt with difficulties on many fronts.[197]

Liang "Pau Pau" Yee Dai, Miao Ying's mother.

Miao Ying gave birth to her eighth child, a son named Philip, in September 1943, about six months after Clifford was taken away by the Japanese.[198] Through pregnancy and childbirth, Miao Ying kept up all her efforts to make sure that her own mother, her niece, and her five other children would survive in Shanghai despite constant threats posed by Allied bombings, armed Japanese sentries, and widespread starvation. For the sake of her family, she refused to give up or give in to despair. She relied on her inner strength and innate intelligence and ingenuity to keep her family safe.[199] But the stress took a toll on her and showed on occasions when her usual constant composure seemed to lapse. For example, once when she was heavily pregnant, a moving vehicle nearly struck her. Charlie, who was only 10 at the time, saw the danger in time, pushed her out of the way, and saved her life.[200]

Feeding a hungry family in the midst of war shortages was challenging, but somehow, Miao Ying always managed to put food on the table, even if it was just one small meal for the day. "We never would go without for any period of time," Chuck recalled later.[201]

Through a friend of Clifford's, Miao Ying learned that the Swiss Consulate was acting as intermediary for families of U.S. citizens in Shanghai. Ever resourceful, she managed to secure ration coupons that could be redeemed for food – albeit food that was neither part of the typical Chinese diet nor

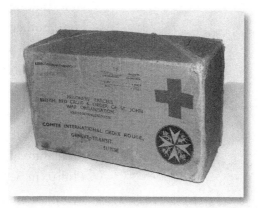

A box of food rations similar to what the family received periodically during the war.

suitable for Chinese cooking.[202] Rations might include loaves of bread, powdered milk, flour, and canned and dry goods including potatoes and sauerkraut, although initially, Miao Ying threw out the large cans of sauerkraut because the taste and smell convinced her they were spoiled.[203]

Miao Ying and Pau Pau would improvise using these ingredients; on the rooftop terrace, they would mince and dry some of the bread to make dumplings. Miao Ying also would arrange for Edward and YaoTim to sell extra loaves of bread to relatives in exchange for money to buy rice, vegetables, or small amounts of meat. She was forced to be creative in her cooking since the quantities and types of available food were inconsistent. For

From left: Choi Yiu Ki "Ah Kai," Miao Ying's nephew; Ho Wai Ying "Ng Yee," Miao Ying's younger sister; Robert Lumsdaine; and Ng Yee's husband, Choi Yuk Chuen

long periods, potatoes and flour were the only ingredients available. Still, the children were constantly hungry, so they ate whatever was available.[204] Although the meager rations kept starvation at bay, malnourishment took its toll. Philip was not able to walk until age 3, possibly because of a lack of nutrients; much of the time, no milk was available, so his baby bottle was filled with rice water.[205]

The logistics of securing food and bringing it home was challenging; the rationed food was distributed from the American School, which was almost seven miles away. Miao Ying, who was pregnant with Philip part of the time, and 10-year-old Charlie carried sacks of food weighing 30 to 50 pounds those many miles. Even 50 years later, Chuck remembered how he cried as a child as he helped his mother carry the weighty sacks that great distance.[206] He had been too young at the time to understand that money was scarce, and they could not afford to pay streetcar fare to take them and their heavy loads home.[207]

Despite her best efforts, Miao Ying had difficulty keeping her charges from starving. Out of necessity, she borrowed money, usually from her sister Ng Yee, whose husband, Choi Yuk Chuen, was a well-paid ship's engineer and instructor.[208] This cost Miao Ying dearly in terms of humiliation, or "losing face," but it would not be the last time she would need to borrow from her younger sister.[209]

At one point during the war, YaoTim was hospitalized for about a month. Thanks to Clifford's U.S. citizenship, she received free medical care from American doctors and free hospital care. YaoTim was fed well as she recovered in the hospital. Knowing how desperately her family needed food, she would pack away some of her hospital meals for Miao Ying or Charlie to take home and share with the family. After she was released from the hospital, YaoTim received extra rations of a pint of milk and one egg each day to maintain her health. Miao Ying watched over YaoTim as she drank the milk and ate the egg to make sure she would not share it with the other children.[210]

5

PEACE AND PROSPERITY, ALMOST

CLIFFORD GOES HOME

J apan surrendered to the Allies on August 15, 1945, but almost two weeks passed before the war prisoners gradually were released in Shanghai.[211] For Clifford and others in the concentration camps, those two weeks were perilous. Prisoners who dared celebrate were subjected to torture or even death; as an adult, Chuck recalled his father telling him of a harrowing event:

> *"... [A]t the end of the war, when they heard the Allies won, the prisoners went nuts and opened the gates on the compound ... some of the Japanese soldiers just mowed them down, just drove over them, killed them."*[212]

It was August 26, 1945, before Clifford was allowed to go home.[213] Lingering Japanese troops in Shanghai made any celebration of their surrender unwise.

Earlier in the war, Charlie and Edward had painted a large U.S. flag on a piece of fabric and displayed it on a wall inside the house until Miao Ying wisely told them to take it down. On August 16, 1945, emboldened

51

by news of the surrender, they attached the homemade flag to a pole and stuck it out the attic window in a show of jubilation. Miao Ying was horrified and rebuked them exclaiming, "Do you want to die? Do you want the whole family to die?"[214] She understood the full horrors of war and occupation and realized that her children's antics could jeopardize the entire family's safety.

Clifford after his release from the Japanese concentration camp, 1945

Charlie and YaoTim were 11 and 9 years old, respectively, when Clifford was released from the Japanese concentration camp.[215] They recalled later that when their father returned home after 2½ years of imprisonment, he was not the same man that they remembered. Edward, who was 5 when his father was taken away, did not remember Clifford at all from before his incarceration. He did not recognize the "very skinny white man" who returned home in 1945 as his father.[216] Clifford never told his children much about his treatment in the camps.[217] Perhaps the look in his eyes and on his

The Lumsdaine family in the summer of 1946, not long after Milly was born in May. Clockwise from top: Clifford, YaoTim, Robert, Philip, Miao Ying holding Milly, George, Edward, and Charlie.

Clifford, c. 1946

face spoke more clearly about what the years of imprisonment did to him than any words ever could.

Clues about what may have happened to Clifford in the Japanese prison camps came from his older children's observations of him before and after his imprisonment. Before his captivity, he was talkative with his children, engaging them in play, taking them for walks, and even being silly with them. Afterward, he was much quieter; he would respond when talked to but did not initiate conversation. He became unusually reserved in speech, even taciturn, and sat in the same chair for hours, saying and doing virtually nothing. Milly recalled later:

> *"Dad sat in that chair a lot, not reading or doing anything but just sitting in silence. Mom would tell me not to bother him, just leave him alone. At one point, she told me he was not the same as he was before the war."*[218]

Before incarceration, Clifford was not prone to anger. If he was mad, he never displayed it. And he never, ever yelled in anger. He epitomized the loving, doting father who "would let you get away with anything."[219] After being released from the prison camp, Clifford was occasionally short-tempered and quick to show anger, and when he was angry, he occasionally yelled. Miao Ying took to cautioning the children not to upset their father as this could make him angry.[220]

Clifford's buoyant personality before the internment is a side of him that some of the Lumsdaine children, especially those born after 1940, never experienced. Milly, for example, was born in May 1946, eight months after her father came home from the Yangshupu Camp. Milly never knew the talkative, playful Clifford from before the war; she only experienced the moody and occasionally short-tempered Clifford post-incarceration. She recalled Clifford spanking her as a punishment for running around his chair screaming as her brothers teased her.[221] Milly, an unusually (at least among the Lumsdaine children) obedient child, was shocked.[222] She had never been spanked before, unlike almost all of the other children. Edward also recalled once being spanked by Clifford merely for playing a radio too loudly.[223] This was a huge change from the father who had previously left discipline to Miao Ying and Pau Pau and had been a "pushover for his children."[224] At the time, post-traumatic stress disorder was unknown. In retrospect, it's almost certain that Clifford was suffering from it.

Despite the challenges and changes, one positive was that the family once again had a wage-earner to provide for the growing, 11-person household of three adults, a teenage niece,[225] and seven children from newborn to age 12. Clifford soon found work in a motor pool driving U.S. Army officers around in a Jeep. He was employed as a driver until November 1945, but after that, he did not find full-time employment again until May 1946, when he was hired by an established shipping company, American President Lines (APL).[226]

While he was working full-time at APL, Clifford also brought home accounting work supplied by friends and acquaintances. He normally worked six days a week, Monday through Saturday, and took Sundays

Employee Christmas party at American President Lines (APL), a Shanghai shipping company where Clifford (kneeling, far right), worked from May 1946 to July 1951

off to go on long, leisurely walks with his YaoTim.[227] As none of the other members of the household brought in wages, when daughter Dolly was born in May 1948,[228] the financial pressures on Clifford and Miao Ying must have been immense.

Clifford quickly rose through the ranks at APL. His strong work ethic and bilingual and biliterate abilities – he was well-versed in Cantonese and Mandarin and could write in Chinese at the grade-school level – likely helped him get steady promotions. Between May 1945 and February 1951, he rose from secretary to bookkeeper to accountant for the company's Shanghai office. With full-time employment at APL plus his side jobs, Clifford was finally able to ensure that his family did not go hungry, as they often had during the war. The family did not live in luxury during those post-war years, but there was finally enough money to buy food, put the older kids in school, and even take into their home people who were impoverished and homeless to help with household work.[229]

THE PRIMACY OF SCHOOLING

Miao Ying and Clifford prioritized their children's education and found ways to pay their tuition; education was second only to keeping them healthy and fed. In 1938, when Charlie, was only 5 years old, they enrolled him in an English and Chinese elementary school.[230] In the 1940s, they enrolled the six older children in Catholic schools operated by the Jesuits and other religious orders because those generally were considered the best schools.

Starting in 1946, Charlie, Edward, and George attended Collège Sainte Jeanne d'Arc,[231] a Roman Catholic elementary and junior high school for boys that was run by French Jesuit missionary brothers.[232] Charlie, who was 12, had previously attended Chinese school through sixth grade.[233] Edward, who was 11, was 5 when his father was taken away in 1943 and

English and Chinese elementary school that Charlie attended in Kowloon, Hong Kong in 1938

likely received little formal education until he enrolled at the Catholic school. George, 6, likely entered first grade.[234] For each of the brothers, the school provided different opportunities and challenges.

Ste. Jeanne d'Arc enabled Charlie to finish high school and excel in athletics. He was a fast runner and once won second place in a school-wide race despite having pneumonia. However, his participation in sports later brought about a lengthy hospitalization after an injury that nearly killed him.[235]

For Edward, Ste. Jeanne d'Arc unfortunately marked the beginning of his impulse toward gambling. He met other kids there who not only became gambling partners but also encouraged him toward serious gambling with cards and dice.[236] Edward missed school frequently because he was gambling or playing with friends. Miao Ying was unaware until the principal called her in for a visit, at which time she was unhappy to be informed that Edward was being expelled for absenteeism and other transgressions.[237]

Edward's gambling partners had wealth that he did not possess. Consequently, he was always raising money to pay off his gambling debts. He used the bus money Miao Ying gave him and engaged in numerous money-making schemes, including scalping theater tickets and soliciting his younger siblings to buy and resell discounted school supplies and other sundries.[238] Edward's reputation as a troublemaker traveled with him from Ste. Jeanne d'Arc to his next school, St. Francis Xavier, where his truancy and gambling continued, and he became progressively less manageable for Miao Ying.

George was a good student and rarely got into trouble.[239] He did not spend much time with Charlie, likely because of the seven-year age differ-

Class photo at Collège Sainte Jeanne d'Arc School in Shanghai. Charlie (Chuck) is in the back row, sixth from left. He was the second tallest student in the class.

Clockwise from top left: school-age Charlie, YaoTim, Edward, and George, 1947-1948

ence, nor Edward due to the latter's penchant for truancy and gambling. Instead, George, Robert, and Philip usually hung around together, going to school, playing, and getting into fights with other kids (although they never fought each other; that was expressly forbidden by their mother. "Family needs to stick together," Miao Ying was fond of saying.)

Fighting with other children, especially Chinese children, was practically unavoidable for the Lumsdaine boys during their years in Shanghai. Their Eurasian looks made them stand out, which subjected them to being singled out by bullies. Their American heritage further decreased their popularity, especially after the communist takeover of China in 1949 and during the Korean War from 1950 to 1953. These events precipitated strong anti-American sentiment,[240] and in this environment, even gentle George was pulled into many a conflict alongside his younger brothers.

Robert started at Ste. Jeanne d'Arc in 1950, and by September 1951, Philip had joined him, Edward, and George at the school.[241] Philip, and likely also

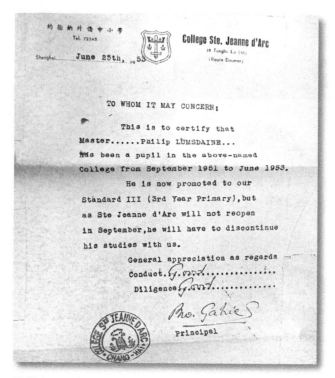

Philip's certificate of completion of third grade at Ste. Jeanne d'Arc, June 1953. The certificate notes that the school will not reopen for the next term; the communist government forced the closure of all religious schools.

Robert, had attended one year of Chinese school before entering Ste. Jeanne d'Arc.[242] George completed sixth grade; Robert, fourth grade; and Philip, third grade, before the communist government closed all religious schools in Shanghai, including Ste. Jeanne d'Arc in 1953.

The only schools that remained open were so-called "people-run schools" that had been nationalized by the communist government. The new government emphasized Maoist ideology; traditional school texts were abandoned and replaced with a curriculum focusing on Mao's works and other official Communist Party doctrines.[243] Miao Ying realized that these schools presented a hostile educational environment for her American-Chinese children, especially since China was battling U.S. capitalist imperialism both in public propaganda and on the battlefields in Korea. Rather than putting the boys in the Communist Party-run schools, she kept all three home and didn't enroll Milly and Dolly in school until the family reached the British-controlled colony of Hong Kong in 1955.[244] Years later, Miao Ying told Milly that putting her children in Communist Party-run schools would have been "going against your American father."[245]

SCHOOLS AND RELIGION

Because the children attended Catholic schools, they tended toward conversion to Catholicism, although neither Miao Ying nor Clifford was Catholic.[246] However, the Catholic schools were considered the best in Shanghai[247], so Clifford and Miao Ying even sent their eldest daughter, YaoTim[248], to Catholic school, despite the traditional Chinese prejudice against educating women.[249]

As it had been when Miao Ying was in school 25 years earlier, many Chinese in the 1940s still considered educating YaoTim – and girls in general – as misguided, foolhardy, and completely contrary to Chinese beliefs and customs because of the belief that literacy morally corrupted them, making them unsuitable as good wives.[250] Neighbors, relatives, and even YaoTim's own grandmother repeatedly questioned Miao Ying as to why she would "waste money" on educating a girl beyond second grade, especially when money was tight, and tuition had to be paid.[251]

To not lose face[252] among her relatives and friends, Miao Ying fabricated the excuse that YaoTim's education was at the insistence of her daughter's American father, and she could not refuse her foreigner husband's wishes. The truth was that Clifford never pressed this or any other serious issue without Miao Ying's consent.[253] Miao Ying and Clifford repeatedly told YaoTim that she could do anything that the boys could do. In this and many

Miao Ying, c. 1949

other ways, Miao Ying showed that her thinking was as progressive and Westernized as Clifford's was.[254]

Before Clifford was taken prisoner in 1943, YaoTim attended a Chinese school. When Clifford returned home in 1945, YaoTim told her father that she wanted to learn English. He enrolled her at Saint Sophia, a Russian Greek Orthodox girls' school. There, the nuns changed her name to the "more Christian" Maria because they considered the name YaoTim "too pagan."[255] YaoTim did not get along with the nuns at Saint Sophia, so she convinced Clifford to transfer her to Loretto School in Shanghai, which was run by the Sisters of Loretto of the Cross.[256] YaoTim found the American nuns at Loretto School to be much kinder. She flourished there and happily stayed at Loretto School for the next six years.[257]

YaoTim was so impressed by the teachers' and the nuns' kindness that in April 1948, she became the first in the family to convert to Catholicism. She then received her first communion with help from her third-grade teacher, a laywoman. Her teacher's special kindness[258] so sparked YaoTim's path of evangelization that she endeavored to make sure all her siblings also were eventually baptized Catholic.[259] Charlie and Edward were soon baptized [260]; later, after emigrating to the United States, YaoTim had her friend Theresa Negris arrange for the baptisms of George, Robert, and Philip at Christ the King Church in April 1954, and Milly, Dolly, and Joseph Albert before 1955.[261]

Miao Ying and Clifford always deferred to Pau Pau as the eldest family member; therefore, YaoTim's conversion was problematic. Miao Ying was open-minded about accepting Clifford's Western ways, including when it came to religion. But Pau Pau was a devout Buddhist, and it angered her that YaoTim wanted to become a Catholic, so they kept certain issues away from her as much as possible.[262] Pau Pau had a makeshift shrine where she put statues with food before them. She frequented the Buddhist temple, often with one of her grandchildren – mostly YaoTim – bringing food and incense for praying to the gods and honoring ancestors.[263] Pau Pau adhered strictly to certain Buddhist traditions, such as not wearing white clothing or white shoes except when attending funerals or mourning the dead.[264]

Miao Ying and Clifford eventually overcame Pau Pau's objections to YaoTim converting to Catholicism, but there was no avoiding the conflict between deep-seated Chinese and Buddhist tradition and Catholic custom when it came to YaoTim's first holy communion.[265] She wanted to wear a white dress and shoes, but as YaoTim was ironing her white first-communion dress, Pau Pau caught sight of it and was enraged. Miao Ying interceded and told YaoTim that she had to hide the dress until the church service and that she could not buy YaoTim white shoes and socks for the occasion.[266] With that admonition, Miao Ying took no further steps to impede either YaoTim's conversion or that of the rest of her children.

Although Clifford was baptized Catholic as an infant, he converted to his father's religion, Presbyterian, sometime after his mother died. He had occasionally taken his children to a Christian church, especially during Christmas, where they had witnessed a baptism.[267] Despite their differences, Catholics and Presbyterians are both Christian sects, so it presumably was less difficult for him to accept his children's conversion to Catholicism than it was for Pau Pau.

People's Liberation Army troops marching into Shanghai on Nanking Road, May 23, 1949

COMMUNIST RULE COMES TO SHANGHAI

Peace was brief in China after the Japanese surrender in late 1945. The armies of the Chinese Communist Party and the Nationalist Party had suspended hostilities between each other in order to battle the Japanese. By the end of 1946, they had resumed their savage civil war.[268] Shanghai, China's largest and most prosperous city at the time, was firmly in the control of the Nationalist Party until the Communists' Shanghai Campaign began on May 12, 1949.[269] Eleven days later, as the older Lumsdaine boys watched, the Communist People's Liberation Army marched into the heart of Shanghai on the former Bubbling Well Road, which had been renamed Nanking Road.[270] The campaign only lasted 21 days, but the battle between the Nationalists and the Communists over the city of Shanghai was fierce as the Nationalists ferociously bombed the city. Charlie was terrified, afraid of losing his dad amidst all of the bombs.[271]

The Communist takeover of Shanghai and the establishment of a Communist government by Chairman Mao Zedong on October 1, 1949, caused a plethora of problems for the Lumsdaine family. To tighten its grip on the populace and prevent a return of the Nationalists, the Communist government began purging Shanghai of Chinese and Western spies and other perceived enemies of the state. This resulted in daily arrests, trials, imprisonments, and executions, often on the same day for the accused. It was

*Communist propaganda poster equating
U.S. imperialism with Nazism.*

difficult, especially for the older Lumsdaine boys, to escape witnessing the Communist takeover and the aftermath. Every day, open trucks crammed with prisoners scheduled for execution rolled down the street in front of their home. "I will never forget the look of horror on the faces of some of the prisoners," Chuck would recall later.[272]

Anti-American sentiment was already strong at the grassroots level of the Chinese Communist Party, even before October 1949,[273] but anti-Americanism intensified substantially – and was pervasive in party propaganda

*Poster depicting the Chinese people defeating
American aggression in Korea*

65

– after the start of the Korean War in June 1950. Soon, anti-Americanism swept through the general populace, and resisting U.S. imperialism became a popular mantra. What Americans called the "Korean War" was known in China as the "War to Resist America and Aid Korea."[274] The Chinese narrative, then and now, is that the war resulted from the invasion of North Korea by U.S. imperialistic forces with the ultimate goal of destroying the newfound People's Republic of China.[275] By July 1950, anti-Americanism was the main Communist Party propaganda pitch to the Chinese people.

Widespread anti-American propaganda in China was evidenced by the numerous public posters that flourished. As in other parts of China, demonstrations, marches, and posters stoking anti-American fervor permeated the public areas of Shanghai.[276] The pervasive anti-Americanism translated into emotional distress, public taunts, and neighborhood fights for the Lumsdaine children. For Miao Ying and Clifford, it was a constant cause of worry, anxiety, and trauma.

DEPRESSION, RESILIENCE, A BIRTH, A DEATH

Saying that 1950 was an eventful and emotional year for the Lumsdaine family would be an understatement. Clifford suffered a nervous breakdown after the Communist Party took over Shanghai.[277] Sometimes he awoke in a cold sweat in the middle of the night, grabbing onto a window grille, like a prisoner looking out from between the bars of a jail cell.[278] Occasionally his children heard him scream in his sleep, fearfully yelling the words, "They are coming for me!"[279]

Clifford's depression and breakdown in 1950 might have been an after-effect of his earlier incarceration. Although he had been freed from wartime captivity more than four years earlier, he was once again facing the prospect of arrest, imprisonment, separation from his family, and possibly death.[280]

Miao Ying and Clifford also were experiencing an increase in financial stress due to the lengthy hospitalization of their eldest son, Charlie.[281] The year before, Charlie had been playing football (soccer), when he was hit hard in the torso by a kicked ball. No one knew anything was wrong until Charlie developed a fever and was hospitalized with an infection in mid-1949. That's

Clockwise from top left: Edward, Charlie (Chuck), YaoTim, George, Milly, Joseph Albert, Dolly, Philip, and Robert surrounding Clifford and Miao Ying, c. early 1951

when doctors discovered that one of his lungs had collapsed. Charlie would spend much of the next two years in the hospital, and several times doctors believed he would die from the infection, but he survived.

Then, in the spring of 1950, Miao Ying's mother and the children's beloved grandmother, Pau Pau, died quietly and unexpectedly in her sleep at age 72.[282] She had been well-respected by her daughter and son-in-law. She did all the washing and most of the cooking, especially during the war years. She cared for the children as babies and toddlers.[283] Pau Pau taught her grandchildren many things. She tried to teach her granddaughter YaoTim how to cook and sew. Although her sudden death was especially distressing to her favorite grandsons, Edward and Philip[284], it also badly shocked Miao Ying and Clifford at an already deeply distressing time in their lives.

In the midst of all this, Clifford and Miao Ying had their last baby, Joseph Albert, in July 1950.[285] In 17 years, from 1933 to 1950, Miao Ying endured 11 pregnancies and births; two of the children died in infancy. The family of Clifford Vere and Miao Ying Lumsdaine was now complete.

Joseph Albert was born barely a week after the start of the War to Resist America.[286] Anti-American zeal had permeated even the small residential neighborhood at 1168 Bubbling Well Road, which the Lumsdaine family called "our lane." Teenage young men demonstrated noisily; some even volunteered to fight in the war against the U.S. aggressors.[287] Insults, taunts, and occasional fights ensued, especially between neighborhood bullies and Chuck, Edward, and George. Perhaps the bullies thought of themselves as patriots.[288]

By February 1951, Clifford had lost his job with APL, which was forced to close by the Communist Chinese government. The company was unable to pay its employees the wages it owed them for many months after its closing,[289] and Clifford was devastated by his termination, the loss of income, and the lack of future prospects. His mood was reflected by a sarcastic poem he wrote after he lost his job and prepared himself for the likelihood that he would have to leave China and go to the United States:

> "Midnight fell on APL,
> Because on 2/28 they got rid of CVL.
> What do I care if they all went to hell;
> I'm going back to the land of ding-dong bell." [290]

With APL's closure, the couple had exhausted all their resources. Miao Ying once again had to borrow money from Ng Yee and Choi Yuk Chuen, her sister and brother-in-law, to pay for Charlie's costly medical bills and contin-

Miao Ying, front right, often borrowed money from her younger sister, Ng Yee, front left, and brother-in-law, Choi Yuk Chuen, back left. Because Clifford was American, he had trouble finding and holding jobs after the Communist Party took power in China.

ued hospitalization for his collapsed lung. Miao Ying was greatly embarrassed to have to borrow frequently from her younger sister, but she had little recourse. For her oldest child to survive, she had to make this sacrifice because they had no medical insurance or other resources to fall back on.[291]

Clifford could not pay bills or repay outstanding loans. His severance pay from APL would not arrive until August 1951, six months after his termination.[292] As a 41-year-old American in communist Shanghai, he had little chance of future employment.[293] There was no social safety net – no unemployment insurance, no food assistance, no aid to children. Clifford's inability to provide for the family he loved so dearly weighed heavily on him, but he needed to persevere, and he did, buoyed by his wife's unwavering love and strength.

If Miao Ying was troubled by the family's many misfortunes after the communists took over Shanghai, she didn't let it show. Through the extreme trials and tribulations, she continued to provide stability for her nine children as she helped her husband through his emotional distress and trauma. The older kids still received necessary schooling and discipline, especially her rambunctious boys who regularly managed to find trouble ("One time, George, Ed, and Chuck bricked up the front entrance to a bully's residence," Philip recalled later).[294] The younger kids were clothed and fed.

As pressures continued to mount, it became clear to Miao Ying that the family's road to survival would lead once again to separation: Clifford would have to leave China to avoid arrest – or worse – by the communist government, as well as to earn income. The four oldest children, who had U.S. and British citizenship papers,[295] would go too. The family could only survive financially if the five of them found work and sent money back to Miao Ying and the rest of the children. The political situation in Shanghai continued to worsen for foreigners, the Korean War raged on, and their ability to borrow from relatives had reached its limit. Splitting the family in half between China and the United States was the only way forward.

6

SEPARATION, AGAIN

*Clifford in Hong Kong en
route to the United States,
August 1951*

THE FIRST DEPARTURES

Clifford was reluctant to leave China. He'd spent most of his adult life there. He'd met his wife there. All of their children were born there. And he had no money to take his family with him.[296] But by July 1951, he had no other choice. It was impossible to find any work, and his life and liberty were in constant jeopardy.

Miao Ying's repeated urging finally persuaded him to go. Clifford borrowed enough money to take his eldest son, 18-year-old Charlie – who had been discharged from the hospital earlier in the year – with him to the United States in hopes that the two of them could earn enough money to support the rest of the family and eventually bring them from China to the U.S.[297]

The Chinese government might not have allowed the entire family to leave regardless because Miao Ying and the five youngest children were Chinese nationals. The Communist government would have had to issue passports in order for them to leave. However, Clifford and Charlie were registered as U.S. citizens so they were able to get U.S. passports. (The next three older children – YaoTim, Edward, and George – also were considered U.S. citizens at birth by virtue of Miao Ying and Clifford's wedding at the U.S. Consulate.) Still, the main, insurmountable obstacle to the family leaving Shanghai together was the lack of money.

Robert, Philip, Milly, Dolly, and Joseph Albert were considered "stateless." This may have been because their births were not recorded in a timely manner with the U.S. Consulate or because U.S. citizenship laws changed in 1940 or perhaps both.[298] In "normal" times, sorting out such legalities might have been possible. However, the social and political situation in communist-ruled Shanghai in 1951 was anything but normal.

Miao Ying and Clifford hoped that the family would be reunited quickly. It is doubtful either of them expected that nearly a decade would pass before they saw each other again.

COPING WITHOUT CLIFFORD

After Clifford and Charlie left Shanghai, Miao Ying was once again a single parent. This time, she was the sole adult caring for eight children between the ages of 1 and 15. Unlike during the war when Clifford was imprisoned she had neither her mother nor her oldest son to help her. With her second-grade education and the help of her oldest daughter, 15-year-old YaoTim, Miao Ying had to navigate school, banking, and other family and financial affairs on her own.

YaoTim was her mother's translator when dealing with English-speaking school or bank officials. She also maintained the family expense ledger that Clifford had meticulously kept. Every day, Miao Ying would recount the expenses to YaoTim to keep the ledger up to date. Together, they would visit the British Consulate to get a monthly check for $100, the maximum amount Clifford could send from the United States.[299] They would then go to a bank and immediately cash the check, which had to suffice for a month's worth of rent, food, and school tuition until the next check arrived. As Milly recalled later:

> *"Mom and I would go to a restaurant that, before the communists came, she and Ng Yee would patronize. With the owner's permission, Mom and I would sort through their discarded vegetables that were in cartons."* [300]

Miao Ying enlisted the help of her older children for household chores and care of the younger kids. YaoTim and 5-year-old Milly helped with 1-year-old Joseph Albert.[301] To lighten the financial strain, Miao Ying decided to send her youngest daughter, 3-year-old Dolly, to live with her sister Ng Yee's family. Her four older sons – Edward, George, Robert, and Philip – were responsible for some household chores and school but were otherwise left to their own devices, sometimes with unplanned and unwanted results.[302] These were some of Miao Ying's survival strategies during this most difficult time period in Shanghai.

Dolly lived with her aunt and uncle's family for most of the Lumsdaine family's remaining years in Shanghai. It helped the family's financial situation, but it also may have helped Ng Yee satisfy her deep desire for more children, as she had only been able to conceive one son. Dolly was chosen because she was "chubby and cute." Milly was not an option because she got sick almost every time she went to stay with Ng Yee's family.

The separation was very difficult for both mother and daughter. Miao Ying clearly understood how hard it would be for her 3-year old daughter,[303] and Dolly, even at that age, could tell that she was no longer living with her own family.[304] Dolly did have monthly visits with her mother and siblings at the family home, and occasionally the family visited her at Ng Yee's house. This separation left Dolly with only a few recollections of interactions with her own family during that time.[305]

One of Dolly's strongest recollections was when she was 6 years old and had been living with her aunt's family for about three years. Dolly, Miao Ying, Ng Yee and Yuk Chuen were socializing at a dance hall when a glass

of scalding water spilled on Dolly's chest, causing her to wail in great pain. Miao Ying carried the crying Dolly in her arms all the way home, talking to her in a comforting voice. As tough and unshakable as Miao Ying was, she had no qualms about bringing out her softer, nurturing side for her children.[306]

Miao Ying relied on Ng Yee, both for taking Dolly into her home and for lending Miao Ying money, but it came at significant personal cost. Miao Ying was greatly embarrassed by the obvious disparity in wealth, and her younger sister was not always gracious about lending her money, sometimes belittling her in the process.[307] YaoTim remembered one occasion when her mother gave her a small, filigree gold ring. When Ng Yee learned of it, she questioned her sister about how she could afford to buy such a ring for her daughter while finding it difficult to repay the money Ng Yee had loaned her. Miao Ying took the gold ring back from YaoTim – it was one of the rare occasions when YaoTim ever saw her

A day in the park: Top, Miao Ying and 3-year-old Dolly; center, sisters Ng Yee and Miao Ying; bottom, Ng Yee and Dolly. For several years after Clifford and Chuck left for the U.S. Dolly lived with her aunt and uncle and their family.

mother cry – sold it, and gave the money to her sister, bringing young YaoTim with her for a lesson on maintaining dignity despite poverty.[308]

... AND THEN THERE WERE SEVEN

In December 1951, five months after Clifford and Charlie left, Miao Ying decided that she would try to get the rest of the family out of China, despite the financial and political difficulties.[309] The family barely had enough money each month to survive. Also, the United States no longer had an embassy or consulate in Shanghai at which to obtain the necessary passport and exit visa for leaving China.

Miao Ying began the process by sending 15-year-old YaoTim to the British Consulate in Shanghai. Because she had dual citizenship – U.S. because Clifford was American, and British because she was born in Hong Kong while it was a British colony – YaoTim was able to obtain a British passport and exit visa to leave China for Hong Kong. Then, once in Hong Kong, she could exchange her British passport for a U.S. passport and join her father and older brother in the United States.[310]

Miao Ying did not want her teenage daughter traveling to Hong Kong alone, so she decided to accompany YaoTim and stay with her in Hong Kong until she could board a ship for the United States.[311] Miao Ying found reliable care for her other seven children while she would be away and then set about planning their trip.[312]

YaoTim's passport showing admission to the U.S. in February 1952

Having already pushed the limits of her sister's generosity by borrowing large sums of money for Charlie's hospitalization, Miao Ying had to find another loan source to cover her and YaoTim's fare for the train trip from Shanghai to Hong Kong, a distance of more than 1,200 miles. The kind sister of YaoTim's teacher, Mrs. Lueck, made the substantial loan, which Miao Ying repaid on her return to Shanghai.[313]

Miao Ying's good friend and benefactor in Hong Kong, Hun Tse (Ah Hun), who also was Charlie's godmother

Government or railroad regulations at that time required that Miao Ying, a Chinese national, ride in the third-class section of the train to Hong Kong. YaoTim, with U.S./British citizenship, was relegated to ride separately in second class. Throughout the trip, Miao Ying was cautious not to show any connection between herself and her daughter; she was afraid of arousing suspicion from the Chinese government officials or even the police. Miao Ying boarded the train separately and carefully approached YaoTim's seat only a couple of times to check on her and provide instructions on what to do when they reached Canton. She warned her daughter not to visit her third-class section of the train but assured YaoTim that she would always be watching over her from a distance. YaoTim sensed her mother's worry and concern, even though Miao Ying was trying to display calm for her daughter's sake. Miao Ying's tone and manner conveyed to YaoTim that this trip was deadly serious and that the slightest misstep could be disastrous.[314]

Once during the trip, Chinese officials took YaoTim and the other foreigners to be interrogated by soldiers, but then she was released. When the train stopped in Canton for the night, Miao Ying rented a room for herself and YaoTim, but they did not enter the room together. The room was reserved for foreigners, so Miao Ying waited and snuck in much later.[315]

When they reached Hong Kong, Miao Ying and YaoTim stayed with Miao Ying's good friend Hun Tse, also known as Ah Hun. The wife of a wealthy Hong Kong merchant, Ah Hun was forever grateful to Miao Ying for looking out for her and giving her financial help when she was a teenager.[316] It took Miao Ying and YaoTim nearly a month to arrange for YaoTim's departure on a ship bound for the United States.[317] During that time, they had to raise all the money for YaoTim's voyage to the U.S. and Miao Ying's return train ticket to Shanghai, as well as money to repay what she borrowed for their train tickets from Shanghai to Hong Kong.[318] Miao Ying was becoming increasingly worried about, and anxious to return to, the seven children she had left behind in Shanghai.[319]

But Miao Ying's most difficult obstacle in Hong Kong was saying goodbye to her eldest daughter. She looked forward to rejoining her other children, but she was heartbroken at having to say goodbye to YaoTim, who would travel 7,000 miles away, to another continent on the other side of the world. Miao Ying lectured YaoTim repeatedly about staying safe while traveling; about not leaving the ship until it arrived in the United States; and about "becoming a woman," knowing that her teenage daughter would mature into adulthood without her guidance. For all of her strength, Miao Ying's softer side broke through, and she cried uncontrollably. A friend finally had to force her from the ship as embarkation approached at midnight.[320]

Miao Ying needed that inner strength when she returned to Shanghai to deal with her cunning, rambunctious, and self-described "unmanageable" second-oldest son.[321] In the year after Clifford and Charlie left for the U.S., 14-year-old Edward had run-ins with gangsters, was twice questioned by the police, and once needed to be bailed out. He was disciplined repeatedly for fighting and finally was expelled from school for truancy and other bad behaviors.[322] Both Miao Ying and Edward realized it would be best for him to leave Shanghai before he got into more serious trouble with the law.[323] The Communist regime was not particularly kind to rebellious teenagers like Edward who, despite his youth, stood 5-feet, 10-inches tall and could easily be mistaken for an adult.

So, at the end of July 1952, Edward was ready to leave Shanghai and all the troubles it contained for him. He borrowed some money from a kindly Catholic priest to pay for the train fare to Hong Kong. Miao Ying met him at the station and gave him a four-canister metal food bucket with pork, rice, vegetables, and dessert. She told him not to eat all of the food at once since it would be a two-day trip. She also put a note in his food bucket wishing him well on his journey and urging him to leave his troublesome past behind and make something of his life. With that, Edward was more than ready to begin his journey to the United States.

In the span of just a year from 1951 to 1952, the Lumsdaine family in Shanghai shrank from 11 people to seven, with Clifford and the three oldest children having left China for the U.S. The six remaining children, ages 2 to 11, were still quite a handful for Miao Ying, but she perservered, as was her character.[324]

Managing the children also involved managing their mischief and its consequences. One incident involved her overly clever son Robert and her otherwise well-behaved daughter Milly. The story became legendary and laughable among Lumsdaine family members,[325] but in communist Shanghai 1952, it must have caused Miao Ying substantial anxiety and stress.

Late one afternoon, she left the two children at home to take naps while an older woman, possibly a neighbor, babysat them. The babysitter must have left the house at some point because Robert and Milly awoke in the dark, scared and alone. Robert, who was 10, convinced 6-year-old Milly that someone was hiding in the large armoire where their mother stored most of the family's household goods. To discover who might be hiding inside, the children yanked forcefully on the door, dislodging the mirror on the front.[326] The mirror fell to the floor and shattered, much to the children's surprise and shock.

Fearing Miao Ying's expected anger and punishment, Robert cleverly devised a plan to lay blame on alleged burglars and avoid personal responsibility. He persuaded Milly to help him scatter belongings from drawers and overturn pots and pans to set the scene.[327] The children then told the neighbors their home had burglarized, and the neighbors called the police. The

*A mirrored armoire similar to the one Robert and Milly
broke and then tried to blame on burglars*

police examined the scene and told Miao Ying to bring Robert and Milly with her to the police station the next day. That night, Robert carefully rehearsed with Milly the made-up story of the burglary and threatened her not to confess the truth, lest they suffer their mother's discipline. However, when the police separately questioned the two of them the next day, Milly confessed that they broke the mirror and staged the burglary. Unbeknownst to the children, however, much more was at stake than a broken mirror: Miao Ying had hidden in the house the family's most valuable remaining possessions – a small amount of jewelry and gold. Had the police found out, she could have been subjected to arrest, imprisonment, and confiscation of her property.[328]

Clockwise from top left: Philip, Miao Ying, Robert, Milly, Joseph Albert, and Dolly around the time of their departure from China. George is absent perhaps because he was an American citizen, and this was an official exit photo for the Chinese government.

Another incident involved George, Robert, and Philip. A cat often slept near the stove and would hiss if the boys, while trying to keep warm, approached the stove. To persuade the cat to leave, the boys tipped over a pot of hot water that sent the cat off screaming in pain and removed a patch of fur from its skin. Miao Ying was displeased when she found out and chased the three of them around with a feather duster as they tried to escape, running around and jumping from bed to bed.[329] Ultimately, they all received punishment from the hard, bamboo side of the feather duster and made the customary and proper apology to their mother, which involved bringing her hot tea on their knees while verbally apologizing for their transgressions.[330]

Joseph Albert rides a toy tractor in a Shanghai park.

With six active, imaginative children came many more mischievous escapades, some stereotypically childish and others completely outlandish, such as removing and selling some of the house's copper wiring.[331] Still, the children were well cared for and even enjoyed some regular childhood pleasures, such as Joseph Albert riding a toy tractor in the park.[332]

But Miao Ying never lost sight of her goal of taking her children out of China and reuniting them with their father and older siblings in the United States. From 1951 through 1953, she worked tirelessly to obtain exit visas from the Communist Chinese government for all of the family members still in Shanghai, but her requests were repeatedly rejected. Many times, she returned home from the government offices frustrated and tearful, although she tried not to show it in front of the children.[333]

By 1953, Miao Ying had deduced that the government's reluctance to issue exit visas to the family might have been due to Clifford's monthly $100

Clockwise from top left: George, Miao Ying, Philip, Robert, Milly, Joseph Albert, and Dolly, summer 1954

81

check.[334] Communist government officials may have wanted the continued inflow of U.S. currency into their economy, or they may have seen no need to let her leave as long as she and her children had money to live on. Regardless, Miao Ying concluded that Clifford needed to stop sending money if the family was to be allowed to leave China. However, she could not simply write this in a letter because she knew that all of her incoming and outgoing mail was monitored by government officials. Instead, she devised a plan whereby a friend of hers who was traveling to Hong Kong would send a letter to Clifford explaining that he would have to stop sending Miao Ying money if he ever wanted to see her and the children again.[335]

Clifford received her message and stopped sending the monthly payments. Miao Ying began selling off her personal property to support the family. Seemingly destitute, she approached the government officials once again to request exit visas to Hong Kong, telling them that she and her children could be taken care of if only she could leave China so her husband could support them. At first, the bureaucrats were reluctant, claiming that the Communist government would take care of its own people and that they would approve public assistance to support her and the children. But public assistance lasted less than a week.

Three days later, Miao Ying and her six children finally received their exit visas to leave Shanghai. The date was July 4, 1955 – Independence Day in the United States.[336]

LAST TRAIN TO HONG KONG

Before leaving Shanghai, Dolly, who was still living with Ng Yee, came down with a fever, and Miao Ying asked the government for a delay. The government then threatened to cancel the visas, so the family could not wait. Their departure was tearful and traumatic for Miao Ying, who had spent most of her adult life in Shanghai, and for the children, all of whom were born and lived their entire lives there. Ng Yee and Yuk Chuen took Dolly to the Shanghai train station, where the two adults had a heated discussion; Ng Yee wanted to keep Dolly in Shanghai, while Yuk Chuen insisted that Dolly board the departing train.[337] Yuk Chuen persevered, and Dolly

A passenger train similar to the one taken by the Lumsdaine family operating on the Canton-to-Kowloon line in the 1950s.

rejoined her birth family. Some of Miao Ying's other relatives also met them at the train station. All were crying as the seven Lumsdaines boarded the train and finally left Shanghai.[338]

The trip to Hong Kong would detour through Canton. Although the family had exit visas from the Chinese government, they still needed entry visas from the British government to enter Hong Kong.[339] One of Miao Ying's friends told her it would be easier to obtain entry visas in Canton than in Shanghai; the friend also told her the family would be welcome to stay with his brother's family in Canton.[340] Miao Ying and the children spent the entire 1,100-mile trip from Shanghai to Canton in the train's third-class section, the only mode of transportation the family could afford. They only had room to sit; none of them could lie down to sleep. Because the family left in haste, they took with them no more than the bare necessities – literally only what they could collectively carry.[341] For Miao Ying, this meant leaving behind a lifetime of accumulated possessions and tangible memories. Even the children's trophies were left behind.[342]

After the family arrived in Canton, they stayed with Miao Ying's friend's brother and his family for almost a month as they waited for their Hong Kong entry visas to be issued by the British Consulate. The upstairs apartment where the family stayed was quite spacious and had a small balcony overlooking the street. The hosts must have been people of some substance, as Miao Ying's friend took her and Dolly to an opera during their stay in Canton.[343]

As was often the case with those who were better off in 1950s China, the family was, unbeknownst to the Lumsdaines, being investigated by the Communist Chinese government. The man of the house had been a member of the Nationalist Government's army before the Communist Party takeover in 1949. He apparently had failed to disclose that fact to the new government, and they caught up with him while the Lumsdaines were staying with his family.[344]

Philip recalls that he answered the front door one afternoon to find three police or army officers, two of whom had pistols drawn.[345] The officer in charge asked to enter. He then asked Philip where the man of the house was. Philip responded that the man was in the kitchen. One of the officers went to the kitchen and brought the man out. He had been working on the stove and begged for the opportunity to clean off the soot that covered him. They told him no, handcuffed him, and brought him into a large room where those in the house, including Miao Ying and the children, were told to sit in chairs near the walls. While one of the officers read the charges against the man from a scroll, the other two officers stood by the doorway, still holding their pistols, with the man standing in between them.[346] After reading the charges, they left, taking the man with them. His wife, who had been out shopping, later told Miao Ying that her husband was convicted and sentenced to five years in prison for not having disclosed his involvement with the Nationalist army.[347]

Aside from the trauma Miao Ying and the children sustained from witnessing the man's arrest by armed officers, further collateral damage was to come. The man's wife told her neighbors that her husband's arrest was "because of the Americans" who were living with them. With that turn of events, Miao Ying decided it was best to move the entire Lumsdaine family out to a small room in a bargain Canton hotel that she could barely afford. It was very cramped for seven people, but fortunately, the stay was brief. Shortly thereafter, the family received entry visas allowing them to leave for Hong Kong.[348]

The border crossing at Lo Wu as it appeared in 1950s

The train from Canton took approximately 3½ hours to travel 90 miles to the Lo Wu border crossing into Kowloon, which at the time was part of the British-controlled territory that included Hong Kong. Because Miao Ying could not afford seats for the entire family, some of the children had to sit on the floor.[349] This would not be the most eventful part of the journey, however, as a truly traumatic experience awaited the family at the border.

CROSSING TO FREEDOM

In 1955, the Kowloon-Canton Railway Corporation still owned and operated the train route, as it had since 1910. However, since the Communist Party takeover of China in October 1949, the train no longer allowed passengers to travel continuously from Canton to Kowloon. All passengers had to get off the train at Lo Wu station, where the Lo Wu Bridge marked the border between Communist-controlled China and British-controlled Kowloon.[350] After disembarking, passengers would undergo inspection and interrogation by armed Chinese soldiers before crossing over the bridge on foot, carrying all their possessions with them.

Years later as an adult, Philip recalled in detail the frightening ordeal he experienced as an 11-year old boy:

> "Most of our belongings were in a small wooden basket, the same
> one that hung in the loft in Shanghai. The officials took Mom some-
> where to search her. Mom was worried about her six children
> being left there with the Communist officials. She later told us that
> they searched her, and they even went through her hair. But Mom
> had hidden anything of value – rings, jade, etc. – in pockets sewn
> into the inside of George's, Robert's, and my pants, near the belt
> area. None of us were searched." [351]

Milly also had precious contraband – several gold chains – sewn into her clothing, but she also was not searched by the soldiers.[352]

While only Miao Ying was subjected to a physical search, the border guards did look through all of the family's belongings for items of significant value that they could confiscate, Philip said:

> "All of us were scared and in shock but not crying. The Commu-
> nist officials asked about Dad's stamp book and took out some of
> the stamps. They searched the wicker basket and found a brush
> that a housekeeper had used in the hotel. It was a cleaning brush,
> somewhat larger than a paintbrush but smaller than a broom.
> The Communist officials questioned us kids about whether we
> had stolen it. They asked us because Mom was still away being
> searched separately. We told them that we did not know how the
> brush got there…We were shocked by the search, by Mom being
> gone, and by the brush questioning." [353]

The soldiers found no contraband or items of significant value, so the family was allowed to proceed across the Lo Wu bridge into British-controlled Kowloon. Still scared from the searches and interrogation, the children looked to their mother and felt reassured by her confidence. Fulfilling the first part of a goal that she had been working toward for years – at great personal risk but with the future of her family in mind – Miao Ying started walking and bravely led her children across the bridge and out of Communist China.[354]

7

ARRIVALS

THE HONG KONG YEARS, PART 2

After the family crossed the border, a bus took them all to downtown Kowloon.[355] Upon arriving, all of the children were distressed and hungry. Since leaving Canton early in the morning, they had not eaten. Miao Ying was keenly aware of her children's plight, but she simply had no money to buy food on the journey, having spent all she had on the Canton hotel and the train fares.[356]

In Kowloon, they were met by Miao Ying's niece, Bieu Tse, who had lived with them as a child. She was dressed in her nurse's uniform and was on her way to work. Miao Ying tried to explain to Bieu Tse that the children hadn't eaten all day and were famished, but Bieu Tse didn't grasp the urgency of the situation and left for her job after a quick greeting. This treatment greatly upset Miao Ying, who had taken Bieu Tse into her family back in Shanghai when Bieu Tse had been orphaned.[357] It was a very unpleasant surprise that left her wondering how she would find food and shelter for her six tired, hungry children. But as usual, Miao Ying took control of the situation. She contacted a lady friend who lived in Kowloon, and when the family arrived at her apartment, the friend immediately offered food to the six extremely hungry children.[358]

The simple food she offered was a delicious repast for the ravenous family and soothed their acute hunger pangs. As Milly remembered later:

Undated photo of Miao Ying with her six younger children after escaping Communist China to British-controlled Kowloon, near Hong Kong. Clockwise from top left, Philip, George, Robert, Milly, Dolly, and Joseph Albert

"This lady asked if the kids were hungry, and we said yes. The lady then went to a bakery nearby to get loaves of bread. It was white bread, and we put butter and white sugar on it. We were starving, so we ate several loaves of it. Her place was an upstairs flat, and you could smell the bakery nearby." [359]

Milly's siblings similarly remember this momentous meal, their first in this new land away from the only home they had known.

The generous friend also offered to let the family stay in the apartment where she lived with her husband and two daughters. While the Lumsdaines were grateful to have shelter, it was quite crowded for them and their hosts. There were no extra beds, so the family slept with blankets on the floor. [360] Fortunately, after a month or two, Miao Ying finally found a place they could call their own, with the financial assistance of her two oldest sons.

When the family first arrived in Hong Kong, Ed was in the U.S. Air Force, and he was able to obtain free passage to the island through the military. When Ed saw his mother for the first time, she was "beside herself because the family had just gotten to Hong Kong from Shanghai and had no money." [361] Later, Chuck, who was in the U.S. Army, also was able to take leave and secure passage to Hong Kong through the military. The two of them provided the money that Miao Ying used to buy the family's first groceries and a place for her and the six children to live in Hong Kong. [362]

Eventually, money would come from Clifford and YaoTim as well, but the amounts did not allow for much more than paying rent and school tuitions and buying groceries on a month-to-month basis. Clifford and the three older children did not lack the desire to provide more money for the rest of the family, but they also were living from month to month after sending whatever money they could.

SAI YEUNG CHOI STREET HOME

It was challenging for Miao Ying to find a place to stay in 1950s Kowloon with little money, an absent spouse, and six young children. The prevailing

Charlie, left, and Edward – who went by Chuck and Ed after moving
to the U.S. – had joined the military and were able to visit their mother
and siblings shortly after the family arrived in Kowloon. Miao Ying's two
oldest sons provided funding for the apartment on Sai Yeung Choi Street
and the family's first groceries after escaping China's Communist regime.

biases in that era in Hong Kong likely worked against her. Biracial children had a harder time in Hong Kong because they weren't fully accepted by the British or the Chinese.[363] Undaunted, Miao Ying proceeded with her housing search by going alone or taking only two or three of the six children with her.[364]

She finally found a landlord, Ho Tek Fong, who was willing to rent her a room in a flat on Sai Yeung Choi Street. The flat was located off of Boundary Street, the main road separating Kowloon's New Territories in the north from older, downtown Kowloon in the south.[365]

"Mom only brought three kids with her to see the landlord and later brought the rest of the kids," George said later. "However, Mr. Ho was a really nice man and said OK to all six kids."[366] The family and Mr. Ho eventually became close friends; Miao Ying even helped him find a spouse. Years later, he stayed briefly with the Lumsdaine family in the United States when he immigrated in the 1960s.[367]

Although the Lumsdaine family home in Kowloon would seem inadequate by U.S. standards, it was considered an above-average residence by Hong Kong standards. The entire home consisted of a large corner room, punctuated by many windows allowing for plenty of light and air circulation. It was adjacent to the entryway on the ground floor of a multistory apartment building.[368] The flat's other rooms were occupied by Mr. Ho and several other tenants.[369]

The room measured approximately 15 feet by 20 feet, and in that space, Miao Ying and the six kids ate, slept, did their homework, and kept all their earthly possessions. George, Robert, and Philip slept in bunk beds[370] while Milly, Dolly and Joseph Albert slept next to their mother in one large bed, which consisted of a flat sheet of wood on which bedding materials were laid out at bedtime.[371] This same sheet of wood may have been used by the entire family for eating, homework, mah-jongg, and other activities.[372] For storage, there was a 5-foot-tall cupboard with a set of cane or wire double doors, where food was kept beneath in drawers. The family's cooking pots and pans were kept in the communal kitchen shared by Mr. Ho and all of his tenants who lived in the ground-floor flat that he owned.[373]

The landlord and all tenant families shared one bathroom, one toilet area, one kitchen, and a courtyard with a small wooden door that led to Poplar Street.[374] The single bathroom consisted of a sink and a bathtub that was separated from the toilet area by a door. One can only imagine the difficulties for the 14 occupants of the flat – seven adults, three teenage boys, and four younger children – to share one bathroom and one toilet. Still, everyone appears to have generally cooperated with each other in peace and harmony, albeit with some stretching of the virtues of patience and tolerance.[375]

By all accounts, Landlord Ho was an extremely kind man whose generosity showed itself in a number of ways. He took the Lumsdaine children to parks and on other outings. Sometimes, he bought them treats.[376] When money ran short for Miao Ying at the end of the month, Mr. Ho allowed her to pay the rent late.[377] He also hired Robert and Philip to work at a small tie shop that he owed in downtown Kowloon off of the main commercial thoroughfare of Nathan Road.[378] This was usually during busy seasons such as at Christmas,

Safely out of China, Miao Ying and Robert were all smiles in front of the Sai Yeung Choi Street house in Kowloon.

*Clockwise from left: the family's landlord in Kowloon,
Ho Tek Fong; Robert, George, Philip, Milly, Joseph
Albert, and Dolly*

when Robert and Philip were able to work and earn some spending money
of their own, as their mother did not insist on them turning the money over
to her even if the family budget was otherwise stretched thin.[379]

Mr. Ho also had to tolerate some stereotypical children's shenanigans.
On one occasion, he allowed young Joseph Albert to play a martial arts
contest with him using a long stick as a pretend weapon. Unfortunately, in
his exuberance, Joseph Albert poked Mr. Ho in his ribs with such force that
it caused him serious pain. Still, Mr. Ho walked away without complaining.
When Miao Ying learned of the incident later – as siblings are perennially
prone to tattle on each other – Joseph Albert had his turn with his mother's
"feather-duster discipline."[380]

On another occasion, Mr. Ho's German shepherd dog had the misfortune
of lying under the table where Dolly wanted to put her feet. Dolly could see
nothing wrong with simply kicking the animal to get him to move. The dog
reacted instinctively, biting Dolly's offending leg and drawing blood with

93

two deep puncture wounds that required a doctor's attention. The doctor filed a report with the authorities, who forced Mr. Ho to take his dog to the pound to be put to sleep.[381] Surprisingly, the good-natured landlord made no reprisals against Miao Ying or her children for this unfortunate turn of events.

MIAO YING: COPING IN KOWLOON

The years in Hong Kong passed relatively uneventfully. Miao Ying made do with what little financial and social resources she had in order to provide food, shelter, and schooling for her six children. With very limited income and no other financial assets, she once again had to rely on her courage and cunning. Most importantly, the family was safe, and all

Clockwise from top left: Dolly, Milly, Miao Ying and Joseph Albert (holding toy pistol) in the single-room Kowloon home on Sai Yeung Choi Street

From left, Robert, Philip, Milly, and Dolly next to the fence around the Hong Kong Police Recreation Area across the street from their house

six Lumsdaine children went to school, where they performed well and avoided any serious trouble.

In the fall of 1955, the year the family arrived in Hong Kong, Miao Ying enrolled all the children – except the youngest, Joseph Albert – in school. Milly and Dolly attended St. Francis of Assisi Primary School. This was the first time either of them had received any formal education. At 7, Dolly was a year older than most of her peers when she started first grade. Milly, who was 9, also started first grade, albeit in a different classroom than Dolly.

In 1957, Miao Ying enrolled Joseph Albert in first grade at St. Francis of Assisi, also at age 7. The delay likely was due to the financial strain of already paying tuition for five children in private school. No free schooling was available to the Lumsdaines in Hong Kong.[382]

Meanwhile, George, Robert, and Philip all enrolled at St. Francis Xavier's College, the equivalent of an American secondary or high school.[383] George started in eighth grade and had completed 10th grade by the time he left Hong Kong for the U.S. in 1958. Although they had only finished fourth

95

and third grade, respectively, in Shanghai, Robert and Philip started in seventh grade in Hong Kong. Despite this seeming disadvantage, Robert did quite well in school, remaining first or second academically in his class of 43 students. Philip held his own but was admittedly an average student compared to his older brother.[384]

St. Francis Xavier's was known less for its academic prestige than for its acceptance of boys with different racial backgrounds, from underprivileged homes, or with disciplinary problems. One notable student who attended while George, Robert, and Philip were there was a young Bruce Lee, who later became an actor, director, and perhaps the most famous martial artist in history.[385]

Both St. Francis of Assisi and St. Francis Xavier's were close enough to home that all six children could easily walk to school.[386] While expensive

The family's landlord sometimes hired Robert, pictured, and Philip to work in his downtown Kowloon tie shop.

*Miao Ying and Joseph Albert in the open courtyard next to the kitchen of
the house on Sai Yeung Choi Street*

to attend, the private schools did give tuition breaks to the family.[387] Miao Ying occasionally reminded the children that it was their duty to study and work hard at school because their tuitions were a monthly financial hardship for the family.[388]

Miao Ying constantly struggled to cover their monthly expenses. After paying for rent and groceries, little remained to pay the children's tuitions.[389] Thankfully, she and the children, now between the ages of 5 and 15, no longer suffered from the food shortages they had experienced in Shanghai. However, aside from occasional and meager charity, the only steady support they received was the money Clifford, Chuck, YaoTim, and Ed sent from the U.S.[390]

For Miao Ying, earning income in Hong Kong would have been difficult, if not impossible. Unlike in Shanghai, she no longer had help with child care or household duties. These daily responsibilities would have made working outside the home infeasible, even if there had been gainful employment opportunities for a 45-year-old woman with a second-grade education.[391] However, Miao Ying was a very strong and resourceful woman who loved her children beyond measure. She also had hope for the future and worked tirelessly in her efforts to bring the entire family back together again in the United States, where she dreamed that they could all prosper.[392]

CLIFFORD: CONDEMNED IN CALIFORNIA

Contrary to the America of Miao Ying's dreams, the country Clifford and Chuck had encountered in 1951 did not welcome them with open arms upon their arrival in California.

The Korean War had begun the previous year, and the U.S. supported South Korea. North Korea was backed by the Soviet Union and Communist China, meaning the U.S. was at war with the country Clifford and Chuck had just left.

America was boiling over with "McCarthyism,"[393] the popular anti-communist campaign propagated by Joseph McCarthy, a Republican U.S. senator from Wisconsin, and anyone who had any past or present association with any communist group or communist country was deemed a suspected communist.

Above, St. Francis Xavier's College school picture; Philip and Robert are in the second row from top, fifth and sixth from left. On the front row on the far right is one of the school's most famous alumni, actor and martial arts expert Bruce Lee. At left, Joseph Albert in uniform of St. Francis of Assisi Primary School

In the eyes of his fellow U.S. citizens, Clifford had three strikes against him: He had just returned from China, he also had lived most of his adult life there, and his Chinese wife and half-Chinese children still lived there. Even American-born Chinese found themselves associated with "communism, a doctrine considered by most Americans to be the height of treason,"[394] between 1950 and 1954, when Senator McCarthy was publicly accusing government officials, university professors, actors and directors, and many other Americans of being communists.

Chuck did not fare much better, given his Eurasian looks and his birth in China. Joining the U.S. Army softened the blow; he was sent to Hawaii, where he received a steady paycheck, and many people mistook him for a Hawaiian local.[395] Also, Hawaii was not yet part of the U.S.; it would not achieve statehood for another eight years.

Clockwise from top left: Robert, George, Miao Ying, Philip, Dolly, Joseph Albert, and Milly standing in front of the fence around the Hong Kong Police Recreation Area across the street from their home in 1955.

Life would not go easily for Clifford, who felt a keen responsibility to support his wife and children back in China. He first applied for work at American President Lines, the company at which he had so successfully risen through the ranks while in China.[396] He was told flat-out that as long as he was married to a Chinese woman, he would never get a job there.[397] This disappointing response was followed by a disheartening succession of unsuccessful attempts to secure employment.[398] While he occasionally found work, opportunities were few and far between. One prospective employer told him his application had to be processed by the United States Federal Bureau of Investigation (FBI).[399]

In fact, Clifford was investigated by both the FBI and the Central Intelligence Agency (CIA). This was not because he was a high-profile or notorious target; it resulted from anti-Communist hysteria – the "Red Scare" that McCarthy perpetuated.[400] Despite Clifford's lifelong lack of interest or involvement in political matters, parties, or organizations; his unfamiliarity with any of Marx, Lenin, or Mao's works; and his repeated protestations to the contrary, a CIA memorandum dated three days after his arrival in San Francisco lists him as "a Communist sympathizer" with an "outlook that is more Chinese than American."[401] Within three months, the CIA had referred his case to the FBI, noting Clifford's "obvious Communist sympathies" and considering him "an indoctrinated Marxist, if not an active Communist in the accepted sense."[402]

The preposterousness of such allegations, aside from any lack of supporting evidence, is made more transparent by other obvious falsehoods in those documents, including the erroneous assertion that he was born on Nov. 6, 1901, in Washington, D.C. (the month and day were accurate, but the year was 1909, and the city was Seattle) and the incorrect statement that he "was not interned by the Japanese during their occupation of Shanghai."[403]

After receiving the CIA's referral, FBI agents regularly made surprise visits to interrogate Clifford, both at his residence and in public. They visited his workplaces and interviewed his neighbors, co-workers, and employers.[404] Their harassment was so pervasive and palpable that Clifford twice sent written complaints to FBI headquarters. His attempts to curb their intrusive activities were unsuccessful.[405] Clifford also was confronted by Chinese caricatures in the newspapers and at work.[406] Coworkers sometimes taunted and teased him at the workplace and in the lunch room. Their harassment took its toll psychologically.[407] Often, Clifford's intense honesty and fierce loyalty to his family caused him to lose his usual reserve and self-control, and he would retort angrily and sarcastically.[408] All of this made it nearly impossible for Clifford to find gainful employment, much less to keep a job for any length of time.[409]

(7-30-45)

Federal Bureau of Investigation
United States Department of Justice

au 67C

COMPLAINT FORM

CLIFFORD LUMSDAINE
Subject's Name and Aliases

SHARP & DOHME 132 2nd. St.
Address of Subject
INTERNAL SECURITY- C
Character of Case

Name of Complainant
SHARP & DOHME 132 2nd.
Address of Complainant
EX 2-5085
Telephone Number of Complainant.
4/14/52   2:50pm
Date and Time Complaint Received

DESCRIPTION OF SUBJECT: 36-Ht. 5ft. 8,Wt.-thin, Hair-Brown, Eyes-Blue. Married and has

8 children.

FACTS OF COMPLAINT: Complainant states subject has been employed by the Company for three

months and is Cashier and Personal Asst. to   Subject came

from China and constantyl condemns everything US and professes to be a Communist.

Subject is endeavroing to return to China and states he is going by way of MOSCOW.

A 1952 complaint by an unnamed co-worker of Clifford's to the San Francisco office of the FBI alleging that Clifford "professes to be a Communist"

This difficult situation was problematic for his family back in Hong Kong, and his lack of employment formed a significant stumbling block in Clifford and Miao Ying's plan to reunite the entire family in the U.S. as soon as possible.[410] After Miao Ying and the six children arrived in Hong Kong in 1955, their biggest obstacle was the lack of money for airplane or ship fares to the United States.

The family had few assets to fall back on. Clifford and Chuck had needed to borrow money to get out of China in 1951, and they left Shanghai with little more than the clothes on their backs. Then, after they arrived in the U.S., the loan had to be repaid.[411] Similarly, when YaoTim left in 1952, Miao Ying and Clifford borrowed, and eventually repaid, money for her transit. Although Ed left Shanghai with money given to him by a Catholic priest, he had to make his own way to the U.S. by working on a ship.[412] Upon arriving in the U.S. in 1952 and 1953, respectively, YaoTim and Ed had few possessions, and given their ages – YaoTim was almost

15½, Ed was three months short of 15 – little ability to immediately earn significant income.

Eventually, Clifford, Chuck, YaoTim, and Ed were able to earn enough money to support themselves and send money to the rest of the family in Hong Kong. However, it was difficult to accumulate enough money to bring the rest of the family from Hong Kong to the United States.[413] What Clifford and Miao Ying had hoped would be a quick family reunification in the U.S. would end up taking several years, with many hardships along the way.

Clifford, age 42, and YaoTim, age 15, in San Francisco in May 1952, shortly after YaoTim arrived in the United States

8

REUNION IN A NEW WORLD

A FAMILY MYSTERY SOLVED

In Hong Kong, Miao Ying worked with the U.S. Consulate to procure entry visas for herself and her five younger children, who were considered "stateless." George did not need a visa because he was considered a U.S. citizen at birth and had an automatic right to enter the country, but the entry visas for the other children required a signed immigration petition from Clifford. In the U.S., YaoTim worked through the immigration bureaucracy and beginning in 1955, attempted to get her father to sign the necessary petition.[414] However, Clifford inexplicably refused her repeated requests for his signature.[415]

On his mother's behalf, George wrote directly to his father in 1957, asking for his cooperation. He also wrote to YaoTim, encouraging her to persevere in her efforts to obtain Clifford's signature.[416] On the surface, Clifford's reluctance to cooperate may have seemed uncaring and perhaps even cruel. However, closer analysis of what he experienced at the time, coupled with his profound love of and loyalty to his wife and children, paints a very different picture.

McCarthyist harassment from the U.S. government and the public had made Clifford's return to his homeland a seemingly never-ending nightmare. Consistent with the mores of "the Greatest Generation,"[417] Clifford was silent about his suffering during that period and his underlying concerns about his family coming to the United States. He did eventually sign the petition, but the way it came about indicates the trauma he was experiencing at the time.

After Miao Ying and the six younger children escaped Communist China for Hong Kong in 1955, YaoTim asked Clifford about bringing the

rest of the family to the U.S. Clifford, who had been in the country for four years at that point, responded with "They're better off there." When YaoTim persisted, he became increasingly angry and dismissive, repeating that the rest of the family would fare better by staying in China.[418]

In 1956, the FBI visited YaoTim at home late one night. During their interrogation, they advised her that the rest of her family in Hong Kong could easily travel to the U.S. as Clifford's family members on a "non-quota" visa.[419] Despite this seemingly good

Miao Ying in her 1957 travel visa photo taken in Hong Kong

news, 20-year old YaoTim's persistent efforts to have her father sign the petition for the visas were rebuffed, and occasionally accompanied by angry exchanges between the two of them. Whether in frustration or desperation, YaoTim brought her parish priest with her, along with the papers to be signed, on her next visit to Clifford.

When the priest asked him why he would not sign the petition papers, Clifford once again replied with "They're better off there." The priest argued that even if it were the case that Clifford's family members were better off in Hong Kong, they wanted to come to the U.S., so he should respect their wishes. Clifford reluctantly signed the papers, but YaoTim's strong-arm tactics opened a rift between them, and Clifford would not speak to his eldest daughter or return any of her phone calls for the next two years.[420]

Clifford never explained his reluctance to signing the petition, so for most of their lives, the reason remained a mystery to the Lumsdaine children – except for Dolly, to whom Clifford revealed his motive when she asked him about it in 1972.

Clifford confided to her that after his experience with McCarthyism and the accompanying harassment from the government and the public, he feared that his family would be treated horribly in this country,[421] and he did not want them subjected to such prejudice and discrimination – or worse.[422] Perhaps he also held onto some lingering hope that world events would somehow change so he would be able to rejoin his wife and children in their homeland instead of the country of his birth, which he now found inhospitable and cruel.[423]

Far from being uncaring or apathetic, Clifford's reluctance to bring the rest of his family to the U.S. reflected his love and commitment for them and his need to protect them from a 1950s America that seemed so hateful of anything Chinese. For a man as devoted to family as Clifford was, the choice must have been as heart-wrenching for him as it was confusing and hurtful for the children, most of whom were unaware of his 1972 conversation with Dolly until she was interviewed in 2017 for the writing of this book. Clifford may have had conversations with Miao Ying about his reasons for not signing the petition earlier, but most of his children didn't know for certain for more than 60 years.

SIBLING SACRIFICES

In April 1958, after Clifford signed the petition, Miao Ying received entry visas to the United States for herself and the children. By then, the Lumsdaine family had also raised enough money to pay for the passage of at least two family members. The choice of sending George and Milly reflected the family's economic pragmatism.

George was almost 18 years old and presumably could get work and help earn the money needed to bring the rest of the family to the U.S. He accepted and understood his position as the oldest of the siblings still in Hong Kong as well as his responsibility to find a job in the U.S. Indeed, he would later

Milly and Philip at the Hong Kong airport in 1958 before Milly and George's departure for the U.S.

be instrumental in helping fund the passage of his siblings and mother to the United States.[424]

Milly was 11 years old and did not understand why she was being "picked on."[425] She did not want to leave her mother and siblings in Hong Kong to go live in the U.S. with her sister YaoTim, whom she barely remembered; Milly was 5 when YaoTim left for the United States. Why did she have to go instead of, say, Dolly? she asked Miao Ying. She felt that "she was being sent away to a stranger"[426]

At the airport, Miao Ying took great pains to explain everything to Milly. She crouched down to Milly's level and told her that she was a big girl now and that her older sister is not her mother, so she would need to be responsible for herself. Miao Ying also told Milly that she was chosen because she was the oldest daughter, but at 11 years old, she was still young enough to get a less expensive fare.[427] This was the most traumatic event that Milly could recall up to that point in her life, but she boarded the plane without resistance or loud protest, accepting – though not liking – the sacrifice of separating from her mother.[428]

When George and Milly arrived at San Francisco International Airport, they were met by their brother Ed and their uncle, Arthur Allen Lumsdaine. Ed was in the U.S. Air Force and had caught a flight to San Francisco; Arthur Allen, Clifford's biological half-brother – Arthur Henry's son with Gerry Strayer – lived in Berkeley. The two of them took George and Milly to stay with Hayden Schofield, an unusually kind and generous man who had been one of Chuck's older co-workers in San Francisco. Unfortunately, after just a few days, they had to leave because Mr. Schofield's neighbors "complained about the two Chinese kids" living there.[429] They had to move out quickly.

Urgently, Chuck called Gerry, Clifford's beloved stepmother, who drove down to San Francisco from Seattle. Gerry put George and Milly up in a hotel until other family members could come to the rescue.

Gerry was kind to them, treating them as her own grandchildren and helping them improve the little English they had learned from their schooling in Hong Kong.[430] Her generosity allowed YaoTim and her husband, Bob – whom she'd married in 1953 – enough time to relocate to Califor-

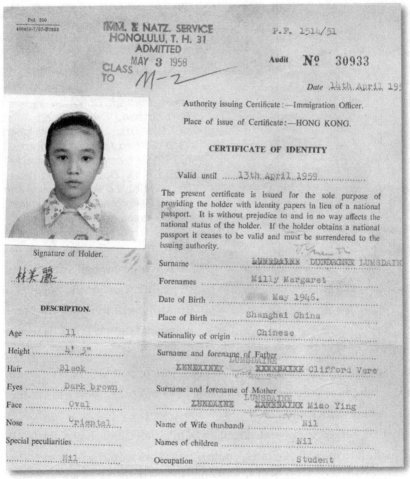

Certificate of Identity showing Milly's entry into the U.S. on May 3, 1958

Above, from left: Bob Allen, Yao-Tim's husband; two unnamed friends; YaoTim holding baby Robert "Bob" Clifford Allen, and Clifford, c. 1956. At left, clockwise from top left, YaoTim, Milly, Bob Allen, and Yao-Tim and Bob's children Theresa and Robert Clifford Allen in 1958 in front of the Truman Boyd apartments

nia from Kansas, where they had been living near Bob's mother and stepfather. YaoTim and Bob picked up Milly and took her into their home at Truman Boyd American Gold Star Homes, a large, government-sponsored housing campus in Long Beach; as a U.S. Navy veteran, Bob was eligible for government housing.[431] Chuck took George to Ventura, Calif., where Chuck and Ed shared an apartment.

By 1958, seven years after Clifford and Chuck left China, half of the family had made it to the United States; another two years would pass before Miao Ying and the four youngest kids were able to join them. Meanwhile, Chuck, YaoTim, Ed, George, and Milly worked diligently to take care of themselves, as well as to accumulate enough money to bring the rest of the family to the United States. Clifford was still struggling to find and keep meaningful employment as a result of the sham CIA and FBI investigations.[432]

The California Lumsdaines made substantial personal sacrifices in their housing, lifestyles, and work lives to save enough money to bring the rest of the family over from Hong Kong. Many of their daily sacrifices went unmentioned, perhaps forgotten through the passage of time or maybe because they wanted to remember only the happier events in their lives.

Chuck was four months shy of 18 years old when he left Shanghai for the U.S. with his father. They escaped China with so few possessions that Chuck had to borrow appropriate clothing for job interviews when they arrived in San Francisco. He was accepted for matriculation at the University of California, Berkeley, but he dropped out in order to work so he could send money to his mother in Hong Kong. Eventually, he joined the U.S. Army and sent Miao Ying most of his paycheck to support her and his siblings.[433]

As the oldest child, Chuck also took on the responsibility of collecting whatever money he could from Ed, YaoTim, and eventually George, to support the family in Hong Kong and save for their eventual travel to the United States.[434] Without his efforts, the rest of the family would not have made it to America.[435]

YaoTim was 15½ years old when she first set foot in the U.S. in 1952. After spending some time with her father and her brother Chuck in San Francisco, she married Bob Allen, whom she'd met at a movie theater while he was on shore leave from the Navy. They started their own family shortly thereafter.

In 1958, when Milly came to live with Bob and YaoTim, the couple already had two young children: Robert Clifford, who was 4, and Theresa, who was almost 1. At that time, YaoTim could not contribute financially toward bringing the rest of the family over from Hong Kong, but she did do all the paperwork for the family's immigration and travel arrangements.[436] All of these contributions – the financial, the bureaucratic, and the logistical – were indispensable to the family's ultimate reunion in the U.S.

YaoTim and Bob eventually took out a loan and gave the money to Chuck to complete the funding for bringing the rest of the family to the U.S. YaoTim never forgot the words her mother spoke to her, and likely to Chuck and Ed as well, before they left China: "Don't forget, your brothers and sisters are counting on you to bring everyone to America."[437] This admonition guided their lives, and later George's, for the years they lived and worked in U.S. until the family finally reunited.

Ed had worked a number of jobs and handed as much money as he could over to Chuck to support their family in China. After he entered the Air Force in 1954, Ed allocated a portion of his pay, with a matching portion contributed by the Air Force, to support Miao Ying and the kids, whom he signed on as his dependents.[438] After being honorably discharged from the Air Force, Ed moved in with Chuck and continued to hand over most of his earnings to fund the rest of the family's passage to America.[439]

George would become the final diligent wage-earner working toward helping the family reunite in the U.S. He, Chuck, and Ed shared the small apartment in Ventura, and Ed and George worked full-time at the Land Air Corporation at Point Mugu, Calif.[440] George also attended Ventura College full-time to obtain his Associate of Arts degree. Sometimes fatigue caught up with him, and he would take naps in the campus infirmary.

George handed over his entire paycheck to Chuck, who relentlessly pursued accumulating enough money to bring the family's Hong Kong contingent to the U.S.[441] Years later, Ed recalled that there was so little money left over for groceries that they would buy the cheapest bulk food, such as wheat germ, and eat only that for an entire week. When they ran out of money at the end of the month, their understanding landlord gave them permission to pay the rent late.[442]

By April 1960, through their frugal tenacity and self-sacrifice, Chuck, YaoTim, Ed, and George finally amassed enough money to buy passage for Miao Ying and their four youngest siblings to the United States.

A SLOW BOAT FROM CHINA

Miao Ying, Robert, Philip, Dolly, and Joseph Albert packed everything they owned and left Hong Kong on April 1, 1960, for the 19-day trip aboard the American President Lines ship *SS President Wilson*.[443]

Postcard depicting the SS President Wilson, *the ocean liner that carried Miao Ying, Robert, Philip, Dolly, and Joseph Albert to the United States.*

They slept in bunk beds in one small cabin, which despite its size did not feel crowded because they had shared one room for the six years they lived in Hong Kong.[444] The cabin had no windows; it was on one of the lowest decks of the ship. This was still better than the accommodations of many other Chinese passengers; they slept in a dormitory-style room on bunk beds or cots along with their luggage. The upper levels of the ship were reserved for the more well-off passengers, but Dolly and Joseph Albert found ways to sneak up to the upper decks, as Joseph Albert recalled:[445]

> *"I watched the ocean – there was no view from our deck below*
> *– threw bread and orange pieces to flying seagulls, which would*
> *catch them in the air. Found other kids to play with. Sixty years later,*
> *I still remember that vividly, especially just watching the ocean go*
> *by and feeling the breeze – still my favorite activity on cruises."*

First-time experiences for some of them aboard the ship included eating with a fork instead of chopsticks; having readily available fresh fruit, such as apples and oranges; and enjoying the taste of dry cereal with cow's milk.[446] Most of these experiences were likely new to Miao Ying as well. All of them made friends with other Chinese people aboard the ship. Miao Ying found people to play mah jongg, and Robert and Philip found other kids to play cards.[447]

The ship stopped at two ports in Japan. In Yokohama, Miao Ying took a taxi on shore with Robert, Philip, and Joseph Albert, leaving Dolly behind in the cabin because she had thrown a temper tantrum.[448] In later years, none of them could recall much of that onshore excursion except that it was a quick driving tour by taxi without stopping to eat or walk around much on shore. Perhaps memories of the war with Japan, which ended only 15 years earlier, were still too fresh for Miao Ying. It's possible that she still harbored resentment because of how Japanese soldiers had tortured her brother and imprisoned her husband as well as other hardships that she personally, and the Chinese people generally, suffered during the years of war and occupation.[449]

On April 14, 1960, the *SS President Wilson* entered its first U.S. port: Honolulu, Hawaii. There, the family was examined by medical and immigration

Piers 31 and 29 on San Francisco's Embarcadero, as they appeared from 1934 to 2008

April 19, 1960: In a waiting area on San Francisco's Embarcadero, Miao Ying, second from right, has a big smile after finally reaching the United States. At left are Hayden Schofield, a friend of Chuck's; George; and Chuck. Milly is at right.

officials.[450] Miao Ying took all of them on shore, and the family spent the entire day eating hot dogs at tables with linen, visiting a Catholic church on Fort Street, and attending the Kodak Hula Show on Waikiki Beach.[451] Miao Ying splurged on her kids that day, celebrating their first experience of an American city.

Five days later, the ship docked at its final destination: one of the historic piers along the Embarcadero in San Francisco.[452] This was the first time that Miao Ying, Robert, Philip, Dolly, and Joseph Albert had seen or set foot on the U.S. mainland.

Exiting the ship, the Lumsdaines found themselves and their luggage inside a cavernous warehouse almost three football fields long. A chain-link fence separated the arriving passengers from those who came to greet them. Miao Ying and the kids had anticipated Clifford, YaoTim, Chuck, and

George meeting them upon their arrival in this new land. To their shock and dismay, not a single one of their stateside family members was at the dock building in the early morning when they first arrived.

Chuck and George had planned to be there when the ship docked. Milly rode along with them; she was anxious to see her mother. Chuck was going to drive all night in his Volkswagen Beetle, from Ventura to San Francisco. The trip along U.S. Highway 101, the most direct route in 1960, would take seven hours. Separately, Bob and YaoTim picked up Clifford and planned to drive all night from Long Beach for what they expected would be an eight-hour trip to San Francisco. None of them could afford an overnight stay at a motel; driving all night was their only option.

Although Chuck's Volkswagen and Bob and YaoTim's six-passenger car were in good working order, both were older cars. Unexpectedly, both vehicles broke down on the way to San Francisco – Chuck's in Salinas and Bob and YaoTim's in Gilroy. Neither one knew that the other's car had broken down, and in the days before mobile phones, they had no way to contact each other.

In Bob and YaoTim's car, Clifford became overwrought that after 10 years of separation, he would not be present for his wife's arrival. YaoTim tried to calm him by mentioning that Chuck had left earlier and would be the familiar face and reassuring voice for Miao Ying.

Ever resourceful, Chuck had located a phone and called Hayden Schofield, his friend in San Francisco, and asked him to meet Miao Ying and her children at the dock. So, to Miao Ying's surprise, instead of their stateside family, an unfamiliar white man stood waiting for them on the other side of the chain-link fence.

Many of the Lumsdaine children thought this man was their dad – an understandable mistake given that it had been 10 years since any of the children had seen their father. Hayden Schofield introduced himself as Chuck's friend and told them Chuck had asked him to meet them at the dock.[453] He helped the family retrieve their luggage and pass through Customs inspections, which took most of the morning. Later that day, Chuck, George and Milly reached the port, much to Miao Ying's relief.

The ever-hospitable Mr. Schofield welcomed everyone to his San Francisco apartment to await the arrival of Clifford, YaoTim, and Bob. He had a small studio apartment that he shared with a roommate. It consisted of a single bedroom that also functioned as a living room, plus a small bathroom and kitchen area. With three Lumsdaine adults and five children, the studio became uncomfortably crowded. When the rest of the family arrived, there was standing-room only for the 12 people gathered in that small space. Instead of a joyful, long-dreamed-about reunion, the encounter was strained and stressful. Everyone was tense and fatigued from their long journeys. There was no time or inclination for extended greetings or conversation; Chuck, George, Bob, and YaoTim needed to get back on the road and drive all night, again, because they had to work the next day.[454] So instead of a celebratory reunion, all the family members packed themselves and their luggage into two small cars and began the long journey home.

Still, an undercurrent of joy and excitement permeated the difficult circumstances because the family finally was together again. From 1951 to 1960, Miao Ying and Clifford had lived an ocean apart on two different continents and lacked the money to visit or even telephone each other.[455] Their first meeting in the U.S. was undoubtedly stressful, perhaps even traumatic, although neither one ever said so. None of the children can clearly recall what their parents said or did during their long-awaited reunion that went so awry or the long car ride home.

Clifford and Miao Ying Lumsdaine, center, with their children and grandchildren in Southern California, July 1960; Clockwise from top left, Chuck; YaoTim; Robert; Philip; Milly; George; Joseph Albert; YaoTim's children Monica (on Miao Ying's lap), Robert, and Theresa (on Clifford's lap); and Dolly. Ed and his family were in Tennessee and are not pictured.

9

LIVING IN AMERICA

A typical Truman Boyd American Gold Star Home apartment building as it appeared in 1958

FIRST HOME: LONG BEACH

In April 1960, Miao Ying, Clifford, Dolly, and Joseph Albert moved into a small, ground-floor apartment at Truman Boyd American Gold Star Homes in Long Beach, in the same complex where YaoTim, Bob, and Milly lived.[456]

The apartment was fairly small, but the grounds surrounding the buildings were covered with spacious lawns. For a short time, Robert and Philip lived in Bob and YaoTim's apartment[457] after Milly, who missed her mother greatly, moved out to live with her parents. Miao Ying and Clifford continued to make their children's education a primary focus. They made sure

119

that their three youngest attended public school from April to June 1960 to finish out the school year and even enrolled Joseph Albert in summer school to improve his English skills.[458]

Due to their proximity in the same housing complex, Bob and YaoTim visited often. Miao Ying had never met Bob before coming to the U.S., but she took to him easily. He would sometimes drop by the apartment on his

Clifford and Joseph Albert on the lawn in front of their apartment building in 1960

motorcycle; this reminded Miao Ying of her youth, when she would ride on the back of her Chinese boyfriend's motorcycle.[459] As Bob did not speak Chinese, and Miao Ying did not speak English, they would communicate through gestures, and sometimes other family members would interpret.

None of the Lumsdaine children could ever recall hearing their parents raise their voices at each other, let alone argue, when they lived in China and Hong Kong.[460] However, Clifford and Miao Ying experienced some difficulties adjusting to each other in their first year back together in Long

Beach. Communication didn't always go smoothly, and faintly raised voices sometimes could be heard from behind closed doors.

On one occasion, after an argument with her husband, Miao Ying walked out of the house. She strode past an open field to a bus stop. Upon seeing that her mother had left in anger, Dolly ran after her and asked where she was going. Miao Ying said she did not know, but she just needed

Joseph Albert and Miao Ying in front of their Truman Boyd apartment building in 1960.

to leave. Dolly reminded her, "You can't even read a bus schedule. How will you know where to go?"[461] Eventually, she convinced Miao Ying to walk back home.

Joseph Albert recalled an instance from that first year in Long Beach when his father took him on a long walk to a convenience store. Although Joseph Albert didn't witness an argument, Clifford was upset after exchanging some words with Miao Ying. Clifford became quite fond of these walks, but 10-year old boys haven't the life experiences yet to appreciate a long walk's benefits, so for Joseph Albert, the walk just felt LONG. However, at the convenience store, Clifford rewarded him with a large Milky Way candy bar, which Joseph Albert had never tasted before. This special treatment by his father, whom he barely knew at the time, as well as his first taste of chocolate, created a fond memory Joseph Albert never forgot.[462]

The Lumsdaine family did not own a car while they were living in Long Beach. In 1961, bus fare was 15 cents per person for the 1.4-mile ride from home to St. Lucy's Catholic School, which the three youngest children attended after the brief stint in public school. Sometimes, even this small fare was unaffordable, and Milly, Dolly, and Joseph Albert would walk to and from school; this was just accepted as a fact of life.[463] They benefited from a generous program that gave vastly reduced tuition to families enrolling multiple children, and the children felt privileged simply to be able to attend a private Catholic school.[464]

To help translate and carry bags of groceries for their mother, some of the children regularly accompanied Miao Ying on the long walk to the nearest supermarket, McCoy's, which was 1.2 miles away in the same direction as St. Lucy's school.[465] Sometimes Clifford shopped with her, but more often, he stayed home, and she took one of the children with her.

Miao Ying needed an assistant, especially during her first year in the U.S., because she did not speak English, and the store personnel did not understand any of her several Chinese dialects. At the supermarket, she would have the child accompanying her ask the butcher for chicken feet, gizzards, or beef bones. At the time, those items were either given away for free or discarded,[466] and Miao Ying continued to use her penchant for and skill at conserving limited resources to make delicious meals from anything edible, just as she had done in China.

THE VENTURA YEARS

In the summer of 1961, Miao Ying and Clifford moved to a rental house on Wall Street in Ventura, Calif., with Milly, Dolly, and Joseph Albert. George, Chuck, and Ed were still living in Ventura, while Robert and Philip mostly lived at the Ojai Valley Inn, about 10 miles away, where they worked as

Joseph Albert on the front porch of the Lumsdaine family home on Wall Street in Ventura with Milly, left, in 1961 and with Miao Ying, right, in 1962

busboys and then as waiters. All five of the older boys moved around as they made their way through school, jobs, or the military,[467] but they all continued to visit their parents' home to play mah jongg,[468] eat their mom's delicious home-cooked meals, or just spend time with the family.

Chuck, George, Robert, and Philip continued contributing money to sustain the family members living in Ventura after 1961. Each gave Miao Ying whatever earnings were left over after they put aside money for basic living expenses.[469] Clifford did find some late-night shift work at a local laundromat in Ventura.[470] He mopped floors, wiped down machines, and kept the laundromat clean. Eventually, he was promoted to the day shift, where the owner entrusted him with collecting the money from the machines and making bank deposits. These responsibilities were in addition to his duties keeping the laundromat clean. However, he was not paid enough to support the family members still living at home.

Miao Ying found occasional part-time work cleaning tables or washing dishes at a Chinese restaurant or taking in sewing, but their combined

123

Miao Ying watches George; Pang, a family friend; Robert, and Philip playing mah jongg in the living room of the family home in Ventura.

incomes still proved insufficient for subsistence.[471] Consequently, and without complaint, the older children contributed greatly to the monthly family budget, accepting it as their duty as sons and daughters. Even after Robert, Milly, and George got married, their spouses consented to continuing the contributions with whatever they could afford to give.[472]

In 1963, when Joseph Albert turned 13, he was allowed to work with his father at the laundromat in the mornings before school. There, he helped mop floors and wipe down machines. Clifford kept meticulous records of the hours that his son worked and paid him by the hour for his efforts. He also helped his youngest child open his first bank account.

Although Clifford was typically reticent while they worked, this time together gave Joseph Albert an opportunity to learn discipline from a regular work schedule, the value of money, and a glimpse into his father's life. He recalls seeing not only how hard his dad worked but also how strong he was. Clifford regularly lifted large bags of salt weighing around 50 lbs.

up to chest height before dumping the salt into a tall water softener in the laundromat's utility room.[473]

Miao Ying and Clifford raised their last three children in the house on Wall Street from 1961 to 1969. Milly left in 1963 to live with YaoTim and Bob and finish her last years of high school before getting her own apartment in Orange County.[474] Dolly and Joseph Albert left to attend college in the San Francisco Bay Area in 1967 and 1969, respectively.[475] During the intervening years, Miao Ying continued adjusting to life in the U.S., and she and Clifford continued adjusting to life with each other after so many years of separation. Both of them continued to ensure that the last of their nine children did well in school and learned the lessons that would help them lead happy and productive lives.

George showing off his new sports car to his mother in the driveway of the Ventura home, c. 1963.

Two photos from a day in 1963. Above, Clifford and Miao Ying with their nine children: top row, from left: Robert, Philip, Chuck, Clifford, Miao Ying, Ed, YaoTim, and George; bottom row, from left: Dolly, Joseph Albert, and Milly. Below, they are joined by Ed's wife, Monika, holding their baby son, Andrew (in front of Ed); YaoTim's husband, Bob (between Miao Ying and YaoTim); YaoTim and Bob's son, Robert (in front of Clifford); their daughters Monica and Theresa (between Joseph Albert and Milly); and their daughter Donna (between Milly and Dolly.)

Miao Ying did her best to adapt to the language, customs, and people of her new homeland, but things did not always go smoothly; for example, at Dolly's first piano recital at Holy Cross School, the private, Catholic grammar school that she and Joseph Albert attended. Miao Ying was obviously proud of Dolly; she bought her a pretty, new dress and attended the recital with her.

It's unknown whether Miao Ying was treated poorly, stared at awkwardly, or simply felt out of place, but afterward, she decided not to attend any more of Dolly's school functions, including graduation from high school. When Dolly brought home friends that made fun or complained of the smell of Miao Ying's cooking, she forbade Dolly from inviting them to the house again.[476]

After about three years in the U.S., Miao Ying felt homesick for the land of her birth. She had spent the first 50 years of her life in China, and her only sister, Ng Yee, still resided in Hong Kong. Miao Ying told YaoTim and Milly that she wanted to visit Ng Yee and asked them to help finance the trip, telling them this would be the only time she would ask them for financial assistance for this purpose. She kept her promise, although she would travel to Hong Kong, and also Taiwan and Japan, several more times. Despite not having a lot of financial resources, Miao Ying purchased jewelry on her trips there and sold it for a profit in the U.S. to finance her additional travels.[477]

In 1966, she again traveled to Hong Kong to visit her sister. Because the trip was costly and lengthy, even by plane, Miao Ying usually would stay for at least two months. Sometimes, however, she would stay much longer. This was especially true of her 1966 trip. She went for George's wedding in December but did not return to California until the summer of 1967 so she could accompany George's wife, Elaine, back to the U.S.[478]

Miao Ying's trips away from home were especially hard on Dolly, although Clifford was not happy about these absences either. Joseph Albert had left for the seminary, and George was living in Lompoc, Calif., so they only came home on weekends. Dolly was stuck with cooking and cleaning, and apparently her methods and results were not up to her father's expectations, and he told her so.[479]

Miao Ying did accommodate some very American customs and practices. Christmas is not a holiday in China and is not even celebrated, but she

LAST OF NINE — The Lamsdaine children, last of nine in the family to arrive from China, pose for their picture after taking oath of allegiance in naturalization ceremonies at the Ventura Courthouse yesterday. From left, Mildred, Joseph and Dorothy.

Ventura County Star-Free Press *newspaper clipping dated March 4, 1963*

allowed Christmas decorations at the house in Ventura. She even bought an ornamental, aluminum Christmas tree with rotating, colored lights that was popular in the early 1960s.[480]

Miao Ying also readily adapted to the American practice of watching TV shows with her family. Her favorites included several westerns popular at the time, but she also enjoyed game shows and the nightly news.[481] Although Miao Ying rarely spoke English and professed to have a limited understanding of it, she laughed at the right times during the shows and sometimes got upset at game-show contestants when they gave the wrong answer. It was obvious that she understood a lot more English than she claimed.[482]

It also was clear that both Miao Ying and Clifford wanted their children to be fully initiated as Americans in their new world. For example, they made sure that their last three children became naturalized United States citizens soon after they arrived. This occasion was memorialized in an article in the local newspaper. And when Joseph Albert won a citywide "Americanism

*Clifford, with Joseph Albert in his seminary uni-
form, in the kitchen of the Ventura home, 1965*

Essay Contest" in 1965, Clifford walked with him to the awards dinner at
the Ventura American Legion Hall.[483]

Sometimes Miao Ying had trouble accepting her children's desires to move
in directions that were contrary to traditional Chinese mores or concepts.
She found it difficult to let Dolly leave home to attend college hundreds of
miles away. Traditionally, a Chinese girl did not leave home until she got
married.[484] It also was hard for her to comprehend, let alone acquiesce to,
Joseph Albert going to a seminary to study for the priesthood. In Miao Ying's
mind, he would be leaving home to shave his head, don an orange robe, and
never return home, as was the custom for Buddhist monks.[485]

Both of these events – an unmarried daughter leaving home and a son
"joining a monastery" – upset Miao Ying tremendously because they
were completely foreign concepts to her. But in neither instance did Clifford contradict her.[486] He withheld his approval and support of Dolly
and Joseph Albert's plans until his wife relented, at which point Clifford

helped both Dolly and Joseph Albert, respectively, to complete the necessary paperwork and scholarship applications for attendance at college and seminary.[487]

Miao Ying did hold fast to some of her Chinese customs and practices after moving to the U.S. Virtually all family meals were traditional Cantonese fare. White rice was always present along with cooked vegetables and

Miao Ying and Dolly in the driveway of the Ventura home, c. 1967

meat or fish.[488] She still liked to cook freshly slaughtered chicken. In Hong Kong, she raised and butchered her own. Now, however, she went to a butcher shop in Los Angeles's Chinatown, where she would select the live chicken to be slaughtered.

These Chinatown outings left lasting impressions, especially among her non-Chinese daughters-in-law, for whom witnessing such a ritual was a highly unusual event.[489] Cooking Chinese food was more than just a way of putting food on the table; it was her favorite pastime.[490] Miao Ying also found new Chinese friends in Ventura who could join her in her other favorite pastime: playing mah jongg.[491]

In other ways, Miao Ying and Clifford settled into a stereotypical suburban American life during those years in Ventura. They allowed Joseph Albert to have a pet cat because he said he would take care of it. They also allowed him to train and care for a ferocious German Shepherd dog named Rocky because they thought he would be a good guard dog. The pets ate leftover Chinese food, as was customary in China, rather than the typical cat and dog food American pets receive.

Miao Ying also was able to garden outside, which her previous crowded urban environments in Shanghai and Hong Kong did not permit.[492] She became so adept at planting rose cuttings that Joseph Albert once counted 42 rose bushes along the driveway and garden surrounding the rental house in Ventura.[493]

MORE SIBLING WEDDINGS

Miao Ying and Clifford witnessed the weddings of several of their children during the years they lived in Ventura. The first was Robert, who married Joycelyn "Joyce" Pang in an Orange County Catholic church in July 1964.

Joyce came from an upper-class Chinese family from Hawaii. While she was ethnically Chinese, Joyce's mannerisms and language were more characteristic of American-born Chinese. Still, her in-laws did not have trouble accepting Joyce into the family. Joyce, in turn, survived the all-night family mah jongg sessions and crowded, boisterous gatherings that characterized the Lumsdaine household in Ventura.[494]

Miao Ying and Clifford did not make any pretense as to who they were; they were neither rich nor culturally refined. They were unpretentious people who brought their large family through unimaginable circumstances to a land where their children would have the opportunity to succeed and thrive.

Above, Robert and Joyce at their wedding reception in July 1964. At left, Clifford and Miao Ying in front of the St. Iranaeus Church in Cypress, Calif., where Robert and Joyce were married

At Robert and Joyce's wedding reception, Milly and her boyfriend, Marcel Ratermann, separately approached Clifford and Miao Ying on the topic of getting married themselves. Miao Ying asked Milly only two questions: "Are you going to go to college?" and "Do you love him?" Milly answered with yes, she would go to college "some day, but not right away" and yes, she loved him. With that, Miao Ying gave her consent and accepted Marcel into the family.[495]

Before Milly and Marcel's wedding in November 1965, Miao Ying gave Milly this sound, motherly advice about relationships with in-laws: "You both love the same person. A boy that loves his mother would also love you. Don't do anything to hurt them (Marcel's parents) because…it would hurt Marcel deeply."[496] Miao Ying clearly had a firm grasp on familial dynamics and in-law interactions.

During her long stay in Hong Kong in 1964, Miao Ying met George's future spouse, Elaine. Miao Ying stayed with her sister, Ng Yee, who was a family friend of Elaine's family.[497] Elaine's mother would visit Ng Yee and

Clifford, Marcel Ratermann, Milly, and Miao Ying at Milly and Marcel's wedding, November 1965

play mah jongg with Miao Ying, and Elaine accompanied her mother on those visits. While she did not join the mah jongg games, she watched the other women play and formed a favorable impression of Miao Ying, who also apparently formed a favorable impression of Elaine.[498]

In 1966, when George accompanied Miao Ying to Hong Kong, he met Elaine at a family party. Later, they went on a date, and after George

Elaine and George at their wedding reception in 1966, flanked by her parents on the left and Miao Ying on the right

returned to the U.S., they corresponded with each other for the rest of the year. In December, George and Miao Ying returned to Hong Kong, where George and Elaine married in December 1966.[499]

Miao Ying and Clifford were not present when Philip married Linda Sue Dees in January 1967, in Alabama, near where Philip was stationed while he was in the U.S. Army from 1965 to 1967. Neither parent had any objections when Philip informed them, however, and after his discharge from the Army, they happily accepted Linda and the couple's newborn son, Gregory, into their Ventura home until Philip and Linda found their own place to live.[500]

In December 1968, while attending the University of San Francisco, Dolly announced that she intended to marry a man she had met in the Bay Area. Miao Ying asked YaoTim to go up with her to see Dolly in San Francisco. Her stated purpose for making the trip was to help Dolly with the wedding plans, as it appeared that the wedding would take place in a few months. They asked Philip's wife, Linda, to drive them the 350 miles in Clifford's car.[501]

The three of them arrived at Dolly's Haight-Ashbury apartment late that night, while Dolly was studying for her final exams, and unexpectedly met Dolly's boyfriend at the apartment. What happened next is not entirely clear, but Miao Ying became extremely upset, started crying, and tried to convince Dolly not to marry her boyfriend.[502] After what seemed like hours of everyone crying and arguing, nothing was resolved, and Miao Ying, YaoTim, and Linda drove back to Ventura the next day.

Dolly did not end up marrying the boyfriend, but she did move with him out of California. This unfortunate series of events led to more than three years of almost complete estrangement between Dolly and her parents, from December 1968 until early 1972.[503]

AT HOME AT 'LA HOMA'

In May 1969, shortly before their youngest child, Joseph Albert, graduated from high school, Miao Ying and Clifford moved from their house in Ventura to a small, two-bedroom house on La Homa Street in the Orange County, Calif., town of Cypress. They already knew that Joseph Albert would be moving to the Bay Area for college during the summer of 1969. The timing of their move was likely in anticipation of no longer having any school-age children living at home.

Miao Ying and Clifford's house was near the homes of YaoTim, Milly, and later, Philip. George, YaoTim, and Milly made the downpayment and continued to pay the mortgage, property tax, and insurance for the house, while their parents paid the utilities.[504] These were sacrifices that the children made willingly, even while raising their own young families. It wasn't Miao Ying and Clifford's style to be effusive with gratitude, but the warmth in their welcome whenever their children visited showed their deep appreciation in a way that words never could.[505]

Miao Ying and Clifford had more leisure time and fewer worries while living at La Homa than at any previous time in their lives. The last of their nine children had reached maturity and left for college. For the first time in 35 years, they had an "empty nest." La Homa was only the second time that had lived together without any children since 1934 when Chuck was born. They baby-

Clifford, Miao Ying, and Joseph Albert at his graduation from St. Bonaventure
High School in Ventura, June 1969

Clockwise from left, Clifford; Miao Ying holding baby Arnold, Ed's youngest son; Andrew, Alfred, and Anne, Ed's other three children; Greg, Philip's son, in the front yard of the house on La Homa, summer 1969

Family portrait, summer 1969: Back, from left, Philip, Joseph Albert, Chuck, Milly, George, Robert, and Ed; front, from left, Dolly, Clifford, Miao Ying, and Yao Tim

Clifford holding Philip's son, Greg, at La Homa, July 1970

sat their grandson Greg during the week for Philip and Linda, both of whom worked outside the home. However, it was much different being a grandparent than being a parent. Miao Ying enjoyed teaching the grandkids some Chinese phrases, and Clifford liked walking Greg to the nearby schoolyard.[506]

They occasionally babysat Milly's sons Michael, Mark, and Matthew. Both Milly and YaoTim visited often; Milly lived close enough that she and her mother would take her sons in strollers and walk between their houses.[507]

Miao Ying delighted in spending more time teaching her daughters and daughters-in-law the art of Chinese cooking.[508] She and Clifford loved gardening in their large yard. The 3½ years they spent at La Homa may well have been their version of the "golden years."[509] They even had time to travel independently, Miao Ying to Hong Kong, and Clifford to South Dakota to visit Ed; his wife, Monika; and their four children.[510]

The kids and grandkids visited frequently, including lengthy visits from Ed and his family during Ed's summer work in California.[511] Although they still occasionally worried about money, the years that Miao Ying and Clifford spent at La Homa were marked by relative peace and tranquility. The move from Ventura to Cypress cost Clifford his steady work managing laundromats, and his efforts to find meaningful work in Cypress were largely unsuccessful, so he spent most of his time gardening and attending to other needs of his household and his wife.[512] Clifford became Miao Ying's chauffeur and companion when she wanted to go shopping or play mah jongg with her friends in El Segundo.

Miao Ying did earn some money by taking fabric "piece work" for sewing at home or by playing mah jongg. Sometimes she stayed overnight at a friend's house and did sewing work for the friend's family's garment busi-

Miao Ying holding Milly's son, Matthew,
with Milly in front of La Homa, 1970

ness in El Segundo.[513] However, Miao Ying and Clifford still needed substantial support from their children to manage financially. Robert and Ed, and occasionally Chuck and Philip, helped with their monthly expenses.[514] Even Joseph Albert contributed when he could, before he started college.[515]

Joseph Albert with his cat, Zeus, and dog, Jingo, in Berkeley, 1972

Although Miao Ying and Clifford's lives were far from lavish, for the first time since the end of World War II in 1945, they no longer had to worry about a place to live or enough money to feed themselves and their children.

In early 1972, Joseph Albert came home from college at the University of California, Berkeley, with his girlfriend, Dianne, and Dianne's toddler niece, Cindy. Joseph Albert's hair was long and flowing, down past his shoulders, as was fashionable among young people at the time. Shortly after their arrival at La Homa, Miao Ying walked over to the couch where Joseph Albert sat, placed a pair of scissors on the coffee table, and said, "I am going to cut your hair because it is too long."

Her youngest child reacted with angry defiance, retorting in an overly loud voice, "If you try it, you'll never see me again!"[516] A few moments of tense silence elapsed as Joseph Albert and his mother stared each other down, and Dianne walked out of the house with the now-crying toddler. Then Miao Ying simply stood up from where she sat next to Joseph Albert, left the scissors on the coffee table, and walked to the kitchen to make lunch.

Clifford had watched the entire scene without speaking a word, then he followed Dianne out of the house. He then did his best to pacify the crying baby and comfort his son's stunned girlfriend. When calm settled, Clifford led them both back into the house, where Miao Ying was preparing to serve lunch. Miao Ying never again broached the subject of Joseph Albert's long hair with him – but Joseph Albert never got the opportunity to apologize for disrespecting his mother.[517]

In September 1972, Joseph Albert returned home from college with what he perceived would be happy news for his parents: He and Dianne were engaged. The young newlyweds-to-be, who were 22 and 21, respectively, drove south from Berkeley, stopping first at Philip and Linda's new house, which was near La Homa. From there, Joseph Albert telephoned his mother and told her his girlfriend had something to tell her. Dianne got on the phone and, reading from a note on which Joseph Albert had written phonetically, told Miao Ying in Cantonese "We want to marry!"

A long, awkward silence followed until a perplexed Dianne handed the phone back to Joseph Albert. On the phone, Miao Ying told Joseph Albert that she believed he should wait to get married until after graduation. Joseph Albert told his mother that he did not intend to wait, but he did intend to graduate from college after their wedding.

What Miao Ying did the next day astounded Dianne and Joseph Albert.[518] She suggested that Joseph Albert drive her to go shopping in Chinatown and that they should pick up Dianne, who was at her parents' house in Bellflower, on the way. Dianne sat in the front seat between Joseph Albert and Miao Ying.

Joseph Albert's handwritten note in Cantonese that Dianne used to tell Miao Ying that she and Joseph Albert intended to get married

While Joseph Albert was driving, Miao Ying reached over without a word, grasped Dianne's left hand, slipped a beautiful diamond and jade ring onto her ring finger, and then withdrew it. Seeing Dianne's surprise and bewilderment, she explained to Joseph Albert in Cantonese that she wanted to size Dianne's ring finger so she could surprise Dianne with the ring as a wedding present.[519]

The entrance to Miao Ying's favorite restaurant, Golden Dragon in Los Angeles' Chinatown, where she took Joseph Albert and Dianne after their engagement announcement.

The rest of the day was equally memorable for Joseph Albert and Dianne. Miao Ying took the three of them to her favorite restaurant, the Golden Dragon in Chinatown, for dim sum. She delighted in seeing Dianne enjoy traditional Cantonese dishes that were new experiences for her; dishes such as turnip cake, taro root dumpling, and stuffed bell pepper slices in black bean sauce, the latter of which Miao Ying would later cook for Joseph Albert and Dianne at La Homa.[520]

The young couple was happy and surprised by how welcoming Miao Ying was to Dianne as well as her acceptance of their impending marriage despite her initial reservations. Neither of them, nor any of Joseph Albert's siblings, had any idea that Miao Ying was seriously ill.

10

FINAL SEPARATION
AND ETERNAL REUNION

EARTH AND HEAVEN

Miao Ying generally did not discuss her health issues with her children. Occasionally she complained about stomach upset or pain, but that was attributed to indigestion.[521] But everything changed one day in October 1, 1972.

That evening, Clifford called Milly, telling her "Mom has a terrible stomach pain." Milly called YaoTim, and the three of them took Miao Ying to the emergency room of La Palma Intercommunity Hospital, less than a mile away. By then, Miao Ying was in excruciating pain and was immediately admitted to the hospital.[522] The preliminary diagnosis was a "possible dissecting aortal aneurysm."[523]

News of Miao Ying's condition spread quickly among her children and their spouses, and nearly all of them made their way to the Los Angeles area within the next two days.[524] From the time Miao Ying was admitted, at least one of her children – and often more – was always at the hospital, keeping her company and translating whatever the medical staff was saying in English into Cantonese so she could understand what was happening. Most of her children were able to visit with her over the next few days.[525]

Ho Miao Ying Lumsdaine, summer 1969

After more tests, cardiologist Robert Touchon, MD, decided that Miao Ying needed surgery that could not be performed at La Palma. Her aortic aneurysm was complicated by obstruction of both the renal artery and the abdominal aorta, and the doctor recommended that she be transferred to Santa Ana Community Hospital for surgery by a vascular specialist.[526] On the afternoon of October 4, 1972, they began Miao Ying's transfer, but didn't inform the family ahead of time. Fortunately, Dolly saw them moving her mother to an ambulance and hurriedly jumped into the front seat. The driver allowed her to remain, but he then got lost on the way to Santa Ana Community Hospital, upsetting Dolly even further.[527]

After an overnight stay, Miao Ying's surgery to repair cardiovascular aneurysms and arterial blockages started at 10:30 a.m. on October 5, 1972.[528] Clifford was at the hospital along with all nine adult children and some of their spouses. Everyone fully expected Miao Ying to survive the surgery.[529] Some of them even went out for lunch and brought back sandwiches for the others that stayed in the hospital waiting room.[530] At times, their chatter grew so noisy that Robert had to caution his siblings to be quieter lest they disturb others in the waiting area.[531] When the surgery seemed to take longer than expected, some of them started to feel concerned, but none doubted that their mother would pull through.

Before the surgery began, Miao Ying's doctors gave her a 40% chance of survival, which Joseph Albert took as an overwhelmingly positive prediction of success.[532] He was not alone in his confidence; the children's universal optimism was buoyed by the fact that their mother was one of the strongest people they had ever known. Her entire life was marked by resilience and overcoming seemingly impossible odds.

Years later, Milly recalled a hospital conversation during which her mother pointed to a person in a wheelchair and stated that she did not want to live confined to a wheelchair after surgery. Milly told her that she would be fine; she would survive the surgery and not be in a wheelchair. Milly was assured by Miao Ying's strength, which seemed indomitable.[533] YaoTim's confidence in her mom's survival was bolstered by the fact that all nine of Miao Ying's children were present at the hospital; years earlier, a fortune-teller had told Miao Ying that one of her children would not be present at her death.[534] Confidence was running high – until 3 p.m., when two somber-looking surgeons entered the waiting room.

The family listened in disbelief as the surgeons told them that three hours into the surgery, Miao Ying's heart went into cardiac arrest. They spent more than an hour trying to resuscitate her but were not successful. She was pronounced dead at 2:35 p.m. on October 5, 1972, a Sunday.[535]

The surgeons' words were spoken in plain English, but their message was practically incomprehensible to the shocked family. Until that moment, they had believed that this enduringly strong woman – wife, mother, grand-mother, matriarch – would overcome this obstacle as she had so many others in her life. When asked years later, none of the Lumsdaine children could remember hearing any words spoken in the aftermath of the doctors' devas-tating news except by Miao Ying's firstborn, Chuck, who, after a seeming eternity of stunned silence, softly uttered "Damn."[536]

Miao Ying died suddenly and unexpectedly at age 62. Less than four days had elapsed since she went to the emergency room of the local hospital, complaining only of stomach pain. During those four days, despite her pain, she reinforced to her children her foundational values: education, feeding one's family, and courage under pressure. When Dolly and Joseph Albert visited her in the ICU, she asked why they were not in school.[537] Although she was in pain and hooked up to IV bottles, she wanted to ensure that her college-attending children knew how much she and their father valued and had sacrificed for their education.[538] She asked Joseph Albert to put away the barbecued pork that had been left on the kitchen table when she and Clifford had hurriedly left for the hospital.[539] She never forgot the struggles to provide food for her family during the many difficult years of deprivation, and she reinforced for her youngest child the value of not wasting food. And when Milly, on the morn-ing of the surgery, held her mother's hand and asked if there was anything at all that she needed, Miao Ying simply and quietly answered, "No." She was strong, determined, and uncomplaining, right to the end.[540]

From the doctors' announcement of Miao Ying's death, through her funeral, burial, and wake, Clifford was even quieter than usual. He responded to most questions with only a soft "I don't know."[541] His children stepped in to help, as they made all of the decisions and arrangements for their mother's interment.[542] As the oldest child, Chuck took charge of everyone and everything. He was even the "informant" on Miao Ying's death certificate, a role normally reserved for the spouse of the deceased.[543]

Chuck made the arrangements for mortuary and burial at Forest Lawn Memorial Park in Cypress. He signed contracts for and largely paid for the plot, the undertaking, the funeral service, and the burial.[544] The one week between Miao Ying's admittance to the hospital and her burial was a blur for the family; as his siblings were mostly in a daze, Chuck stepped up for them all.[545]

FINAL SEPARATION

On October 7, 1972, Ho Miao Ying Lumsdaine's family buried her in the Ascension Gardens section of Forest Lawn Memorial Park in Cypress, Calif. Many people attended the memorial service, including the extended Lumsdaine family, their spouses and significant others, Miao Ying's Chinese friends, and friends and co-workers of her children. Clifford's brother, Arthur Allen, flew down from Seattle to be with his half-brother in what Clifford later described as the saddest time of his life.[546]

After his wife's death, Clifford seemed totally lost.[547] Unlike their previous separations, there was no hope of physical reunion this time. They had been married for nearly 40 years. Now Clifford and Miao Ying were separated for the last time.

Clifford was despondent and depressed for most of the year after Miao Ying died.[548] In the first few months after her death, he did not seem to care much about anything. He needed prompting, even to eat.

Clifford allowed his children to make virtually all his decisions,[549] including what to do with Miao Ying's personal effects. Just as their eldest son, Chuck, had taken charge of his mother's funeral arrangements, their eldest daughter, YaoTim, handled the clearing of Miao Ying's clothing and other possessions from the house.[550] Clifford did not seem to care about his wife's possessions, or much else, during the months after her death.[551]

147

Miao Ying kept a substantial collection of jewelry. She seldom wore any of it; instead, she sold it to finance her trips back to Hong Kong. YaoTim obtained an appraisal of the jewelry, then organized its sale to her siblings in order to keep the items in the family – and to provide some money for Clifford to live on.[552] At Clifford's request, the diamond and jade ring that his wife had briefly slipped on Dianne's finger would not be sold. Just as Miao Ying had intended, Clifford wanted to give Dianne the ring at her wedding.

After the saddest event of Clifford's life, the family questioned whether they should put him through Joseph Albert and Dianne's wedding, which was scheduled for November 25, 1972, only 50 days after the death of his beloved wife. Clifford didn't seem to care much either way. His preferred response at that point was simply, "Tell me what to do."[553]

Whether or not the wedding should proceed posed a difficult choice for the rest of the family. The wedding date fell within the traditional 100-day Chinese

Church of Our Fathers

A new commandment I give unto you,
That ye love one another.
—from John 13:34

In the belief that a heart filled with love knows no separation from those who live on in memory, these words are inscribed above the chancel of the Church of Our Fathers in Forest Lawn Memorial-Park, Cypress. Reproduced from St. John's Church in Richmond, Virginia where Patrick Henry climaxed a speech with the historic declaration "... but as for me, give me liberty or give me death," it is a memorial to the courage and faith of the Virginia patriots who risked their fortunes and their lives to make our country free.

© Forest Lawn Memorial-Park Assn.

A Service of Memory

For

Miao Ying Lumsdaine

Announcement of Miao Ying's memorial service, October 7, 1972

At The

Church of Our Fathers

mourning period for a deceased parent; in addition, sons of the deceased should not get married for six months after a parent's death.[554] Joseph Albert, however, felt strongly about the wedding proceeding. After a traumatic summer separation from each other, he and Dianne were determined to seal their renewed commitment to each other as soon as possible. Ultimately, the family reached a compromise: The large wedding and banquet hall reception was exchanged for a small gathering at Dianne's parents' home for immediate family and a half-dozen close friends.[555]

Although Clifford was clearly depressed in the months immediately after Miao Ying's death, he remained ever the gentleman, kind and thoughtful.[556] Less than two months after his wife's death, he participated in Joseph Albert and Dianne's wedding celebration. Five days after the wedding, he sent his newest daughter-in-law a birthday card that read, "May your troubles all be brief, May your blessings never end."

Church of Our Fathers

Forest Lawn Memorial-Park
Cypress, California

Born	July ▨ 1910 Canton, China
Passed Away	October 5, 1972 Santa Ana, California
Services Held	October 7, 1972 12:00 Noon
Services Conducted By	Rev. Frank Newbern First Congregational Church Buena Park, California
Organist	Mr. J. DeWitt Schwab
Organist Selections	"Medley of Hymns"
Funeral Director	Forest Lawn Mortuary-Cypress
Interment	Forest Lawn - Cypress Cypress, California

As their father's depression continued, the siblings believed that it would be best for him to temporarily leave the La Homa house. In early 1973, Clifford took several trips with YaoTim and Milly and spent substantial amounts of time visiting his other children, especially those outside of Southern California. He visited George and Elaine in Lompoc, as well as Ed, Monika, and their four children in their spacious Knoxville, Tennessee, home for several extended periods.[557]

Clifford returned to the La Homa house for the summer of 1973 and lived there with Joseph Albert and Dianne. They shared expenses while Joseph Albert saved money to attend law school in the fall.[558]

During that summer, it was clear to his nine children that Clifford no longer wanted to live in the house he had shared with Miao Ying.[559] In late August 1973, after Joseph Albert and Dianne left for law school and college, the family put the furniture and furnishings in storage and rented out the La Homa house.[560] Clifford boarded a train for Atlanta, where Ed picked him up and drove him to Knoxville.[561] Clifford spent the next eight months

Joe and Dianne are in love so they are getting Married

Harry and Clara Niethamer
and their daughter
Dianne
and
Clifford and Miao Ying Lumisdaine
and their son
Joseph Albert
want you to celebrate with them
this pledge of love and fidelity
on November 25, 1972
6:00 o'clock in the evening
Woman's Club of Bellflower
8402 Oak Street
Bellflower, California

After his mother's death less than two months before his wedding, Joseph Albert and his fiancée, Dianne, decided to forgo their large wedding for a smaller celebration. Their wedding invitations were never mailed.

Clifford with Dianne and Joseph Albert at their 1972 wedding reception

with Ed, Monika, and their children, who distracted him from his grief with family activities, outings, trips, and many books.[562]

Clifford's visits to Tennessee after Miao Ying's sudden death were undoubtedly well-needed respites that helped him grieve, but he never intended to live there permanently. He wanted to return to California, so at the family's suggestion – and with George and Elaine's invitation – he moved to Lompoc.[563]

LIFE IN LOMPOC

Clifford arrived in Lompoc on a Greyhound bus in April 1974. He stayed with George and Elaine for a couple months until he found a suitable place of his own – an apartment on W. North Avenue, which he moved into in June 1974.[564]

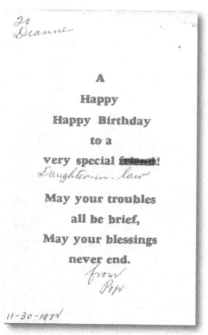

The inside of the 1972 birthday card Clifford sent to Dianne

Clifford lived there for 9½ years, until November 1983. In Lompoc, he seemed to adapt to life as a single parent and grandparent. During that time, he appeared to move past his earlier depression and develop a life of relative well-being and happiness. He gained many new friends and had many new experiences while he maintained strong family ties with his children and grandchildren.

Clifford's years in Lompoc were marked by frequent visits with family members. He often had meals with George and Elaine, visiting with them and their children, Christopher and Agnes.[565] As his apartment was

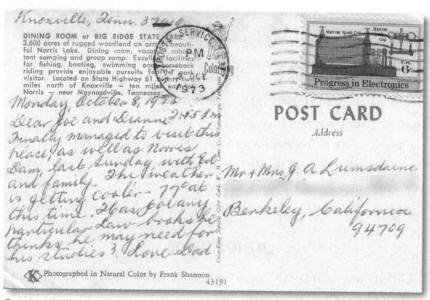

October 1973 postcard from Clifford to Joseph Albert and Dianne in which he discussed visiting Big Ridge State Park and Norris Dam with Ed and his family

only five miles from George and Elaine's house, when Christopher got old enough, he would ride his bicycle to his grandfather's apartment and spend time there. Clifford always mentioned to his other children how he enjoyed Christopher's frequent visits.[566]

Clifford's children from Southern California visited often, and they would usually bring their children with them to visit their Grandpa. Sometimes they would stay overnight at George and Elaine's or at a nearby hotel to make a visit last longer.[567] Those who visited Clifford in Lompoc saw that he was genuinely pleased with life there. He told them how he liked his apartment, with its easy walking-distance access to his bank, shopping, and other things.

Although he liked his quiet life in the small town, Clifford also enjoyed traveling to spend time with other family members. He would go north to Placerville or south to San Diego, and Downey and Cypress in between,

Clifford with Ed and Monika's children in Tennessee, spring 1973: From left, Andrew, Anne, Arnold and Alfred

for family celebrations, birthdays, anniversaries, and christenings. He took road trips, including one with Milly, Marcel, and Marcel's parents in a motor home to see the giant sequoias in northern California.[568]

Family trips were just part of Clifford's many travels during the years he lived in Lompoc. He quickly made many new friends at the apartment complex, at the senior community and nutrition centers, and at his local Presbyterian church. He went on numerous outings with senior and church groups to nearby cities like Solvang and Santa Barbara, as well as further afield to Los Angeles' Chinatown and Busch Gardens in Van Nuys. They even visited St. Helena in the Napa Valley, and Lake Tahoe.[569]

Aside from group excursions, Clifford also traveled overseas to Scotland for a Lumsden Clan Gathering in 1976, to Hong Kong for a visit with his Chinese relatives and friends, and to Honolulu just for fun.[570] Clifford also was involved in community and civic affairs in Lompoc. He held responsible positions, such as officer or director, at the Lompoc Senior Citizens Club, Nutrition Center, Meals on Wheels, and Tenants' Council.[571] He had a particularly dear friend, "Miss Ann," at the apartment complex with whom he would take long walks as they looked for recyclables together. She also invited him over for his first Christmas day dinner in Lompoc and accompanied him on the Honolulu trip in 1976, although he told Milly the relationship was platonic; in a postcard to Joseph Albert, he made a point of mentioning that they had separate rooms while in Hawaii.[572]

Clifford also appeared to experience a renewal of his faith – or at least a resurgence of his connection with the Presbyterian Church – while in Lompoc. He enrolled as a member of the First Presbyterian Church of Lompoc in October 1974. By 1977, he had been ordained as a deacon there, and in January 1982, he was installed as a member of the Deacon's Board.[573]

Clifford was well known and well liked by the church pastor and parishioners. When he brought George as a guest, nearly everyone took turns shaking George's hand. Even after Clifford moved out of Lompoc to Bellflower, Calif., some of his friends from his former church would travel the nearly 175 miles to look in on him and make sure he was doing well.[574]

Clifford; Philip's wife, Linda; Albert, holding baby Jonathan; Greg; and Dianne at Jonathan's baptism at St. Iranaeus Church in Cypress, March 8, 1975

A NEW RELATIONSHIP CAUSES CONCERN

Clifford flourished in Lompoc until an unfortunate situation necessitated his departure and relocation. In January 1983, about a year after he was installed on the church's Board of Deacons, Helen Hinnrichs, a widow from the church, took an unusual interest in him. Before early 1983, none of Clifford's children, and few of his friends, knew of Helen. But then each of the children received a wedding invitation.

George and Elaine hadn't had the opportunity to meet Helen yet, even though they lived in Lompoc. In a conversation with George shortly after the announcement, on a day when Helen wasn't around, Clifford admitted that plans for the wedding – set for April 30, 1983, only about three months after he and Helen met – were "abrupt." But George and his siblings knew Clifford had seen other women in the 11 years since Miao Ying passed away; he was a gentleman in the classic sense and had many women friends and acquaintances, although his children believed the relationships were mostly platonic. So while they thought the quick marriage seemed somewhat strange, they all wanted their father to be happy.[575]

Their thoughts quickly turned to serious worry. Soon after the wedding, Clifford's children learned that Helen had been widowed not once but four times. To find out what had happened to her late husbands, they hired a private investigator who discovered that all four had died under somewhat mysterious circumstances.[576]

As spring turned into summer, Clifford started becoming increasingly withdrawn and morose; he even stopped attending church. His health had significantly deteriorated, and he was seemingly bedridden on most days. Helen told YaoTim that Clifford did not want to visit or talk to her, and she wrote letters saying that he also did not want to travel to visit his children anymore. She told several family members that Clifford actually couldn't travel safely anymore because of a serious heart problem she claimed he had developed, but a phone call to Clifford's physician confirmed for the children that Clifford did not have any heart problems and there was no reason why he couldn't travel to Los Angeles to visit his family.[577]

Concerned about their father's health and safety, several of his children went together to Lompoc one day in November 1983.[578] After making sure Helen would not be around, they asked Clifford about his general welfare – and his marriage to Helen. Regarding both, Clifford replied "I wouldn't mind leaving." That same day, Clifford's kids helped him leave Lompoc and move to southern California, away from a bad situation he'd felt powerless to deal with.[579]

SERENITY IN BELLFLOWER

Clifford's first stop after leaving Lompoc was Joseph Albert and Dianne's home on Priscilla Street in Downey. Joseph Albert and Dianne got along with Clifford just fine – he was easy-going and grateful for anything done for him. However, they had a small house and three children between the ages of 1 and 7, so it needed to be a temporary arrangement.[580] In December 1983, when Clifford was 74 years old, he moved into a one-bedroom bungalow on Ryon Avenue in Bellflower.[581]

Clifford's years at his Bellflower bungalow were tranquil and conducive to regaining his overall health. He recovered his generally happy disposition and his strong relationships with family, friends, and church. Joseph Albert and Dianne tried to persuade him to quit smoking – a habit he had picked up the 1920s. But his brand of cigarettes offered valuable coupons that he could redeem for small household items, Clifford told them, so the couple offered to pay him $1 a day for every day that he didn't smoke. Clifford must have decided that was a better deal than saving coupons because he accepted their offer. As far as Joseph Albert and Dianne knew, Clifford faithfully kept his promise to not smoke and would "bill" them each month for the appropriate number of days of non-smoking for the rest of his life.[582] It was a bill they were happy to pay.

Clifford also resumed another favorite activity that he'd developed years earlier while living in Long Beach: taking long walks. Granted, it was partly because he no longer drove, or even owned, a car. But he also genuinely enjoyed walking for the exercise. He would walk to his bank and to the nearby grocery store, a round-trip of almost a mile. In January 1984, he joined the Bellflower Presbyterian Church, and sometimes he would walk the half-mile from his home for Sunday services or evening programs. That month, he joined the Bellflower Senior Nutrition Center, where he usually got his lunch, and he would occasionally make the round-trip walk of over two miles. More often, he used the local Dial-A-Ride service or caught a ride from others, at least for the return trips.[583]

Most importantly, Clifford resumed staying in close and frequent contact with his nine children. Several times a week, he would talk with one or more of them on the telephone. Not a week went by without one, and usually two or three, of his children visiting him. (In January 1984, it was noted in Clifford's journal that he had received 23 visits with one or more of his children and 19 telephone calls.[584]). Sometimes they would visit his bungalow, but more often than not, he would join a family meal at one of their houses or at a favorite restaurant.[585] These visits were full of pandemonium due to the presence of several young and noisy grandchildren, but Clifford was ever the unflappable "English gentleman," regardless of the commotion surrounding him.[586]

The 1980s and early 1990s passed with Clifford rarely missing family celebrations or important family events, whether they were close by in Southern California or several hours away in Northern California. He attended marriages, baptisms, birthdays, first communions, confirmations, graduations, singing and theatrical presentations, Girl Scout and Boy Scout functions, baseball and softball games, and many other milestone events for his nine children, 22 grandchildren, and eight great-grandchildren, not to mention in-laws and other members of his sizable extended family.[587]

Clifford clearly enjoyed such festivities and often attended two or three celebrations in the same week. Occasionally, he would attend that many in one day. In addition, he sometimes attended Catholic Mass on Sundays, Christmas Eve, and Easter, either at St. Irenaeus in Cypress with Philip and Linda or at St. Dominic Savio in Bellflower with Joe and Dianne. He also attended church social functions including concerts, fiestas, and luaus.[588] Perhaps during this period of his life, he was catching up for all the years when world events forced his separation from most of his family.[589]

After Clifford moved to Southern California, the biggest annual Lumsdaine family celebration was his birthday every November, when his children, grandchildren, extended family, and friends – usually 25 to 40 people – would gather at one of his children's homes. Sometimes, these celebrations were held at restaurants; in 1986, at a Szechuan restaurant in Downey; the next year, at Charlie Brown's in Anaheim.

The party for his milestone 75th birthday in 1984, which included a live band, was held in the Bellflower Presbyterian Church hall because the family needed a room that was big enough to hold not only his family but also all of the friends Clifford had made at his church and in the community. With good humor, Clifford introduced the octogenarians at the party, proud of the fact that at 75, he was the youngster in the group.[590] On his 80th birthday, more than 65 guests celebrated with him at a Sunday brunch aboard the *RMS Queen Mary*, permanently docked in Long Beach Harbor. His 85th birthday was a weekend getaway at a Laughlin, Nevada, casino hotel, where Clifford received a large bag of nickels to play his favorite slot machine.[591] Other birthday outings included a San Francisco Bay cruise aboard a chartered

60-foot boat in 1988, a Hornblower brunch cruise around Newport Harbor in 1990, and a cruise to Mexico and back on the *Princess Pacific Star* in 1991.[592]

THE MOVE TO THE MANOR

In May 1986, Clifford moved from the Ryon Avenue bungalow to the Bellflower Friendship Manor, a senior living center on Oak Street. Clifford had first looked at "The Manor" in 1984 with Dianne and YaoTim, but at the time, the waiting list for open apartment units extended out two years.[593] The Manor consisted of 144 small apartments dedicated to affordable living for active seniors. It was much closer to the Bellflower Senior Nutrition Center and Clifford's church and offered meal plans, in-house recreation, local transportation, and optional group tours.[594] All of these amenities were more desirable for him than living by himself in a bungalow. On clear days, his new eighth-floor studio apartment gave him a nice view of the San Gabriel Mountains, something that he often commented on in his diary.[595]

Clifford had no trouble making new friends while living alone at the Ryon Avenue bungalow, but the Manor offered even more opportunities for socialization, with its daily group meals, field trips, and other organized activities.[596] He apparently took full advantage of the multitude of opportunities, making many new friends at the Manor.[597]

Howard Bailey was a fellow resident with whom Clifford became friends early on; later, they were frequent companions. Howard lived on the same floor as Clifford and at 77 was almost the same age. On almost daily lunchtime visits to the Bellflower Senior Nutrition Center, they often walked together, or Howard drove them.

Mealtimes at the Manor also presented opportunities for him to meet and become friends with other residents. Clifford could cook in his own apartment, but he frequently ate dinners at the Manor's downstairs dining room, particularly on Tuesday and Thursday nights, after which he walked over to the common area for bingo games, travel videos, or group choir practice.[598] For most of his years there, Clifford embodied the "active senior" on which the Manor's adverting focused.

Clifford continued his community and civic involvement while living at the Manor, just as he had done while living on Ryon Avenue. He served for a time as director, and then president, of the Advisory Council for the Bellflower Senior Nutrition Site and director of an advisory council for the Human Services Association in nearby Bell Gardens.[599] He also remained an active member of the Bellflower Presbyterian Church and continued to serve as a deacon there on most Sundays.[600]

Even with his busy schedule at the Manor, at church, and in his community, Clifford managed to take some longer trips with a few family members. During his years in Bellflower, he sometimes stayed a week or longer with YaoTim in Placerville or with Milly in San Diego on extended visits. Clifford also took some "dream" trips in 1992 and 1993 with his eldest son, Chuck, and daughter, YaoTim, and her husband, Bob. The first was a tour, driving to Seattle, where he was born, and then flying from Seattle to Juneau, Alaska, where he had spent part of his youth.[601] From Juneau they flew to Glacier Bay and then took a cruise to Sitka, Alaska, before flying back to Seattle.[602]

The second trip was a weeklong stay on the island of Maui, one of the Hawaiian islands Clifford had not previously visited. They took a side trip to Oahu, where Chuck drove Clifford, Bob, and YaoTim all around the island and showed them where the Army had stationed him during the 1950s.[603]

Choir practice at the Manor; Clifford is at far left.

Clifford, far left, and his friend Howard Bailey, far right, at the Bellflower Senior Nutrition Center for lunch with a couple of other friends

These two trips would be Clifford's last out-of-state trips; at 84, his advancing age and deteriorating health limited his mobility and activities.

DECLINING HEALTH

In 1993, Clifford suffered some serious health setbacks. He was not eating well and had lost significant weight, gradually declining to 114 pounds from his average weight of 140 pounds. He also was experiencing unexplained blood loss. Clifford was still living at the Manor at the time, but YaoTim offered to take him up to her home in Placerville to see if, with closer monitoring, he could regain his weight and strength. With YaoTim and Bob's attention and some medical procedures, Clifford did begin to eat better.[604] Of the 98 days between January 16 and April 24, he spent 88 in Placerville with YaoTim and Bob.

Aside from gaining vitality during that period, Clifford witnessed two milestone events while up in Placerville. First, he completed editing *The Grandparent Book*, YaoTim's compilation of Clifford's writings, personal commentaries by almost all his living children, and notes and interviews about his genealogy and his life, including the time shared with his beloved wife, Miao Ying.[605] Second, he learned from his oldest son Chuck and

Back row, from left: Joseph Albert, Philip, Chuck, Robert, and Ed; front row, from left: Dolly, Milly, Clifford, YaoTim, and George at Clifford's 81st birthday celebration in Newport Beach Harbor, 1990

Chuck's fiancée, Rhonda, that he would become a grandfather again. Some months later, he would meet Chuck and Rhonda's baby son, Cory, the last of his grandchildren to born during his lifetime.[606]

After staying with YaoTim and Bob, Clifford spent 23 days at Joseph Albert and Dianne's house as his health, appetite, and weight continued to improve. By the time he returned to the Manor in May 1993, his health had recovered so dramatically that he was again participating in group activities there. He even started playing, and winning, in the Manor's Tuesday night bingo games.[607]

By early 1994, however, Clifford's health once again was deteriorating. He had problems with his back from osteoporosis, as well as other issues, including emphysema, and he still was losing blood internally, for reasons doctors never were able to determine. Walking became extremely painful, and he began to spend much more time in bed.[608] He went downstairs less frequently for group activities and often asked for his meals to be brought up to his room. He had stopped going to the Nutrition Center for lunch and made it to church on Sundays only infrequently.

The staff at the Manor and his family agreed that the Manor seemed like it was no longer a good fit for Clifford; he needed more care than the independent-living arrangements offered. His children attempted to locate an appropriate assisted-living facility close to his community and friends that could provide the type of care Clifford needed, but facilities in Bellflower were either inappropriate or unavailable.[609]

In April 1994, the children moved their father to a small, 24-hour care, assisted-living home on Lola Avenue in Stanton, about 13 miles away from the Manor. It was a small-group home for only five clients, set in a quiet residential neighborhood. There, Clifford had a private room, three meals a day, and monitoring of his medications. The Lola Avenue home had the added advantage that the live-in owner, Elena, could take him every Sunday to the same Presbyterian church that she attended, St. Paul's, just a mile away, when he felt well enough to go.[610]

Clifford was generally well-taken care of there. He had to only walk a dozen or so steps out of his ground-floor room to the dining area for all of his meals. Home-health nurses and caregivers regularly visited. But Clifford was never totally happy there. He missed his many friends at the Manor, the Nutrition Center, and the church where he had been a deacon. He no longer had his own studio apartment, and the community television in the group home's common area left much to be desired.

Clifford never complained much, but as his children visited him, they soon learned that another resident there was loud, offensive, and constantly complained. This must have been difficult for a quiet gentleman like him to tolerate without substantial difficulty.[611] Still, he received good physical care around the clock, and his children visited him regularly, sometimes taking him out for meals at home or at restaurants.[612]

It was on one of those visits by Joseph Albert and Dianne on the evening of Father's Day, June 18, 1995, that they found Clifford in extreme physical distress. He was lying in bed, listless, lethargic, and disoriented. They called his doctor, Paul Yoon, MD, who convinced them to immediately take

Top row, from left: Chuck, Dolly, George, and Joseph Albert; bottom row: YaoTim, Clifford, and Milly at Clifford's 86th birthday celebration at Albert and Dianne's home in Downey in November 1995

Clifford to the emergency room at Bellwood Hospital in Bellflower. There, Clifford underwent a series of tests that showed inoperable lung cancer. Although radiation treatment would help extend his life, Dr. Yoon's prognosis was that Clifford only had about six months to live.[613]

After that brief hospital stay in June 1995, he went to live with Joseph Albert and Dianne and their two youngest children, Paul, 14, and Casey, 8. Clifford received consultations at City of Hope in Irwindale and began radiation treatment at Downey Community Hospital's radiology clinic. As in the past – especially in times of crisis – his children came together and collaborated, this time for the acute care Clifford needed during his cancer treatments and his terminal illness.[614] He required 24/7 care even more intensely than what he had received at the assisted-living facility in Stanton.

The nine siblings and their families scheduled contributions of time and money from all who could afford it. They hired a caregiver for eight hours per day during the weekdays while Joseph Albert was at work and Dianne was busiest with the kids. While Joseph Albert and Dianne usually cared for Clifford when the caregiver wasn't there, sometimes Clifford's other children would help. They would come by to sit with him or take him for treatment and medical consultations. Virtually every weekend, one of Clifford's other children and his or her spouse would come to the house to watch over Clifford and give Joseph Albert and Dianne a break. Or, in Milly and Marcel's case, they would take Clifford home with them for the weekend or longer.[615]

Through it all, Clifford generally maintained his gentleness and consideration of others, even in the last months of his life. When he was in extreme pain, he would sometimes get a little grumpy, but mostly he just quietly endured. In July 1995, he underwent regular radiation treatments several times a week. He was extremely tired after each treatment, but he managed to be "charming as usual with the nurses and doctor" the next time.[616] Clifford even managed to sit through what would end up being his final birthday party in November 1995, two days before his 86th birthday.[617]

ETERNAL REUNION

In 1995, Joseph Albert and Dianne planned to spend several days between Christmas and New Year's Day at their second home at Big Bear Lake while Milly and Marcel hosted Clifford at their San Diego home. On Christmas Eve, Milly picked up Clifford in Downey and drove him to San Diego. Clifford appeared quite weak. Perhaps he should not have traveled, but others had made plans, and Clifford didn't complain. He went along with whatever he thought would make his family happy, as he had done most of his life. But two days later, he appeared so weak and ill that Milly took him to an urgent care center, where the doctor advised her to have Clifford admitted to the nearest hospital.[618]

As with their mother in 1972, the other Lumsdaine siblings were quickly notified about their father's failing health. All of Clifford's children, and many of his sons- and daughters-in-law, converged on Sharp Memorial Hospital in San Diego. They took turns keeping vigil, day and night, with their father over the next several days so he would know that each of his children was there with him.

Clifford's condition did not always allow him to verbally respond, but words were unnecessary to make his final moments meaningful.[619] Each of his children had a chance to say goodbye in their own way. At one point, Ed held his father's hand, and Clifford held Ed's hand, something Ed never recalled his dad doing before. On January 1, 1996, after praying the "Our Father" with the hospital chaplain,[620] he told a nurse, with brave resignation, "I'm dying."[621] After 24 years apart, Clifford Vere Lumsdaine then passed on to join his beloved wife, Miao Ying.

Clifford Vere Lumsdaine
1909 – 1996

Clifford's death was neither sudden nor unexpected, but for the family he left behind, it was no less difficult.[622] As with Miao Ying, Clifford's memorial service was held at the Church of Our Fathers in Forest Lawn. It was conducted by a minister from St. Paul's Presbyterian Church in Anaheim, the last church that Clifford had regularly attended. He is buried in Forest Lawn's Ascension Garden, next to Miao Ying. They are united once again, never to be parted.[623]

A Service of Memory
for
CLIFFORD VERE LUMSDAINE
Born November 1909 — Seattle, Washington
Passed away January 1, 1996 — San Diego, California
Service held January 6, 1996 — 12:00 noon
at the
Church of Our Father's
Forest Lawn Mortuary
Cypress, California
Officiating — The Reverend William Halliday
Saint Paul's Presbyterian Church
Anaheim, California

Interment — Ascension Gardens at Forest Lawn
Cypress, California

Afterword

The Legacy of Clifford and Miao Ying Lumsdaine

As I write this epilogue during the 2020 COVID-19 pandemic, many families, including ours, are physically separated as the country, and the world, try to contain this virus. For many people, this year has been one of sacrifice and heartbreak; it has brought into sharper focus the things that really matter. My parents' story took place in the last century, but how they lived their lives exemplifies what it means to be family, to love and support each other, even in the most challenging times.

Clifford Vere Lumsdaine and Ho Miao Ying were two people born on opposite sides of the world and who came from vastly different cultures. They dared to love so deeply that no obstacle was too big to overcome. No separation could keep them apart. They showed their unbreakable commitment to each other and to their children not by hugs and kisses but by how they continued to care for and provide for their family through unimaginable hardship. To them, "love conquers all" was not just a saying. It was their reason for being.

Clifford and Miao Ying left behind nine children, 23 grandchildren, and at the time of this writing, 38 great-grandchildren and 8 great-great-grandchildren. Their legacy is a large and sprawling family that continues to care for and provide for each other, especially in times of trouble and need, despite philosophical, political, or physical separations. I cannot know what will happen after this pandemic ends. What I know with certainty is that the same love, courage, and perseverance that brought and kept Clifford and Miao Ying together will continue through untold future generations.

Joseph Albert Lumsdaine
December 2020
Downey, Calif.

Appendices

Appendices I-VI may be made available with the digital version of INDOMITABLE to family members with permission from the author or his successors and assigns. Appendices VII and VIII are available to anyone with a print or digital version of INDOMITABLE.

Photo credits

All images courtesy of the Lumsdaine family except as noted below.

Page 4: *RMS Niagara:* Wikimedia Commons, https://commons.wikimedia. org/wiki/File:Niagara.gif

Page 7: *Shanghai Maru:* Caledonian Maritime Research Trust, clydeships. co.uk/view.php?ref=15565

Page 9: Map of Shunde District, China, and Pearl River delta area: original author: Croquant. This is a modified map. Wikimedia Commons, https:// commons.wikimedia.org/wiki/File:Pearl_River_Delta_Area.png

Page 11: The Bund, Wikimedia Commons: https://commons.wikimedia.org/ wiki/File:Bund_in_1930_-_Shanghai_Urban_Planning_Exhibition_Center.jpg

Page 12: Shanghai International Settlement: Wikimedia Commons, https:// commons.wikimedia.org/wiki/File:Shanghai_Nanjing_Road_1930s.jpg

Page 13: Map of Shanghai's International Settlement: University of Texas Libraries, "Outline of the Plan of the Foreign Settlements at Shanghai", from Col. A. M. Murray's Imperial Outposts, from a Strategical and Commercial Aspect, with Special Reference to the Japanese Alliance. Published by John Murray (London), 1907. http://www.lib.utexas.edu/maps/historical/ shanghai_1907.jpg

Page 17: Cathay Hotel postcard: *The Newsletter,* International Institute for Asian Studies; https://www.iias.asia/the-newsletter/article/foreigners-treaty-port-china. Original from "All About Shanghai: A Standard Guidebook" by H.J. Lethbridge (1934)

Page 18: Old Jazz Band: https://www.pinterest.com/pin/843369467691251325/

Page 31: Japanese troop carriers: pinterest.com

Page 32: Japanese tanks: https://www.military-history.org/articles/war-zone-city-of-terror-the-japanese-takeover-of-shanghai.htm

Page 33: Japanese troops on streets of International Settlement: https://www.histclo.com/essay//war/ww2/camp/pac/china/city/shang/w2cs-bat37.html

Page 34: Armband: CSUN Oviatt Library Special Collections and Archives - Civilian Internment in China, 1941-1945. https://library.csun.edu/SCA/Peek-in-the-Stacks/civilian-internment

Page 36: Japanese soldier: World War II Database – https://ww2db.com/image.php?image_id=23915

Page 40: Pootung Camp: https://www.globaltimes.cn/content/853558.shtml, courtesy of Greg Leck

Page 48: Red Cross food ration box: https://commons.wikimedia.org/wiki/File:Prisoner_of_War_Parcel,_British_Red_Cross.JPG

Page 64: Chinese troops marching into Shanghai: https://en.wikipedia.org/wiki/Shanghai_Campaign#/media/File:PLA_Troops_entered_to_Nanjing_Road,_Shanghai.jpg

Page 65: Red propaganda poster: http://www.commonprogram.science/art54.html

Page 65: Yellow propaganda poster: Center for Research Libraries holdings, Chinese Pamphlets: Political communication and mass education in the early period of the People's Republic of China (1947–1954). https://www.crl.edu/focus/article/5954. From the website of https://adamcathcart.com/2018/03/19/cruel-resurrection-chinese-comics-and-the-korean-war/

Page 83: Passenger train: http://kfwong2013.blogspot.com/2015/03/blog-post_15.html

Page 85: Lo Wu bridge: https://www.luoow.com/dc_hk/107668918

Page 113: SS President Wilson postcard: Pinterest; https://www.pinterest.com/pin/574490496187113104/?d=t&mt=login

Page 114: Embarcadero piers: Courtesy of the San Francisco History Center, San Francisco Public Library; https://www.inside-guide-to-san-francisco-tourism.com/san-francisco-piers.html

Page 119: Apartment building: https://myemail.constantcontact.com/From-the-heart.html?soid=1102010860910&aid=g_Ig0gRRric

Endnotes

1   Arthur Henry Vere Lumsdaine (hereinafter "Arthur Henry") was born on February 9, 1882, in Burwood, Australia, to Edward Alexander and Florence (Halloran) Lumsdaine. Birth Certificate, Appendix 1, p. 1. He had traveled to the U.S. by way of Johannesburg, South Africa, and Montreal and Vancouver, Canada, to Seattle in 1906. Arthur Henry married Clifford's mother at St. Joseph's Catholic Church in Seattle on March 3, 1908. Marriage Certificate, Appendix 1, p. 2. Email from YaoTim Allen, 10/04/2007, Appendix 3, p. 1-2. Arthur Henry died in England in 1962. Appendix IV, *Transition to the Colony: An Australian Family*, by Geoffrey Lumsdaine, July 2002, at p. 56, Appendix IV. See also Last Will and Testament dated 1/2/1952, Appendix 1, p. 3; Email from YaoTim Allen, 12/8/2010, Appendix 3 p. 3. According to Clifford, Arthur Henry was "a self-made man" who did not smoke or drink." According to Virginia, Clifford's half-sister, Arthur Henry was "a handsome, vain, and brilliant man." *The Grandparent Book* (hereinafter *1995 Grandparent Book*), Appendix 2, Section 2, infra. Clifford's birth certificate incorrectly lists Arthur Henry's age as 28. Appendix 1, p. 5.

2   Mary Ellen Margaret Clifford was born on March 2, 1881, to Daniel Clifford and Mary Ann Bresnahan of Farmington, Iowa. Both the Cliffords and the Bresnahans had emigrated from County Kerry, Ireland. Mary Ellen lived in both Farmington and Fort Madison, Iowa, before moving to Seattle in 1905 to work at Seattle General Hospital. Email from YaoTim Allen, 9/28/2015, Appendix 3, p. 4-5. She died from diabetes mellitus on December 10, 1911. Death Certificate, Appendix 1, p. 4. According to Arthur Henry, Mary Ellen was a "devoted mother who loved him [Clifford] as no other human being could and who watched over him so carefully and tenderly from the time of his birth." *1995 Grandparent Book*, at Section 1 Our Baby Book by Arthur Henry, Appendix 2.

3   *1995 Grandparent Book,* YaoTim (Lumsdaine) Allen, December 20, 1995, at Section 1, Our Baby Book, by Arthur Henry Vere Lumsdaine, November 1909-1913 (hereinafter CVL Baby Book), Appendix 2. He was only 4 pounds at birth and may have been kept at the hospital for 10 days because of pneumonia, *Ibid.* at Section 2, p. 14.

4   CVL Baby Book, *supra.*

5   CVL Baby Book, *supra.* Also see Email from YaoTim Allen, 10/04/2007, Appendix 3, p. 2.

6   CVL Baby Book, *supra*

7   CVL Baby Book, *supra.* Death Certificate, Appendix 1, p. 4.

8   *1995 Grandparent Book*, Appendix 2, Section 2, p. 3 at Question 24.

9   As to the marriage, see CVL Baby Book, *supra.* Gladys Ethel Strayer was born on August 20, 1884, in Swanton, Ohio (Declaration of Margaret M. Strayer dated October 5, 1920) and died in 1961 in Seattle. She preferred the nickname "Gerry" and was called that by her family. Gerry was a schoolteacher and a music teacher, supporting herself

sometimes with the help of her sister, Margaret, who never married and lived with Gerry until Gerry's death in 1961 in Seattle. See Appendix V, Family Background, Johnny Harper Lumsdaine (2019).

10   CVL Baby Book, *supra*. *1995 Grandparent Book*, Appendix 2, Section 4, 1987 Interview of Dad, pp. 2-3.

11   *1995 Grandparent Book*, Appendix 2, Section 2, at p. 2 (question #14). Arthur Allen Lumsdaine (hereinafter "Arthur Allen") was born on November 23, 1913 and died on May 1, 1989 in Seattle. He earned his PhD in psychology at Stanford University and became an applied psychologist researching media and programmed learning and teaching for many years at the University of Washington in Seattle. en.wikipedia.org/ wiki/ Arthur_A._Lumsdaine

12   *1995 Grandparent Book*, Appendix 2, Section 2, p. 5 (question #5).

13   *1995 Grandparent Book*, Appendix 2, Section 4, 1987 Interview of Dad, pp. 2-3. "[T]hey had a brawl or something I don't know...." *Ibid.*, at p. 1. One can only speculate as to why Arthur Henry left the U.S. for Australia at that time and whether it was intended to be only a visit to family or a more permanent separation from his wife, Gerry. In the 1920 U.S. census, Arthur Henry lists himself as residing in his Seattle residence as head of household with Gerry and two sons, Clifford and Arthur, without mentioning his daughter, Virginia. Whether his declaring in 1920 that Clifford, who was then in Australia, was residing in their Seattle residence indicated that Arthur Henry had only intended to have taken Clifford to Australia in 1918 for a short visit, or was a mistake or obfuscation, one can only guess.

14   The *RMS Niagara* was commissioned in 1912 and traveled regularly between Vancouver, BC, Canada, and Australia. It was owned by the Union Steam Ship Company and sank after striking a German mine in 1940. For possible links between the *RMS Niagara* and the spread of the pandemic, see "*RMS Niagara* – the 1918 influenza pandemic" at nzhistory.govt.nz/media/photo/rms-niagara (August 10, 2020).

15   en.wikipedia.org/wiki/Spanish_flu. (August 9, 2020)

16   *1995 Grandparent Book*, Appendix 2, Section 4, 1987 Interview of Dad, p.1.

17   Gladys Valentine Ghys was born on July 15, 1899, in London and would have been 20 years old when she gave birth to Virginia. She married Arthur Henry in 1926, and they were divorced in 1949. She subsequently married William James Gande in 1956. Gladys died in California in 1994. myheritage.com/names/arthur_lumsdaine and myheritage. com/names/william_gande

18   The RMS *Niagara* left Vancouver in October 1918 and docked in Sydney in August 1919. *1995 Grandparent Book*, Appendix 2, Section 4, 1987 Interview of Dad, p.1. Virginia (Lumsdaine) McCutcheon was born about 4 months later in Seattle, on December 23, 1919 (myshanghaifilm.com/my-shanghai-journal) to Arthur Henry, age 37, and Gladys, age 20. Assuming Virginia was not born at less than four months, conception likely took place on the ship sometime between October 1918 and August 1919.

19   "In 1900 and for several decades thereafter, out-of-wedlock births were notorious and rare." pbs.org/fmc/timeline/ddisruption.htm (8/7/2020). There would have been great social pressure to have the woman be married off or leave for a distant community and give the baby up for adoption. Unmarried mothers were considered "ruined" or branded as "sex delinquents" and subjected to the juvenile justice system. encyclopedia.com/ social-sciences/applied-and-social-sciences-magazines/births-out-wedlock (8/7/2020). One can only speculate whether Arthur Henry, not wanting Gladys to be "ruined" and subjected to shame, had taken responsibility for his paternity of Virginia by taking Gladys away from the many Lumsdaine relatives in Australia and going back to the U.S.

20 According to Clifford, Arthur Henry brought Gladys to Seattle, where Arthur Henry's wife, Gerry, helped to take care of both Gladys and baby Virginia after she was born. *1995 Grandparent Book*, Appendix 2, Section 4, 1987 Interview of Dad, p. 1.

21 *1995 Grandparent Book*, Appendix 2, Section 4, at p. 2.

22 Clifford, about 11 or 12 years old at the time, was quite attached to Gerry and was very upset when Gerry and Arthur left Australia. *1995 Grandparent Book*, Appendix 2, Section 4, 1987 Interview of Dad, at p. 3.

23 At different times, Clifford lived in Artarmon, a suburb on the lower North Shore of Sydney, about six miles northwest of Sydney's central business district. He also lived in Lane Cove, another place where Clifford stayed with his grandparents. Finally, he lived for a short time in Manly, when his stepmother, Gerry, and his half-brother, Arthur Allen, came briefly to live in Australia. After that, Clifford again lived in Manly at the house of his uncle, Allen Lumsdaine, before he returned to the United States in 1926. *1995 Grandparent Book*, Appendix 2, Section 4, 1987 Interview of Dad, pp. 1-3.

24 Edward Alexander Lumsdaine was born on May 21, 1848, and died on January 23, 1943, at age 94. He was a solicitor, the equivalent of an attorney in the United States. He was married to Florence Edith Halloran, who was born on November 14, 1850, and died on July 13, 1940, in Sydney, Australia. Appendix IV, *Transition to the Colony: An Australian Family*, by Geoffrey Lumsdaine, July 2002, at p.52 (which incorrectly lists Florence's death as occurring in 1884).

25 *1995 Grandparent Book*, Appendix 2, Section 4, 1987 Interview of Dad, p. 2.

26 "Through the efforts of my grandpa, I got a job at a firm of … solicitors." Ibid. at p.2. It was at the Law Offices of Dodd & Richardson, Sydney NSW, from September 1925 to June 1926. *1995 Grandparent Book*, Appendix 2, Section 2, p. 15. It was at about this time when Arthur Henry sent Clifford to live in Manly with Uncle Allen Lumsdaine, who was married and had children similar in age to Clifford. Allen Lumsdaine was born in 1879 and would have been about 40 years old when Clifford was asked to live with him. Appendix IV, *Transition to the Colony: An Australian Family*, by Geoffrey Lumsdaine, July 2002, p. 56. Manly is a coastal suburb about 11 miles northeast of Sydney's central business district.

27 *1995 Grandparent Book*, Appendix 2, Section 4, 1987 Interview of Dad, p. 2-3, quotes at p.3.

28 treatyportsport.com/lumsdaine--j-l-s--1940-.html

29 *1995 Grandparent Book*, Appendix 2, Section 4, 1987 Interview of Dad, at p. 3. The car they drove was a Rickenbacker, as shown in the photograph on pg. 5 with Arthur seated inside and Clifford standing next to it. *Id.*

30 *1995 Grandparent Book*, Appendix 2, Section 4, 1987 Interview of Dad, at p.4. Arthur Henry was divorced from Gerry and married Gladys (Ghys) Lumsdaine sometime in 1926.

31 Clifford went to Galileo High School and worked at Langley & Michaels, Druggists. *Id.* Clifford was on the SS Oregonian from November 1927 to January 1928. *1995 Grandparent Book*, Appendix 2, Section 2, p. 15 and Section 4, 1987 Interview of Dad, at p.4. The Panama Canal was completed in 1914, and given that the trip took only two months round-trip, Clifford likely made a canal passage.

32 *1995 Grandparent Book*, Appendix 2, Section 2, p. 15 and Section 4, 1987 Interview of Dad, at p.4.

33   *1995 Grandparent Book*, Appendix 2, Section 4, 1987 Interview of Dad, p. 4.

34   The ferries were very active in San Francisco Bay Area before the opening of the Golden Gate Bridge in 1937 and the San Francisco-Oakland Bay Bridge in 1939. Clifford held this job from May 1928 to November 1929. en.wikipedia.org/wiki/South_Pacific_Coast_Railroad

35   Clifford resigned from Southern Pacific on November 30, 1929, and left for Shanghai on December 4. *1995 Grandparent Book*, Appendix 2, Section 2, p. 15, and Section 4, 1987 Interview of Dad, pp.4-5. This would have been right after the "Black Tuesday" stock market crash on October 29, 1929, which launched the Great Depression in the U.S., but before its full impact would have been felt. Scholars have debated whether the Great Depression had as much effect on China, particularly the vibrant city of Shanghai, as it did on the U.S. and other parts of the world. en.wikipedia.org/wiki/Economic_history_of_China_(1912-49); and "A Short History of Shanghai," *The New York Times*, archive.nytimes.com/www.nytimes.com/fodors/top/features/travel/destinations/   asia/china/shanghai/fdrs_feat_145_5.html

36   According to YaoTim Allen, the two characters together, Miao Ying, means "beautiful heroine" or "beautiful slender lady (like a phoenix)." Appendix V, YaoTim Allen Interview, Questionnaire Responses at p. 1, at para. 2. The name "Ying" could also mean "an eagle," "jade" or "victorious," according to thenamemeaning.com/ying/ #ixzz5jcAvFbuO, while the name "Miao" is said to refer to an ethnic group in the part of south China that includes the Guangdong (formerly Canton) province where the Shunde District is located; en.wikipedia.org/wiki/ Miao_people

37   en.wikipedia.org/wiki/Shunde_District

38   Specific dates on the Chinese calendar change every year on the Western (Gregorian) calendar; The Chinese Calendar (timeanddate.com/calendar/about-chinese.html). After Miao Ying came to the United States in 1961, the family celebrated her birthday on a different date each Western calendar year. Several family members began to ask her if she could specify a birth date on the Western calendar for her birthday celebrations. On one of her Hong Kong trips, Miao Ying consulted with an expert who determined for her that the Western calendar birth date was July 23, 1910, using the date on the Chinese (Julian) calendar and converting it to that date on the Western calendar. Appendix V, YaoTim Allen Interview, Questionnaire Responses at p. 1, at para. 1. There are several different dates listed in different documents: July 28, 1910, on her Chinese passport and U.S. Immigration and Naturalization Entry Permit; July 26, 1910, in her 1972 hospital records; and July 23, 1910, on her death certificate. Appendix I, Original Documents, under tab, "Mom."

39   Chinese surnames are generally patrilineal; a descendant's surname follows that of his or her father. The name "Ho" is a Romanized transliteration of the Chinese character shown in the photo accompanying the story. In 2012, there were more than 14 million people named "Ho" in China; it was the 17th most common Chinese family name in 2002; en.wikipedia.org/wiki/He_(surname). Its origin is from the royal house of Ji during the Zhou Dynasty that ruled a large part of northern China from 1046 B.C. to 771 B.C.; en.wikipedia.org/wiki/Zhou_dynasty

40   Appendix V, YaoTim Allen Interview, Questionnaire Responses at pp. 4-5, at para. 7.

41   *Ibid.*

42   If Ho Kok Peh and Liang Yee Dai were about the same age, and she survived him by about 17 years (dying in 1950 at age 72), Ho Kok Peh would have been in his 50s when he died. See Appendix V: Philip Lumsdaine Interview, 2017-06-20, p. 2, para. 3; Milly Ratermann Interview, May 3, 2017, p. 1, para. 1.

43 Appendix V: Philip Lumsdaine Interview, 2017-06-20, p. 2, para. 3; Milly Ratermann Interview, May 3, 2017, p. 1, para. 1.

44 Appendix V, YaoTim Allen Interview, Questionnaire Responses at p. 3, para. 5. A bronze temple incense burner in Foshan City had many "Ho" names inscribed on it. *Ibid.*

45 Appendix V, YaoTim Allen Interview, Questionnaire Responses at p. 2, para. 4. See "Women's Education in Traditional and Modern China," Wong Yin Lee (1995), *Women's History Review*, 4:3, 345-367. It was widely believed that "A Woman's Strength Lies in Her Ignorance." *Id.* at p. 353. Literacy was associated with moral corruption in women that rendered them unsuitable as good wives. *Id* p. 354.

46 *Ibid.* Miao Ying would also comment on the roughness of her hands in relation to this work she had done. Appendix V: Elaine Lumsdaine Interview, August 31, 2018, p. 5, para. 4; Dolly Lumsdaine Veale Interview, November 1, 2017, pp. 2-3, para. 15.

47 Appendix V: Dolly Lumsdaine Veale Interview, November 1, 2017, pp. 2-3, para. 15.

48 Appendix V, YaoTim Allen Interview, Questionnaire Responses at pp. 1-2, at para. 3.

49 The infant mortality rate in China overall in early 1900s was 42%; ourworldindata.org/child-mortality

50 Chinese art and poetry dates to the earliest dynasties and developed into "the three perfections" of calligraphy, poetry, and painting, often with a painting inspired by poetry and combined with calligraphy. As in many other cultures, Chinese artists and poets made their livings relying on patrons. See, generally, James Cahill, Wai-Kam Ho, and Claudia Brown (1989), *Artists and Patrons: Some Social and Economic Aspects of Chinese Painting* pp. 3-4, 23, Department of Art History, University of Kansas, Kansas City. While none of Ho Kok Peh's artworks are known to exist today, the fact that he was reputed to be at least an artist and a poet makes it likely that he would have attempted "the three perfections" by incorporating calligraphy into his works.

51 Ho Kok Peh's half-brother lived in Shanghai and was quite wealthy, as evidenced by the fact that he had five wives. Presumably, the half-brother would have had access to the "rich and famous" who would be the types to commission art and poetry. This is according to Sai Suk Kung, the half-brother's son; the author has a taped but not yet transcribed interview with Mr. Sai. Still, Miao Ying's family was not rich because Ho Kok Peh chose to only work when he needed money to buy cigarettes and other luxuries. Otherwise, according to Liang Yee Dai, he would turn away work even when it was available.

52 *1995 Grandparent Book*, Appendix 2, Section 4, 1987 Interview of Dad, p. 4.

53 Between 1929 and 1932, global gross domestic product (GDP) fell by 15% amid rising nationalism; en.wikipedia.org/wiki/Great_Depression, en.wikipedia.org/wiki/Nationalism. In contrast, Shanghai was becoming a center of commerce and finance that rivaled New York and a city of fashion, art, and vice that rivaled Paris; theguardian.com/society/2017/mar/11/1930s-humanity-darkest-bloodiest-hour-paying-attention-second-world-war, frommers.com/destinations/shanghai/in-depth/history, "A Short History of Shanghai," *The New York Times*, *supra*, at fn 28.

54 In the 1930s, Shanghai alone produced more than 40% of China's manufactured goods and more than 50% of its textiles, including cotton and silk. The city's population more than tripled – from 1 million to 3.5 million – between 1910 and 1930, with over 40,000 foreign immigrants coming into the city during the 1930s alone. *The Dream and the Reality: Rural-Urban Migration to Shanghai (1927-1937)*, by Lei Shi, Universitat Autonoma de Barcelona (June 2017) ddd.uab.cat/pub/tesis/2017/hdl_10803_455000/lesh1de1.pdf

55 en.wikipedia.org/wiki/Shanghai_International_Settlement (8/12/2020).

56   en.wikipedia.org/wiki/Gweilo_(8/12/2020)

57   Extensive historical research has shown that there was not actually a sign that read "No dogs or Chinese allowed." There was, however, a sign that reserved park use for "the Foreign Community" only – thereby disallowing Chinese use. Another part of the sign prohibited dogs and bicycles. Therefore, while the physical sign did not specifically state "No dogs or Chinese allowed," the two concepts were put together in such a crass way that they essentially provided the same message, fueling the myth; en.wikipedia.org/wiki/Huangpu_Park. This park is now known as Huangpu Park. Ibid. Also see: Bickers, R., & Wasserstrom, J. (1995), "Shanghai's 'Dogs and Chinese Not Admitted' Sign: Legend, History, and Contemporary Symbol." *The China Quarterly*, 142, 444-466. doi:10.1017/S0305741000035001.

58   Jeffrey Hays (2013), "Foreigners and Chinese in the 19th and 20th Centuries," factsanddetails.com/china/cat2/ sub4/item55.html. See also *Chinese Characteristics*, by Arthur Henderson Smith, (New York: Revell, 1894) ISBN 1-891936-26-3, which was the most widely read book on China among foreign residents there in the 1920s, and see current criticism of its treatment of the topic at akarlin.com, "Book Review: Arthur H. Smith – Chinese Characteristics" (March 28, 2013); akarlin.com/2013/03/chinese-characteristics-arthur-h-smith-review

59   *1995 Grandparent Book*, Appendix 2, Section 2, at p. 14 and Section 4, 1987 Interview of Dad, p. 5.

60   According to YaoTim (Lumsdaine) Allen, the tension apparently stemmed at least in part from the fact that Gladys was only about 10 years older than Clifford. YaoTim's ESM Questionnaire, at para. 40, p. 30. One can only speculate as to her reasons, whether because of the small age difference between them or because Clifford represented Arthur Henry's previous marriage to Gerry.

61   *1995 Grandparent Book*, Appendix 2, Section 4, 1987 Interview of Dad, p. 6.

62   *Ibid.*

63   *1995 Grandparent Book*, Appendix 2, Section 4, 1987 Interview of Dad, p. 5-6. The Shanghai Volunteer Corps was first established in 1853 after China lost the First Opium War, and "foreign concessions" were allowed in Shanghai's International Settlement. The Corps consisted, at various times, of volunteers who were American, British, German, and from other European countries. en.wikipedia.org/wiki/Shanghai_Volunteer_Corps

64   Also known as the "January 28 Incident" because it took place between January 28 and March 3, 1932, the First Shanghai Incident was the first of two battles instigated by the Japanese to seek control of Shanghai. The second battle, known as "The Second Shanghai Incident" or "The Battle for Shanghai," occurred in 1937. *Ibid.* en.wikipedia.org/wiki/January_28_incident

65   *1995 Grandparent Book*, Appendix 2, Section 4, 1987 Interview of Dad, p. 6.

66   Sixty years later, when asked what attracted him to Miao Ying, Clifford said, "She was very pretty." *1995 Grandparent Book*, Appendix 2, Section 2, at p. 10.

67   By 1932, more than 1 million Chinese lived within the International Settlement; en.wikipedia.org/wiki/Shanghai_International_Settlement

68   Juliana Batista (2017) "The Confucianism-Feminism Conflict: Why a New Understanding is Necessary"; schwarzmanscholars.org/news-article/confucianism-feminism-conflict-new-understanding-necessary (August 12, 2020)

69   Appendix V, YaoTim Allen Interview, Questionnaire Responses at p. 2, para. 4. Appendix V, Dolly's Interview of November 1, 2017, para. 15, p.3 (August 12, 2020.

70   en.wikipedia.org/wiki/Color_in_Chinese_culture#white (August 12, 2020)

71   Linghua Xu (Spring 2015, University of Iowa) "Rethinking Woman's Place in Chinese Society from 1919 to 1937"; ir.uiowa.edu/cgi/viewcontent.cgi?article=5859&context=etd (August 12, 2020). The concept of companionate pairing or marriage was perhaps first introduced publicly in Shanghai around the time of the 1935 Shanghai Film Festival with the film "A New Woman." *Id.* Whether Miao Ying saw this film or read articles about it would be speculation. That she was "a new woman" of that era is well-evidenced by how she behaved toward her former boyfriend and thereafter toward Clifford.

72   Appendix V, YaoTim Allen Questionnaire Responses at p. 2, at para. 4.

73   Harry Ho was an acquaintance whom Clifford had met in Shanghai. Clifford had received a letter of introduction to Harry from the department store's San Francisco office. Harry had spent about 15 years in the U.S. and was fairly bilingual in Chinese and English. *1995 Grandparent Book*, Appendix 2, Section 2, p. 10, and Section 4, 1987 Interview of Dad, p.6-7.

74   *Id.* at p. 10.

75   "My dad hired a teacher, a Chinese teacher from the Shanghai American School....[It] was the phonetic system, so he taught me to speak as well as copy the sounds so I could read back....[After a while,] we stopped the program." *1995 Grandparent Book*, Appendix 2, Section 4, 1987 Interview of Dad, at p.6.

76   *1995 Grandparent Book*, Appendix 2, Section 2, p. 10.

77   In fact, Miao Ying did not learn to speak English until almost 30 years later, after coming to the U.S., and then only occasional phrases. Later in her life, when asked why she never really tried learning English, she stated that her husband spoke Chinese, and all her children were bilingual, so there was no need. Appendix V, YaoTim's Questionnaire Reponses, p. 4, Question 6.

78   *Id.* Here lies another good example of Miao Ying as much more of the type of "new woman" in 1930s China than the more traditional Chinese woman who practices passivity and demureness. See Linghua Xu (Spring 2015 University of Iowa) "Rethinking Woman's Place in Chinese Society from 1919 to 1937," ir.uiowa.edu/cgi/ viewcontent. cgi?article=5859&context=etd (August 12, 2020)

79   "One time, Mom and Dad met Mom's ex-boyfriend. He threatened Dad with a gun, and Mom had to step in between them and basically tell the boyfriend to go to hell." Appendix V, Dolly's Interview of November 1, 2017, para. 15, p.3.

80   *1995 Grandparent Book*, Appendix 2, Section 4, 1987 Interview of Dad, at p. 7.

81   Clifford had stated that they had obtained a wedding "contract" in "April of '32." When reminded that he had didn't meet Miao Ying until August 1932, he corrected himself, saying "No, it ... wasn't actually that long after [we met]" in August 1932. *1995 Grandparent Book*, Appendix 2, Section 4, 1987 Interview of Dad, at p. 7. Curiously, the U.S. Federal Bureau of Investigation lists their wedding date as April 22, 1932. See Appendix I, "Dad," tab 1, Memorandum to "Director, FBI" dated April 25, 1952, at p. 16. It is more likely that they entered into the wedding contract in April 1933 rather than April 1932. No one in the family has been able to locate a copy of that marriage contract. This is not surprising given the ravages of the many wars and conflicts fought in Shanghai, the destruction of government records, and the family's flight from those conflicts. For a sample of such a marriage contract, see pinterest.com/pin/594686325770433965 (August 14,2020).

82 *1995 Grandparent Book*, Appendix 2, Section 2, at p. 10.

83 *Ibid*. Her father disowning her resulted in Miao Ying being cut off from the rest of the family until after her father's death, when her mother moved in with her after the death of Ho Gai Zien, Miao Ying's brother.

84 On the negative and deeply held biases that the Chinese and Westerners had toward each other, see endnotes 55-58, *supra*, and text accompanying them.

85 "Miscegenation" is defined as "a mixture of races." merriam-webster.com/dictionary/miscegenation

86 Emma Jinhua Teng, *Eurasian: Mixed Identities in the United States, China, and Hong Kong, 1842-1943* (2013), University of California Press, ISBN 978-0-520-27627-7. In China, it was seen by many as "cultural treason" *Id*. at p. 49 and as "racial and national betrayal" *Id*. at 46. See also "How Mixed Chinese-Western Couples Were Treated a Century Ago," Asia Society (blog), asiasociety.org/blog/asia/how-mixed-chinese-western-couples-were-treated-century-ago, reprinted in Appendix VII.

87 *Ibid*. at pp. 13, 33, 36, and 43. In the U.S., it was even more common for such couplings to be viewed as "the pollution of our blood by intermarriage" leading to "congenital degeneracy" and "criminality" of their offspring. *Id*. at p. 35-36 and 92-95. For an example of an American man and Chinese wife being ostracized in their Shanghai expatriate society, see *Id*. at pp. 135-137.

88 Between 1861 and 1939, 15 U.S. states had anti-miscegenation laws that specifically included Chinese marrying whites. Deenesh Sohoni (Sep 2007), "Unsuitable Suitors: Anti-Miscegenation Laws, Naturalization Laws, and the Construction of Asian Identities," Law and Society Review, jstor.org/stable/4623396, pg. 606. Some states made it criminally illegal, either as a felony or a misdemeanor; other states made such marriages void or voidable. *Ibid*. No state court overturned any such state laws until the California Supreme Court did so in 1948. It was not until 1967 that the U.S. Supreme Court held all such anti-miscegenation laws unconstitutional; en.wikipedia.org/wiki/Anti-miscegenation_laws_in_the_United_States. For an example of anti-miscegenation laws in China, see Genet Jacques (1996) A History of Chinese Civilization (2 ed.), Cambridge University Press, p.294 IASBN 978-0-521-49781-7.

89 The History and Context Of Chinese-Western Intercultural Marriage In Modern And Contemporary China (From 1840 To The 21st Century), by Dr. Qin Bo, *supra* at footnote 50, p. 12; *Cf*. Emma Jinhua Teng, *Eurasian: Mixed Identities in the United States, China, and Hong Kong, 1842-1943* (2013), University of California Press, ISBN 978-0-520-27627-7, pp. 135-137.

90 In the 100 years prior to Clifford and Miao Ying's marriage in 1933, out of hundreds of marriages recorded in Shanghai each year, less than one a year was between a Western man and a Chinese woman. "The History and Context Of Chinese-Western Intercultural Marriage In Modern And Contemporary China (From 1840 To The 21st Century)," by Dr. Qin Bo, *Rozenberg Quarterly* (June 2015) ISSN:2212-425X, http://rozenbergquarterly.com/the-history-and-context-of-chinese-western-intercultural-marriage-in-modern-and-contemporary-china-from-1840-to-the-21st-century; reprinted at Appendix VII. *Cf*. pp. 10-13.

91 Not only had World War II started in Europe in September 1939, but Japan occupied much of China, including Shanghai, by the end of 1937. Unlike Chinese citizens, U.S. citizens – particularly those living in the International Settlement – were not considered enemies of Japan until the U.S. declared war on Japan on December 8, 1941, the day after Japanese planes bombed Pearl Harbor in Hawaii.

92   It should be noted that while this wedding occurred at a U.S. Consulate and thus was subject to federal laws and regulations, such a marriage still would have been prohibited in California for another eight years, until the California Supreme Court ruling in *Perez v. Sharp*, 32 Cal. 2d 711, 198 P. 2d 17 (Cal. 1948), which held unconstitutional California Civil Code section 60, the statute that had prohibited biracial marriages.

93   *1995 Grandparent Book*, Appendix 2, Section 4, 1987 Interview of Dad, at p. 11. See also caption to the above picture next page, *Id.* at Section 4, which states, "The 'official' marriage in 1940 as required by the U.S. government so that Charlie, YaoTim, Edward, and George would be considered U.S. citizens." The Chinese marriage contract and ceremony in April 1933 were not considered a legal marriage by the U.S. Consulate. *Id.*

94   Appendix V, YaoTim Allen Interview, Questionnaire Responses at p.33 (answer to question 42).

95   *1995 Grandparent Book*, Appendix 2, Section 1, last page titled "Kinship and Descendants." The name "James" was added when "Charlie" was baptized while attending Ste. Joan D'Arc School. Only later in life did Charlie – whose siblings always called him "Chuck" – use the name "Charles James Lumsdaine." YaoTim email of July 1, 2019. Appendix V, YaoTim's Interview of 11-21-16, p. 2; YaoTim's Questionnaire, para. 7, p.2.

96   Chuck said it best: "[Y]our generation … would never experience the things we experienced, it's so far-fetched, you can't even imagine it." Appendix V, Chuck's Interview by Anne Lumsdaine, early 2000, Tape #1 as transcribed by Dolly, p. 1, line 3-5.

97   The Chinese word (混血) for biracial children can be translated as "mixed blood," a somewhat pejorative term. en.wikipedia.org/wiki/Multiracial_people_in_China and en.wiktionary.org/ki/%E6%B7%B7%E8%A1%80. In that era in China, such biracial children were generally assumed to be the illegitimate offspring of Western sailors and Chinese prostitutes. Andrew & Bushnell (1907), *Heathen Slaves and Christian Rulers*, pp. 7-10, godswordtowomen.org/Heathen_Slaves_and_Christian_Rulers.pdf reprinted at Appendix VII. See also, "Eurasian (mixed ancestry)" en.wikipedia.org/wiki/Eurasian_(mixed_ancestry) at p. 14-15, at Appendix VII; and Eric Fish, "How Mixed Chinese-Western Couples Were Treated A Century Ago," Asia Society Blog asiasociety.org/blog/_asia/how-mixed-chinese-western-couples-were-treated-century-ago, reprinted at Appendix VII.

98   Emma Jinhua Teng, *Eurasian: Mixed Identities in the United States, China and Hong Kong, 1842-1943* (2013), University of California Press, ISBN 978-0-520-27627-7, pp. 86-111. Even noted "criminal anthropologists" such as Cesare Lambroso (1837-1909) argued that those of "mixed races" inherited a propensity for crime and violence through their non-white parent. *Id.* at pp. 94-95.

99   *Ibid.* According to Massachusetts Institute of Technology professor Emma J. Teng, "There was absolutely nationalistic backlash against [Chinese who married foreigners], especially with the emergence of Chinese nationalism in the early 20th century." Fish, "How Mixed Chinese-Western Couples Were Treated A Century Ago," Asia Society Blog, asiasociety.org/blog/asia/how-mixed-chinese-western-couples-were-treated-century-ago (August 17, 2020).

100 *1995 Grandparent Book*, Appendix 2, Section 2, at p. 15.

101 Years later, Clifford told YaoTim about this visit, which would have been around 1934. The two families apparently lost track of each other until after Clifford's death in 1996. Later that fall, YaoTim met up with Virginia in Las Vegas at a convention for a group called "Old China Hands" that consisted of people who had left China sometime after World War II. From then until Virginia's death, there were several contacts between her and family members of Clifford Lumsdaine. When Joseph Albert and Dianne visited with her in 2011, Virginia confirmed having witnessed her mother, Gladys, telling Clifford not to visit them.

102 *1995 Grandparent Book*, Appendix 2, Section 1, last page titled "Kinship and Descendants." While Clifford spelled it "Shum" Shui Po, the name of the district is properly
spelled as "Sham" Shui Po.

103 *1995 Grandparent Book*, Appendix 2, Section 2, at p. 13.

104 At Paramount, Clifford worked part of the time for Anna May Wong, a well-known Chinese-American actress in the 1930s, whose signature movie, Daughter of Shanghai,
was released in December 1937. *1995 Grandparent Book*, Appendix 2, Section 2, p.
16, at number 19. YaoTim's Interview of 11-21-16, at para. 16, pp. 2-3. Anna May Wong:
en.m.wikipedia.org/wiki/Anna_May_Wong

105 *1995 Grandparent Book*, Appendix 2, Section 2, p. 19.

106 YaoTim's ESM Questionnaire, para. 32, pp. 26-27. On August 17, 2020, YaoTim clari-
fied her statement in her questionnaire that "Because of the bad experience with Anne
which resulted in her death, Mom was very cautious about having servants tend to her
babies." Anne was still nursing when Miao Ying became pregnant with YaoTim. It was
common in that era to use a wet nurse to continue breastfeeding for a baby in that
situation because of difficulties with milk production, etc., when a woman is pregnant.
See, e.g., Marygrace Taylor, "Breastfeeding While Pregnant and Tandem Nursing," July
22, 2020, whattoexpect.com/pregnancy/breastfeeding/breastfeeding-while-pregnant
(August 17, 2020).

107 *1995 Grandparent Book*, Appendix 2, Section 2, at p. 19. YaoTim's Interview of 10/16/17,
p.2.

108 *1995 Grandparent Book*, Appendix 2, Section 1, last page titled "Kinship and Descendants".

109 YaoTim recalls being handed over by two women to her father, who was on a ship. She
remembers she started crying but was told by one of the women to "be a good girl." This
took place in Hong Kong, when the family was departing for Shanghai. Interview of October 17, 2017, para. 1, p. 1. A picture of one of the women, Lai Shou Guen – whom the
family called Dai Goo – appears with captions that show she was YaoTim's godmother
and was employed by Charlie's godmother, Hun Zia. Appendix VI, Album, p. 16.

110 Infant mortality rates averaged 35%-50% in Hong Kong during the 1930s. Ian Christopher Petrie (1996), *The Problem of Infant Mortality in Hong Kong, 1886-1937*, University
of British Columbia, Department of History Graduate Program, Master Thesis, open.
library.ubc.ca/clRcle/collections/ubctheses/831/items/1.0099171 (August 17, 2020)

111 Clifford had worked as a secretary for Anna May Wong at Paramount Studios and her
movie, *Daughter of Shanghai,* was released on December 17, 1937. *1995 Grandparent
Book*, Appendix 2, Section 2, p. 16, at number 19. YaoTim's Interview of 11-21-16, at
para. 16, pp. 2-3. Wikipedia, *Daughter of Shanghai*, en.wikipedia.org/wiki/Daughter_of_
Shanghai (August 17, 2020).

112 When YaoTim visited Shanghai in 1984, she met with the former landlord at the Lumsdaine family's former residence on Bubbling Well Road who told her that Clifford had
worked for his textile company in Shanghai. Telephone conversation with YaoTim on
August 17, 2020.

113 Battles between Japanese and Chinese forces in southern China included an Imperial
Japanese bombing raid on Shenzen during which some bombs landed in Hong Kong
territory, destroying a bridge and train station. Wikipedia, Japanese Occupation of Hong
Kong, en.wikipedia.org/wiki/Japanese_occupation_of_Hong_Kong#Imperial_Japa-
nese_invasion_of_China (August 17, 2020).

114 As many as 80,000 Chinese died before Shanghai surrendered to the Japanese on November 5, 1937. An estimated 250,000 to 300,000 Chinese civilians were killed by the Japanese army on its march to and capture of Nanking, with an estimated 80,000 Chinese women raped when senior officers openly allowed the Japanese army to murder and ransack in what historians have referred to as "The Rape of Nanking." C.N. Trueman, "The Japan-China War," historylearningsite.co.uk, 26 May 2015. 6 Mar 2019. James Hart, "The Fall of Shanghai: Prelude to the Rape of Nanking & WWII," October 1, 2018, Warfare History Network, https://warfarehistorynetwork.com/ daily/wwii/the-fall-of-shanghai-prelude-to-the-rape-of-nanking-wwii/print/ (12/6/2018)

115 The International Settlement, or "Foreign Concessions," was largely left alone by the Japanese from November 1937, until December 8, 1941, when the United States declared war on Japan after its attack on Pearl Harbor the previous day. The Settlement became a prosperous enclave amidst the war zones, and 400,000 Chinese refugees settled there during those four years. History of Shanghai – Wikipedia, p. 11/18 en.m.wikipedia.org/wiki/History_of_Shanghai. Edward Lumsdaine (2016), *Rotten Gambler Two Becomes a True American*, pp. 4-5 ISBN 9781523748532.

116 Because Japan was not at war with the Allies (the U.S., U.K., France, and the U.S.S.R.) until December 8, 1941, the International Settlements controlled by those countries were largely left alone by the Japanese, who occupied the rest of Shanghai and surrounding areas, until then. "History of Shanghai" – Wikipedia, p. 11/18 en.m.wikipedia.org/wiki/History_of_Shanghai.

117 *1995 Grandparent Book*, Appendix 2, Section 1, Kinship and Descendants of Clifford/ Miao Ying Lumsdaine [last page of Section 1]. *Id.* at Section 2, at p. 19.

118 Current Shanghai City Map located at https://www.google.com/maps/place/1168+Nanjing+W+Rd,+Nan+Jing+Xi+Lu,+Jingan+Qu,+Shanghai+Shi,+China,+200003/@31.228 7133,121.4557357,18z/data=!4m5!3m4!1s0x35b2701af3201077:0xd343f0559ab5aa5 b!8m2!3d31.228885!4d121.4555299?hl=en&authuser=0 (July 2, 2019).

119 This was "a traditional Shanghainese architectural style combining Western and Chinese elements" called "Shikumen" in Chinese, meaning "stone warehouse gate" and sometimes referred to as "lane houses" in English. By 1939, there were about "9,000 Shikumen-style buildings in Shanghai, comprising 60% of the housing stock in the city." en.wikipedia.org/wiki/Shikumen (July 3, 2019); "Understanding Lilong Housing and Shikumen Architecture," *Shanghai Street Stories*, shanghaistreetstories.com/?page_id=1288

120 YaoTim Allen Interview of November 11, 2016, Appendix V, para. #4, p. 1.

121 Milly Ratermann Interview of May 3, 2017, Appendix V, para. #1, p. 1.

122 YaoTim Allen Interview of November 21, 2016, Appendix V, para. 17, p. 4.

123 "Shikumen" - Wikipedia en.wikipedia.org/wiki/Shikumen (July 3, 2019); "Understanding Lilong Housing and Shikumen Architecture," *Shanghai Street Stories*, shanghaistreet-stories.com/?page_id=1288 (July 5, 2019).

124 Robert Lumsdaine visited Shanghai in 1985 with his wife, Joyce; in 2000 with his daughter, Robin; and in 2005, with Joyce. YaoTim Allen and her husband, Bob, visited in 1987. At some point between YaoTim and Bob's visit in 1987, when they took pictures of the building that are on pages 27-28, and 2000, when Robert and Robin visited, the entire residential compound on Bubbling Well Road was demolished. There are many photos and some good notes relating to the Lumsdaines' Shanghai home and environs from these visits. See Appendix V, Joyce's Interview of July 7, 2018, and Exhibit B.

125 C.N. Trueman, "The Japan-China War," historylearningsite.co.uk. the History Learning Site, 26 May 2015 (March 6, 2019). Mark Felton, February 8, 2013, "WAR ZONE – City of Terror: the Japanese takeover of Shanghai," Military History Matters, pp.6-7/20, military-history.org/articles/war-zone-city-of-terror-the-japanese-takeover-of-shanghai.htm (June 29, 2019). Yang Zhenqi, "Shanghai's war prisoners," September 4, 2014, *Global Times*, globaltimes.cn/content/853558.shtml (July 9, 2019).

126 History.com editors, "The United States Declares War on Japan," history.com/this-day-in-history/the-united-states-declares-war-on-japan (July 9, 2019)

127 Editors of the Encyclopedia Britannica, "Allied Powers," britannica.com/topic/Allied-Powers-international-alliance (July 9, 2019)

128 Mark Felton, February 8, 2013, "WAR ZONE – City of Terror: the Japanese takeover of Shanghai" – Military History Matters, p. 4/20, military-history.org/articles/war-zone-city-of-terror-the-japanese-takeover-of-shanghai.htm (June 29, 2019). There were also 20,000 Jews who had escaped Nazi persecution that were considered enemy civilians by virtue of Japan's alliance with Nazi Germany. *Id.*

129 Wikipedia, Nanjing Massacre en.wikipedia.org/wiki/Nanjing_Massacre (July 10, 2019). Iris Chang (1997), *The Rape of Nanking*, ISBN 0-465-06835-9; available free on Amazon Kindle. Mark Oliver, "27 Rape of Nanking Photos and Facts That Reveal Its True Horrors," allthatsinteresting.com/rape-of-nanking-massacre (July 10, 2019) Warning: photos are graphic and upsetting.

130 Mark Felton, February 8, 2013, "WAR ZONE – City of Terror: the Japanese takeover of Shanghai" – Military History Matters, p. 4/20, military-history.org/articles/war-zone-city-of-terror-the-japanese-takeover-of-shanghai.htm (June 29, 2019).

131 *1995 Grandparent Book*, Appendix 2, Section 1, last page titled "Kinship and Descendants."

132 Bernice Archer (2004) *The Internment of Western Civilians Under The Japanese (1941-1945)* ISBN 0-203-32587-7, pp. 55-56, west-point.org/family/japanese-pow/Internment.pdf. Also see downloaded PDF of book at Appendix VII.

133 Yao Minji (January 9, 2017), Diary of wartime Shanghai gets modern airing, ShanghaiDaily.com, archive.shine.cn/feature/art-and-culture/Diary-of-wartime-Shanghai-gets-modern-airing/shdaily.shtml. Mark Felton, February 8, 2013, WAR ZONE – City of Terror: the Japanese takeover of Shanghai – Military History Matters, pp. 7-10/20, military-history.org/articles/war-zone-city-of-terror-the-japanese-takeover-of-shanghai.htm (June 29, 2019).

134 For Chuck, there were "Japanese soldiers who looked scary with their long swords" and senseless questionings by them even in chance encounters. Appendix V, Cory's Interview of July 7, 2019, para. 2, p. 1. For YaoTim, there were "machine guns," "lots of bombings," "severely injured people, and a severed dead baby." Appendix V, YaoTim Interview of November 17, 2016, para. 4, p. 1. "During the Japanese occupation, even children came to feel that death was only a misstep away," according to Ed. Edward Lumsdaine (2016), *Rotten Gambler Two Becomes a True American*, pp. 10-11, at p. 10, ISBN 9781523748532.

135 For a detailed account of all that Chuck, YaoTim, and Ed recalled of their lives in Shanghai between 1941 and 1945, please review transcripts of Chuck's interviews and notes of YaoTim's and Ed's interviews, all of which can be found in Appendix V. Also, see Ed's book, Rotten Gambler Two, *supra*, especially pp. 4-18.

136 Appendix V, Chuck's Interview by Anne Lumsdaine in early 2000, Tape #1 as transcribed by Dolly, p. 1, para. 1 and p. 4, last para. Appendix V, Cory's Interview of July 7, 2019, p.1, para. 3. Diagram courtesy of Philip Lumsdaine modified at Appendix V, Philip's Interviews, Documents.

137 Appendix V, Chuck's Interview by Anne Lumsdaine in early 2000, Tape #1 as transcribed by Dolly, p. 3, first para.

138 Appendix V, Chuck's Interview by Anne Lumsdaine in early 2000, Tape #1 as transcribed by Dolly, p. 2, first para.

139 *Id.*, at pp. 1-7.

140 Aside from Chuck, YaoTim, Ed and George, Robert was born June 30, 1942 and Philip was born September 20, 1943, both during the Japanese occupation of the International Settlement from December 1941 to August 1945.

141 Appendix V, Chuck's Interview by Anne Lumsdaine in early 2000, Tape #1 as transcribed by Dolly and YaoTim's Interviews, in text and as cited below.

142 Mark Felton, February 8, 2013, "WAR ZONE – City of Terror: the Japanese takeover of Shanghai – Military History Matters," https://www.military-history.org/articles/war-zone-city-of-terror-the-japanese-takeover-of-shanghai.htm (June 29, 2019).

143 Appendix V, YaoTim's Interview of November 17, 2016, para. 4, p. 1 and para. 11, p. 11.

144 Appendix V, YaoTim's Interview of November 17, 2016, para. 9, p. 9; Ed's Interview of December 3, 2017, para. 5., p. 2.

145 In their interviews, Chuck, Ed, and YaoTim all commented repeatedly on the lack of food, not having regular meals, and going hungry often. See, e.g., in Appendix V: Cory's Interview of July 7, 2019, para. 4, p. 1; YaoTim's Interview of November 17, 2016, para. 5, p. 2; Ed's Interview of December 3, 2017, para. 5, p. 2.; Edward Lumsdaine (2016), *Rotten Gambler Two Becomes a True American*, p. 14, ISBN 9781523748532.

146 YaoTim's Interview of November 17, 2016, para. 4-5, pp. 1-2; Ed's Interview of December 3, 2017, para 7., p. 3. Edward Lumsdaine (2016), *Rotten Gambler Two Becomes a True American*, p. 14, ISBN 9781523748532.

147 After dinnertime, the communal charcoal stove would be snuffed out, meaning that if the family needed drinking water, they would have to go out and buy from a vendor. YaoTim's Interview of November 17, 2016, para. 5, p. 2.

148 "Mom affectionately called me AhTim. When she called me YaoTim, I'm in deep kim-chee, which was quite often." *1995 Grandparent Book*, Appendix 2, Section 3, YaoTim at p.5.

149 YaoTim's Interview of November 17, 2016, para. 5, p. 2-3. *1995 Grandparent Book*, Appendix 2, Section 3, YaoTim at p. 2.

150 *Ibid.*

151 Appendix V, YaoTim Interview of November 17, 2017, p. 8, para. 9.

152 *1995 Grandparent Book*, Appendix 2, Section 3, YaoTim at p. 9.

153 Edward Lumsdaine (2016), *Rotten Gambler Two Becomes a True American*, p. 11, ISBN 9781523748532.

154 *Id.* at p. 13. Appendix V, Chuck's Interview in early 2000, pp. 1 & 5.

155 Edward Lumsdaine (2016), *Rotten Gambler Two Becomes a True American*, p. 14, ISBN 9781523748532.

156 New Zealand History: Pacific War Timeline, nzhistory.govt.nz/war/second-world-war/war-in-the-pacific/timeline (July 13, 2019): US defeats Japanese naval forces at Battle of Midway and was gaining ground at Guadalcanal in the Solomon Islands.

157 Mark Felton, February 8, 2013, WAR ZONE, p. 8-9/20, https://www.military-history.org/articles/war-zone-city-of-terror-the-japanese-takeover-of-shanghai.htm (June 29, 2019).

158 Mark Felton, February 8, 2013, WAR ZONE, p. 8/20, https://www.military-history.org/articles/war-zone-city-of-terror-the-japanese-takeover-of-shanghai.htm (June 29, 2019).

159 Ibid. Pudong means, literally, "east of the Pu (Huangpu) river." Appendix V, YaoTim Interview of November 17, 2016, pp. 9-10. Map drawing courtesy of Greg Leck (2006) *Captives of Empire: The Japanese Internment of Allied Civilians in China 1941-1945,* ISBN 0977214109, 9780977214105.

160 Appendix V, Cory Interview of July 7, 2019, para.8, p. 1. Children at home were Chuck, 9; YaoTim, 6; Ed, 5; George, 2; and Robert, 8 months.

161 Norman Cliff, *Prisoner of the Samurai: Japanese Civilian Camps in China, 1941-1943,* p. 28/85, Appendix VII, available as downloadable PDF at http://weihsien-paintings.org/NormanCliff/Books/Samurai/Binder-Samurai(WEB).pdf (July 13, 2019).

162 There were 700 British, 350 American, and 15 Dutch prisoners by March 15, 1941, crowded into dormitories of over 100 men each. There had been attempted suicides, attempted murders, and other acts of violence by a "gang of men" who were left unchecked by the Japanese guards. *Ibid.* Also see generally, Sonya Grypma, China Interrupt (2012) Chapter 7 "The End of the World Has Come – Pudong Camp," pp. 181-222, ISBN 978-1-55458-627-1.

163 Greg Leck (2006) *Captives of Empire: The Japanese Internment of Allied Civilians in China 1941-1945,* p. 604

164 *Ibid.*

165 Appendix V, Chuck's Interview by Anne Lumsdaine in early 2000, Tape #1 as transcribed by Dolly, p. 8, first para.

166 Appendix V, Chuck's Interview by Anne Lumsdaine on in early 2000, Tape #1 as transcribed by Dolly, p. 8, last para; Cory Interview of July 7, 2019, para.8, p. 1.

167 *EXPRESS* (April 21, 2009), "Torture, starvation and hell of Japan's concentration camps," p. 2, express.co.uk/ expressyourself/96232/Torture-starvation-and-hell-of-Japan-s-concentration-camps (August 14, 2017).

168 "The relatively high toll in Japanese camps is partly due to brutal mistreatment and summary execution. Many of the Japanese captors were cruel toward the POWs because they were viewed as contemptible for the very act of surrendering. The guards were conditioned to consider that inhumane treatment was no less than what the POWs deserved; real warriors die." Jeff Kingston, *The Japan Times,* "An account of POWs 'in hell,'" March 31, 2013, japantimes.co.jp/culture/2013/03/31/books/book-reviews/an-account-of-pows-in-hell/ (August 21, 2020)

169 Alexander Mikaberidze (2019) *Behind Barbed Wire: An Encyclopedia of Concentration and Prisoner-of-War Camp,* ISBN 978-1-4498-5761-4, pp. 158-160)

170 See text *infra,* for details as to how his fundamental personality and behavior appears to have changed both after incarceration from 1943 to 1945 and again after the Communist takeover of Shanghai in 1949.

171 Greg Leck, *Captives of Empire: The Japanese Internment of Allied Civilians in China 1941-1945*, p. 604. The site is currently Shanghai Shixi High School. Yang Zhenqi, "Shanghai's war prisoners," September 4, 2014, Global Times, globaltimes.cn/content/853558.shtml (July 9, 2019).

172 Norman Cliff, *Prisoner of the Samurai: Japanese Civilian Camps in China, 1941-1943*, p. 34/85, Appendix VII, available as downloadable PDF at http://weihsien-paintings.org/NormanCliff/Books/Samurai/Binder-Samurai(WEB).pdf (July 13, 2019).

173 Geni, Yu Yuen Road Intern Camp, geni.com/projects/Yu-Yuen-Road-Shanghai-China-Intern-Camp-Japanese-Civilian-Internment-Camp-WWII/33610 (July 15, 2019)

174 Greg Leck, Captives of Empire, *supra*, p. 712.

175 Greg Leck, *Captives of Empire: The Japanese Internment of Allied Civilians in China 1941-1945*, p. 186.

176 Notes from conversation with YaoTim Allen in July 2019. It is unclear whether YaoTim got this information directly from Clifford or indirectly from Miao Ying.

177 YaoTim's Interview of November 17, 2016, para. 11, pp. 10-11.

178 "You could get beaten for moving," Mark Felton, February 8, 2013, "WAR ZONE – City of Terror: the Japanese takeover of Shanghai," Military History Matters, military-history.org/articles/war-zone-city-of-terror-the-japanese-takeover-of-shanghai.htm p. 10/20 (June 29, 2019).

179 YaoTim's Interview of November 17, 2016, para. 11, p. 11; *1995 Grandparent Book*, Appendix 2, Section 3, YaoTim at p. 8.

180 Appendix V, YaoTim Interview of November 17, 2016, para. 8, p. 7.

181 Norman Cliff, *Prisoner of the Samurai: Japanese Civilian Camps in China, 1941-1943*, p. 68/85, Appendix VII, available as downloadable PDF at http://weihsien-paintings.org/NormanCliff/Books/Samurai/Binder-Samurai(WEB).pdf (July 13, 2019).

182 *Ibid.* at p.45-46/85. Appendix V, Chuck's Interview by Anne Lumsdaine in early 2000, Tape #1 as transcribed by Dolly, p. 8, first para. As for Allied bombings in Shanghai, see Greg Leck, Captives of Empire: The Japanese Internment of Allied Civilians in China 1941-1945 (2006), pp. 386-87, 389, and 517; Helen Zia, Last Boat Out of Shanghai (2019), pp. 150-151, 181; World War II Database, Shanghai in W2 History, ww2db.com/event/timeline/ place/china/_shanghai (November 19, 2020); "Target Shanghai B-24 Bombers Drop Payload," youtube.com/ watch?v=rCeKdeC-L4A&list=PLN8shDjpGEvl-MedjKsY2m830DEE8IxN&index=74 (November 19, 2020).

183 Greg Leck, *Captives of Empire: The Japanese Internment of Allied Civilians in China 1941-1945*, p.712. This was the former Sacred Heart Hospital at 41 Ningkuo Road (now Hangzhou Road). While Leck's book states that Clifford was sent to "Yangtzepoo" Camp, other sources refer to the place as "Yangshupu" Camp, located on the modern Yangshupu Road. See Francis Irving, "Child of the atom bomb," flourish.org/2006/05/yangshupu-camp/ (July 15, 2019) and PDF at Appendix VII. Yang Zhenqi, "Shanghai's war prisoners," September 4, 2014, Global Times, globaltimes.cn/content/853558.shtml (July 9, 2019).

184 *Ibid.*

185 "The official daily Japanese ration was down to only 300 calories by June 1945." Yang Zhenqi, "Shanghai's war prisoners," September 4, 2014, *Global Times*, globaltimes.cn/content/853558.shtml (July 9, 2019). On effects of varying caloric intake, see "Is 500 Calories a Day a Healthy Diet?" sharecare.com/health/calories-and-weight-loss/is-500-calories-day-healthy-diet (July 15, 2019).

186   See citations at footnote 183, *supra*.

187   Appendix V, YaoTim Interview of November 17, 2016, para. 11, p.11. Clifford told his
children little about his internment experience, but he did tell YaoTim that Yangshupu
Camp was liberated by Chou En Lai, the first premier of the People's Republic of China, who "spoke to us in English and told us we were free to leave." *Ibid*. On Clifford's
release date, see *1995 Grandparent Book*, Appendix 2, Section 4; 1987 Interview of
Dad, p. 7. For an interesting connection being made between the dropping of the atom
bombs and the survival of the author's father from Yangshupu Camp, see Francis Irving,
"Child of the atom bomb," flourish.org/2006/05/yangshupu-camp/ (July 15, 2019) and
PDF at Appendix VII.

188   See footnote 171, *supra*, and text accompanying same.

189   See Bernice Archer (2004), *The Internment of Western Civilians Under The Japanese
(1941-1945)* ISBN 0-203-32587-7, PP. 55-56, west-point.org/family/japanese-pow/In-
ternment.pdf , downloaded in PDF at Appendix VII. Also see, American Chamber of
Commerce in Shanghai, "Our History, amcham-shanghai.org/en/our-history (July 15,
2019), downloaded in PDF at Appendix VII, pp 9-10/14.

190   Traditionally among the Chinese, a person is not referred to by their birth-given name
but by the name of their relationship to you. Hence, Bieu Tse was so called by the author
and his siblings because she was the daughter of their mother's older brother – their
uncle, Ho Gai Zien; Pau Pau, because she was their maternal grandmother.

191   According to her daughter Oi Lum (Margaret), Bieu Tse was born on July 5, 1928, as
converted from the lunar calendar. WhatsApp message from Oi Lum dated July 22, 2019.

192   Edward Lumsdaine (2016), *Rotten Gambler Two Becomes a True American*, p. 5, ISBN
9781523748532.

193   Appendix V, YaoTim Interview of November 9, 2013, pp. 2-3.

194   Appendix V, YaoTim Allen Interview, Questionnaire Responses at p. 4-5, at para. 8. It
is well-established Chinese custom to be obedient to one's elders and defer to their
wishes.

195   *Ibid*.

196   Appendix V, YaoTim Interview of November 17, 2016, para. 7, p. 5.

197   Appendix V, Elaine Interview of August 31, 2018, p. 4.

198   *1995 Grandparent Book*, Appendix 2, Section 1, last page titled "Kinship and Descendants".

199   Edward Lumsdaine (2016), *Rotten Gambler Two Becomes a True American*, p. 6. ISBN
9781523748532.

200   Appendix V, YaoTim Interview of November 17, 2016, para. 7, p. 6.

201   Appendix V, Chuck's Interview by Anne Lumsdaine in early 2000, Tape #1 as transcribed by Dolly, p. 2, last para.

202   *Ibid*. Appendix V, YaoTim Interview of November 17, 2016, para. 7, pp. 5-6. The ration
was for Clifford's five children, plus one-half for baby Philip. *Ibid*. Miao Ying had to make
do for seven people and a baby out of the ration for only 5½.

203   Appendix V, YaoTim Interview of November 17, 2016, para. 7, pp. 5-6. *Id*. Also see,

Edward Lumsdaine (2016), *Rotten Gambler Two Becomes a True American*, pp. 12-13. ISBN 9781523748532.

204 Appendix V, Chuck's Interview by Anne Lumsdaine in early 2000, Tape #1 transcribed by Dolly, p. 2, para. 2. Appendix V, Ed's Interview of December 3, 2017, para. 5, p.2. Appendix V, YaoTim Interview of November 17, 2016, para. 7, pp. 6-7. At one point, Ed and YaoTim ate so many potatoes that they threw it all back up. *Id.* p. 7.)

205 Appendix V, Philip's Interview of June 28, 2017, p. 3, para. 13.

206 See Appendix V, YaoTim Interview of November 17, 2016, para. 7, p. 6; Chuck's Interview by Anne Lumsdaine in early 2000, Tape #1 as transcribed by Dolly, p. 2, para. 3.

207 *Ibid.* There also was a small monthly stipend that the U.S. government paid to the Swiss Red Cross to be passed on to families of imprisoned U.S. citizens such as Clifford. Appendix V, Ed's Interview of December 3, 2017, p. 2, para. 5; *1995 Grandparent Book*, Appendix 2, Section 3, YaoTim at p. 9.

208 Appendix V, Chuck's Interview by Anne Lumsdaine in early 2000, Tape #1 as transcribed by Dolly, p. 2, last para.

209 Appendix V, YaoTim Questionnaire Responses p. 20, para. 19. "Her husband was kind about it, but Mom's sister would find ways to belittle her (make Mom feel bad) about it." *Ibid.*

210 Appendix V, YaoTim Interview of November 17, 2016, p. 9 at para. 9.

211 en.wikipedia.org/wiki/Surrender_of_Japan

212 "... [Dad] just said that at the end of the war, when they heard the allies won the war, so the prisoners went nuts and opened the gates on the compound...some of the Japanese soldiers just mowed them down, just drove over them, killed them." Appendix V, Chuck's Interview by Anne Lumsdaine in early 2000, Tape #1 as transcribed by Dolly, p. 8 last para. to p. 9, first para.; "Beating, torture and execution were constant threats." *EXPRESS* (April 21, 2009) Torture, starvation and hell of Japan's concentration camps, p.2, express.co.uk/expressyourself/96232/ Torture-starvation-and-hell-of-Japan-s-concentration-camps (August 14, 2017).

213 *1995 Grandparent Book*, Appendix 2, Section 4, 1987 Interview of Dad, p. 7.

214 Edward Lumsdaine (2016), *Rotten Gambler Two Becomes a True American*, p. 14, ISBN 9781523748532 at p. 15; Appendix V, Ed's Interview of December 3, 2017 at para. 11, p. 4; and Chuck's Interview in early 2000, at p.2.

215 *Id.* at p. 16. Appendix V, YaoTim's Interview of July 13, 2019, p. 1.

216 Appendix V, Ed's Interview of December 3, 2017, p. 1, para. 3.

217 Appendix V, Cory Interview of July 7, 2019, para. 8, p. 1. Some 42 years later, when asked, Clifford did not respond to the specific question of how he himself was treated but instead gave a long narrative describing the general makeup of the camps. *1995 Grandparent Book*, Appendix 2, Section 4, 1987 Interview of Dad, pp. 10-11.

218 *1995 Grandparent Book*, Appendix 2, Section 3. Appendix V, Milly's Interview of May 9, 2017, at 2, para. 11

219 Appendix V, YaoTim's Interview of July 13, 2019, p. 1.

220 *Ibid.*

221 For occasion when Dad spanked Milly, seemingly with little provocation, see Appendix V, Milly's Interview of May 9, 2017, at p. 2, para. 11; and *1995 Grandparent Book*, Appendix 2, Section 3, Mildred.

222 After just swatting her twice on her behind, Clifford gave Milly a coin to "go buy myself something at the store." Appendix V, Milly's Interview of May 9, 2017, at p. 2, para. 11. It must have really bothered Clifford because almost 50 years later, in 1995, he asked Milly if she remembered that incident. *1995 Grandparent Book*, Appendix 2, Section 3, Mildred.

223 Appendix V, Ed's Interview of December 3, 2017, p. 2, para. 4.

224 "He was gentle, kind … a real push over for his children." *1995 Grandparent Book*, Appendix 2, Section 3, YaoTim at pp. 2-3.

225 Bieu Tse was born on July 5, 1928 and was 17 at the time of Clifford's release from prison in 1945.

226 *1995 Grandparent Book*, Appendix 2, Section 4, 1987 Interview of Dad, p. 7-8.

227 *1995 Grandparent Book*, Appendix 2, Section 3, YaoTim at p. 3.

228 Clifford allowed for the two younger girls' names to be picked by their older sister Yao-Tim, who chose Milly as she was the heroine in YaoTim's favorite comic book and Dolly, who "with her chubby cheeks looked like the Shirley Temple dolls in the store." *1995 Grandparent Book*, Appendix 2, Section 3, YaoTim at p.4.

229 Appendix V, YaoTim Interview of November 21, 2016, at para. 16, p. 2. Also see *1995 Grandparent Book*, Appendix 2, Section 4, 1987 Interview of Dad, p. 8. So-called "servants" were sometimes homeless "beggars" whom Miao Ying was compassionate enough to take in and feed in return for them doing some household chores. *1995 Grandparent Book*, Appendix 2, Section 3, YaoTim at p. 10.

230 The banner in the left side of the picture has Chinese words which can be translated as "… Road English & Chinese Elementary School." This has been identified by YaoTim as the first school that Chuck attended, although it is nearly impossible to specifically identify Chuck in this picture among the many faces.

231 See British Expat britishexpat.com/expatforum/viewtopic.php?f=110&t=11551 (September 1, 2019). See picture and description at Virtual Shanghai virtualshanghai.net/Data/Buildings?ID=360

232 *Id*. Edward Lumsdaine (2016), *Rotten Gambler Two Becomes a True American*, p. 19.

233 See Appendix V, YaoTim Interview of November 17, 2016, para. 7, p. 5.

234 Edward Lumsdaine (2016), *Rotten Gambler Two Becomes a True American*, p. 19.

235 Appendix V, Cory Interview of July 7, 2019, para.10, p. 1. According to YaoTim, in caption she wrote to photo of APL Christmas party shown in Fig. 59 above, the doctors had not expected Chuck to survive his hospitalization. Chuck's godfather, a co-worker of Clifford's at APL, said a "novena" for Chuck to which Chuck later commented, "I guess he prayed for a miracle and got one."

236 Edward Lumsdaine (2016), *Rotten Gambler Two Becomes a True American*, pp. 19-20.

237 Edward Lumsdaine (2016), *Rotten Gambler Two Becomes a True American*, pp. 34-35. While Ed recalls being dismissed by Brother Gilbert in front of his sobbing mother [Ibid. at p.35], Philip recalls that he, George, and Robert were present when Ed was dismissed publicly, possibly during school assembly, to set an example to others at the

school. Appendix V, Philip's Interview of June 20, 2017, p. 3, para. 5.

238 Appendix V, Philip's Interview of June 28, 2017, pp. 2-3, para. 5. Edward Lumsdaine (2016), *Rotten Gambler Two Becomes a True American*, pp. 1-3, 20-25. Appendix V, Ed's Interview of December 3, 2017, pp. 5-6, para. 14.

239 Appendix V, George's Questionnaire Response #35, p. 4. "One time only, George got into a fight with an older boy who had bullied him couple of times before." *Id.*

240 Appendix V, Philip's Interview of June 20, 2017, p. 2, para. 5. Especially during the Korean War (1950-1953) when Chinese and U.S. soldiers battled each other, anti-American sentiment was rampant. See, e.g., Keun-Sik Jung, "China's Memory and Commemoration of the Korean War in the Memorial Hall of the 'War to Resist U.S. Aggression and Aid Korea,'" *Cross-Currents: East Asian History and Culture Review*, cross-currents.berkeley.edu/e-journal/issue-14/jung (September 24, 2019). Appendix V, Joyce's Interview of July 18, 2018, p. 4. See, e.g., Appendix V, Philip's Interview of July 5, 2017, p. 1, para. 5; Edward Lumsdaine (2016), *Rotten Gambler Two Becomes a True American*, p. 42.

241 Chuck was no longer at the school as he had left Shanghai with Clifford on July 27, 1951, about four months shy of his 18th birthday. *1995 Grandparent Book*, Appendix 2, Section 4, 1987 Interview of Dad, p. 8. Appendix V, YaoTim Interview of November 9, 2013, p. 1.

242 Appendix V, Philip's Questionnaire Response #37.

243 Liqing Tao, Margaret Berci, and Wayne He, *The New York Times*, "Historical Background: Expansion of Public Education," archive.nytimes.com/www.nytimes.com/ref/college/coll-china-education-001.html#peoples1 (August 22, 2020). Communist ideology saw no difference between education and propaganda or indoctrination. Jean-Paul Wiest, "Catholic Elementary and Secondary Schools and China's Drive toward a Modern Educational System (1850-1950)," journals.openedition.org/extremeorient/187, pp. 92-114. (August 22, 2020).

244 Appendix V, Milly's Interview of May 9, 2017, para. 10, p.2; Milly's Interview of May 17, 2017, para. 19, p. 1. Dolly's Interview of November 16, 2017, paragraphs 16 and 25, pp. 1 and 4; Joyce's Interviews of July 18, 2018, p. 1 and July 7, 2018, p.3.

245 Milly's Interview of May 17, 2017, para. 19, at p. 1. As for the Communist takeover and anti-American sentiment, see section titled "Communist Rule Comes to Shanghai."

246 Clifford came from a long line of Presbyterians, and Miao Ying paid dutiful respect to her mother's religiously Buddhist traditions.

247 Formal name of this religious order of the Catholic Church is "The Society of Jesus."

248 Appendix V, YaoTim Interview of November 17, 2016, para. 5, p. 3.

249 See "Women's Education in Traditional and Modern China," Wong Yin Lee (1995), *Women's History Review*, 4:3, 345-367 and footnote 38 above.

250 It was still widely believed, at that time in China, that an educated woman would not easily find a husband as no man would want a wife smarter than he. See "Women's Education in Traditional and Modern China," Wong Yin Lee (1995), *Women's History Review*, 4:3, p. 354.

251 Appendix V, YaoTim Interview of November 17, 2016, para. 12, p. 11-12.

252 "Lose face" is the English translation of the Chinese phrase "tiu lien," meaning "to suffer public disgrace" or humiliation. phrases.org.uk/meanings/lose-face.html

253 Appendix V, YaoTim Interview of November 17, 2016, para. 12, p. 11-12.

254 *Id.*

255 *1995 Grandparent Book*, Appendix 2, Section 3, YaoTim at p. 5; Appendix V, YaoTim Interview of November 17, 2016, para. 12, pp. 11-13.

256 *Id.* The Sisters of Loretto of the Cross have their headquarters and archives in Kentucky. This religious order ran an elementary and high school at Loretto School in Shanghai, from 1933 to 1952. *Christianity in China* (2nd ed. 2009) edited by Xiaoxin Wu, ISBN 978-1-56324-337-0, p. 177. Also see "Lorettine Education in China 1923-1952" (1961), a dissertation by Marie Gutteres.

257 *1995 Grandparent Book*, Appendix 2, Section 3, YaoTim at p. 5. Also see, Appendix V, YaoTim Interview of November 17, 2016, para. 12, pp. 11-13. "They were very kind to Maria [YaoTim], and it is there that she learned most about God and about Catholicism." *Id.*

258 Appendix V, YaoTim Interview of November 17, 2016, para. 13, p.13. For kindness to her exhibited by a priest, Fr. Des Lauriers in Hong Kong, and by Catholic Charities, see Appendix V, YaoTim Interview of November 21, 2016, para. 20, p. 8-9. For charity to YaoTim practiced by Mrs. Lubeck, a laywoman and third-grade teacher, who not only helped her with first communion but later made "a sizeable loan that allowed YaoTim and Miao Ying to leave for Hong Kong," see Appendix V, YaoTim Interview of November 17, 2016, para. 13, pp. 14-15.

259 YaoTim was baptized in April 1948, receiving first communion and confirmation the following month. Appendix V, YaoTim Interview of November 17, 2016, para. 13, pp. 13-15.

260 *Ibid.*, para. 13, p. 15.

261 Appendix V, Philip's Interview of June 20, 2017, p. 7, para. 6 and Philip's baptismal certificate.

262 Appendix V, YaoTim Interview, of November 17, 2016, para. 13, p.13.

263 *Id.* Pau Pau had even dedicated her daughter, Ng Yee, to the Buddhist Goddess of Mercy, which in China is "Guanyin", in fulfillment of the promise Pau Pau had made to that Goddess in return for keeping Ng Yee healthy, as Pau Pau had lost three other baby girls before Ng Yee was born. Appendix V, YaoTim's Questionnaire Response #10, p. 9. Also see en.wikipedia.org/wiki/Guanyin for a detailed explanation of this Goddess of Mercy. Pau Pau was kind-hearted, strong-willed and religiously Buddhist, but acted in many ways "more like a Christian then most Christians because she was kind to every-one and did not have prejudice towards people." Appendix V, YaoTim's Questionnaire Response #10, p. 8. Even when the family had little food to share around, Pau Pau would scrape the bottom of the rice pot to give something to the beggars. *Id.*

264 en.wikipedia.org/wiki/Color_in_Chinese_culture#White (September 9, 2019).

265 Compare *Id.* on the color white in Chinese culture with the Catholic cultural norm of girls being expected to wear white dresses and shoes in first holy communion at blog. beau-coup.com/the-guests-guide-to-a-first-communion-what-to-expect-wear-and-gift (September 9, 2019).

266 Fortunately, YaoTim was able to procure her white shoes and socks with the help of her third-grade teacher, Mrs. Lubeck. Appendix V, YaoTim Interview of November 17, 2016, para. 13, p. 13. This contrasts with Miao Ying procuring a white dress and shoes for Milly's baptism and communion in 1954, long after Pau Pau died. Appendix V, Milly's Interview of May 3, 2017, para. 5, p. 3.

267 Appendix V, YaoTim Interview of November 17, 2016, para.12, p. 13.

268 Chinese Civil War, en.m.wikipedia.org/wiki/Chinese_Civil_War (September 9, 2019); the Chinese Revolution of 1949, history.state.gov/milestones/1945-1952/chinese-rev (September 9, 2019)

269 "Shanghai Campaign," en.m.wikipedia.org/wiki/Shanghai_Campaign (December 6, 2018)

270 Chuck and Ed "observed column after column of soldiers walking through the streets." Edward Lumsdaine (2016), *Rotten Gambler Two Becomes a True American*, at p. 29.

271 "I think the scariest [experience] that I had was … [my dad] was working down the Bund…and [the Nationalists] started bombing the heck out of [the Communists] … I thought something had happened to my dad because he was late coming home … and my mom was frantic wondering what happened. It was probably one of the most frightening things." Appendix V, Chuck's Interview by Anne Lumsdaine in early 2000, Tape #1 as transcribed by Dolly, p. 7.

272 *Ibid.* pp. 28-30. It has been estimated that as many as 2 million people were executed by the purges throughout China between 1949 and 1951. Roberts, J.A.G. (2006) A History of China, p. 257, ISBN 978-1403992758; Maurice Meisner (1999), Mao's China and After: A History of the People's Republic, Third Edition p. 72, ISBN 0-684-85635-2

273 Jon W. Huebner (January 1987) "Chinese Anti-Americanism, 1946-1949," *The Australian Journal of Chinese Affairs*, No. 17, p. 115.

274 See Keun-Sik Jung, "China's Memory and Commemoration of the Korean War in the Memorial Hall of the 'War to Resist U.S. Aggression and Aid Korea'," *Cross-Currents: East Asian History and Culture Review*, cross-currents.berkeley.edu/e-journal/issue-14/jung (September 24, 2019).

275 *Ibid.* at pp. 7-8.

276 Milly vividly recalls standing, with baby Joseph Albert strapped to her, in front of a propaganda poster and being unable to read and fully understand its contents. Appendix V, Milly Interview of May 9, 2017, para. 10, p. 2. Ed recalls frequent "Down with U.S.A." demonstrations and parades showing American "paper tigers." Appendix V, Ed's Interview of December 3, 2017, p. 2; para. 3; Edward Lumsdaine (2016), *Rotten Gambler Two Becomes a True American*, p. 32.

277 The term "nervous breakdown," while not a medical diagnosis, refers to "a wide variety of mental illnesses including depression, anxiety, and acute stress disorder." Annamarya Scaccia, "How to Recognize and Treat the Symptoms of a Nervous Breakdown" (August 13, 2019) healthline.com/health/mental-health/nervous-breakdown#symptoms (September 26, 2019). Symptoms may include insomnia, unexplained outbursts, panic attacks, paranoia, and flashbacks of traumatic events. *Id.* Miao Ying described Clifford's condition after the Communist takeover as a "nervous breakdown." Appendix V, YaoTim Questionnaire Response #8, p.28.

278 Edward Lumsdaine (2016), *Rotten Gambler Two Becomes a True American*, p. 31.

279 *Id.*

280 See Ed's detailed account of the daily arrests, trials, and executions at Edward Lumsdaine (2016), *Rotten Gambler Two Becomes a True American*, pp. 29-30. Miao Ying and Clifford must have seen and known even more of the horrors of that time than what Ed, who was 12, witnessed and clearly recalls.

281 Chuck was hospitalized for about two years. Appendix V, YaoTim's Questionnaire Response #20, p. 19. He suffered a collapsed lung from broken ribs caused during a soccer game where an opponent kicked the ball into his torso. Appendix V, Cory Interview of July 7, 2019, para. 10, p. 1.

282 Ed does not recall 72 year-old Pau Pau being sick, but Philip recalls her coughing a lot. Philip had slept in the same bed and woke up to find her quiet and still before going to get Miao Ying. Appendix V, Ed's Interview of December 3, 2017, para. 9, pp. 3-4; Philip's Interview of June 20, 2017, paras. 2-3, pp. 1-2. Milly's earliest memory of Shanghai was a distinct recollection of seeing Pau Pau's body lying on a bed with her head on a "Chinese pillow" – a square, hollow wood block – looking like she was just sleeping. People were in another room, and Aunt Ng Yee was wailing loudly. Appendix V, Milly's Interview of May 3, 2017, para. 1, p. 1. Milly would have been 4 years old at the time as Pau Pau died in 1950. See footnote 217 *supra*.

283 Appendix V, YaoTim Interview of November 17, 2016, para. 7, pp. 5-6.

284 Ed, and later Philip, were the only grandchildren to have slept in the same bed as Pau Pau, and each received special treats that the other grandchildren did not. Appendix V, YaoTim Allen Interview, Questionnaire Responses at p. 3, para. 15; Ed's Interview of December 3, 2017, para. 9, pp. 3-4; Philip's Interview of June 20, 2017, paras. 2, pp. 1-2.

285 *Author's note:* As it borders on the gauche for me to say that my parents saved "the best for last" when I was born, I will only mention it here, as a footnote. As with several of the other Lumsdaine children, "Joseph Albert" was the name chosen by my oldest sister, YaoTim. Because of the difficulty of the Chinese tongue forming the sound to say the word "Joseph", especially for my Mom, she chose to call me by my middle name, "Albert," and that remained the name by which my siblings address me, such that even their children and grandchildren still now refer to me as "Uncle Albert" rather than "Uncle Joe."

286 North Korean troops crossed over the "38th parallel" into South Korea on June 25, 1950, and U.S. troops entered the war on South Korea's behalf by July. History.com editors, "Korean War," history.com/topics/korea/ korean-war (September 25, 2019).

287 Appendix V, Ed's Interview of December 3, 2017, p. 2; para. 3

288 "In the neighborhood, we got into a lot of fights over Dad (being American)." Appendix V, Chuck's Interview by Anne Lumsdaine in early 2000, Tape #1 as transcribed by Dolly, p. 5.

289 APL was closing because the United States did not recognize Communist China. Clifford lost his job in February 1951 but was not paid until May 1951. *1995 Grandparent Book*, Appendix 2, Section 4, 1987 Interview of Dad, pp. 8-9. See also, Appendix V, YaoTim Interview of November 21, 2016, para. 16, p. 2; Edward Lumsdaine (2016), *Rotten Gambler Two Becomes a True American*, p. 33.

290 Appendix V, Ed's Interview of December 3, 2019, at p. 2. "[L]and of the dingdong bell" appears to be a reference to Clifford having to leave China and go to the United States – land of the Liberty Bell – to find work. See Chapter 6, *infra*. Presumably, Clifford wrote this verse between his termination on February 28 and his departure for the U.S. on August 6, 1951.

291 Appendix V, YaoTim's Questionnaire Response #20, p. 19-20.

292 Clifford had already gotten advances from APL: "I had to have money to buy injections, you know, plasma, so I had to borrow money from the accountant. So of course when I got back to the States, that was deducted [from his unpaid wages and severance pay]." *1995 Grandparent Book*, Appendix 2, Section 4, 1987 Interview of Dad, at p. 9. Clifford did not get fully paid up by APL until after August 1951, after he had travelled to the United States. *Ibid.* p. 12.

293 *1995 Grandparent Book*, Appendix 2, Section 3, YaoTim at p. 1.

294 See, e.g., Appendix V, Philip's Interview of June 20, 2017, p. 3, para. 5. "One time, George, Ed, and Chuck bricked up the front entrance to a bully's residence when they were in Shanghai." Appendix V, Agnes' Interview of August 16, 2019, p. 2.

295 Chuck was born in Shanghai, but had U.S. citizenship because Clifford got married in the U.S. Consulate, and his birth was certified at that time. YaoTim and Ed were born in Hong Kong, which entitled them to British citizenship in addition to U.S. citizenship.

296 As to Clifford not wanting to leave China, see Appendix V, Dolly's Interview of November 16, 2017, at para. 23, p. 3. When asked in 1987 why he left the rest of the family in China, Clifford responded, "There'd be no support in the US. I didn't have a job.... We didn't have the money." *1995 Grandparent Book*, Appendix 2, Section 4, 1987 Interview of Dad, p. 12. Clifford, Chuck, and Miao Ying boarded a train from Shanghai to Hong Kong on July 27, 1951. Miao Ying was held back at the border by Chinese authorities for unknown reasons. Clifford and Chuck entered Hong Kong on July 30 and left for the United States on August 6, 1951. *Ibid.*, p. 8.

297 *1995 Grandparent Book*, Appendix 2, Section 4, 1987 Interview of Dad, pp. 8-9 and 11-13.

298 Only Chuck, YaoTim, Ed, and George were registered as U.S. citizens. This happened in 1940, when Miao Ying and Clifford were at the U.S. consulate in Shanghai for their "official" wedding ceremony. (See end of Chapter 2, *supra*.) Also see e.g. Section 201 of the Nationality Act of 1940, which later was superseded by the Nationality Act of 1952, 8 USC section 1401. Family lore has had it that Clifford needed to have gone to a consulate to record the births in a timely manner, and there was no U.S. Consulate in Shanghai after 1941; alternatively, that Clifford did not reside long enough in the U.S. after age 16. It should be noted that the Nationality Act of 1940, cited by Clifford, did change the residency requirements. See Section 201(g) of that Act.

299 *1995 Grandparent Book*, Appendix 2, Section 3, YaoTim at pp. 11-12. YaoTim sometimes wondered what purpose was served by maintaining Clifford's ledger since Miao Ying could keep track of such information in her head, and Clifford likely would not ever see it again. In fact, at that time, YaoTim doubted that she would ever see her father or older brother again. *Id.*

300 Appendix V, Milly's Interview of May 9, 2017, at para. 8, p. 1.

301 *Author's note:* Milly recalls having me strapped to her back, and YaoTim has reminded me over the years that she used to change my diaper. Appendix V, Milly's Interview of May 9, 2017, para. 10, p. 2.

302 According to Robert, Miao Ying allowed the older boys a lot of independence for the children. He, Edward, George, and Philip would walk from one end of Shanghai to the other. Appendix V, Joyce's Interview of July 18, 2018, p. 1. For results likely undesired by Miao Ying, see the escapades of Ed and Robert in the pages to follow in this chapter.

303 One story told by Milly exemplifies what Miao Ying must have felt knowing that Dolly would no longer be living with her mother and siblings: Likely around Christmas time, Milly had received a doll at a party held by the Jesuits at the boys' school. This was the first doll Milly ever received, and Dolly wanted it. Milly refused, but Miao Ying told Milly to give the doll to Dolly, saying, "You always have me, but Dolly can have this doll to take with her" back to her aunt's house. Appendix V, Milly's Interview of May 3, 2017, para.7, p. 3.

304 Dolly was only 3 years old when she went to live with her aunt, Ho Wai Ying "Ng Yee," and uncle, Choi Yuk Chuen, but she knew she was no longer with her own family. Years later, she would recount how she was treated more like a servant than a daughter by

her aunt. She stayed in the servants' quarters in back instead of the main house where her aunt, uncle, and teenage cousin Choi Yiu Ki "Ah Kai" lived. Dolly had chores like cleaning pigeon cages and feeding the fish, whereas Ah Kai did not. Sometimes she also would be asked to help the servants with cooking or cleaning chores. Still, she was provided food, clothing, and her own bed to sleep in. And Choi Yuk Chuen frequently took her places and brought her back gifts from his travels, at which times she felt more like a daughter, at least to him. Appendix V, Dolly's Interview of October 16, 2017, paras, 1, 6, 7, pp. 1-3.

305   Appendix V, Dolly's Interview of October 16, 2017, para.1, p. 1.

306   Appendix V, Dolly's Interview of October 16, 2017, para. 2, p. 1. Two of Dolly's other recollections also showed the protective yet nurturing side of her mother. One example related to her uncle's "womanizing." Dolly recalled Miao Ying getting into a heated argument and scolding Yuk Chuen for taking Dolly with him to his mistresses' houses, where he stayed overnight. Dolly also recalled her mother showing up to take Dolly off a train where Ng Yee had sent her to accompany a pregnant servant girl who was being sent back to her home village. *Ibid.* at paras. 3, 4, pp. 1-2.

307   Appendix V, YaoTim's Questionnaire Response #20, pp. 19-20. YaoTim considers this as something Miao Ying was most embarrassed about: "Her husband was kind about it, but Mom's sister would find ways to belittle her about it; for example, when Mom had to borrow money because Chuck was in the hospital...." *Id.* For other examples of times when Miao Ying would be embarrassed by her younger sister's actions, see Dolly's account of her aunt taking her to Miao Ying for discipline and punishment at Appendix V, Dolly's Interview of October 16, 2017, para. 5, p. 2; and her "ranting and raving" because Philip dirtied a "polished spittoon" in her house at Appendix V, Milly's Questionnaire Response #8, p. 2, and Appendix V, Philip's Interview of July 5, 2017, para. 15, p. 1.

308   *1995 Grandparent Book*, Appendix 2, Section 3, YaoTim at p. 11.

309   *1995 Grandparent Book*, Appendix 2, Section 3, YaoTim at p. 12.

310   *Id.* Appendix V, YaoTim's Interview of November 21, 2016, paras. 18-19, pp. 4-5.

311   As a teenage girl, YaoTim would have been targeted for kidnapping or worse, since human trafficking was "a trade that has been very prevalent in China for centuries." Appendix V, YaoTim's Interview of November 21, 2016, para. 18, pp. 4.

312   Ed recalls "two goong yan" taking care of the 7 of us during that time. Edward Lumsdaine (2016), *Rotten Gambler Two Becomes a True American*, pp. 36-37.

313   Appendix V, YaoTim's Interview of November 21, 2016, paras. 18, p. 4, and YaoTim's Interview of November 17, 2016, para. 13, p. 14-15. Mrs. Lueck is the teacher who loaned YaoTim the money to buy her white shoes and socks for First Communion, which YaoTim had been paying off by working in Mrs. Lueck's garden. *Ibid.* at p. 14. As for repayment of that loan, see Appendix V, YaoTim's Interview of November 21, 2016, para. 20, pp. 7-8.

314   Appendix V, YaoTim Interview of November 21, 2016, para. 19, pp. 5-6. See also, Appendix V, Talk with YaoTim on November 11, 2013, p.1.

315   Appendix V, YaoTim Interview of November 21, 2016, para. 19, pp. 5-6.

316   "Mom had known her [Ah Hun/HunTse; also spelled "Hon Jie" by YaoTim and "Hung Tser" by Ed] as a teenager when, in the early years, they had lived in Hong Kong [1934-1939]. Ah Hun's father was a gambler, lost a lot of money, and was in serious trouble. Ah Hun did not have an education; therefore, it was very difficult for her to find work to

help her parents. So Mom took Ah Hun under her wings. Mom sold her watch to give money to Ah Hun to take dancing lessons in order to become a dancer – a very legitimate profession, not an exotic dancer. It would provide her a better income than working at a factory or such. Eventually, Ah Hun became the fourth wife of a very wealthy man and lived richly ever after that but did not forget what Mom had done for her. Although Ah Hun was the fourth wife, she was this rich man's favorite wife." Appendix V, YaoTim Interview of November 21, 2016, para. 19, p. 5. Author's notes are in brackets.

317 They left Shanghai by train on December 13, 1951. Arriving in Hong Kong three days later, YaoTim obtained an U.S. passport on December 20, 1951, boarded a ship on January 20, 1952, and arrived in San Francisco on February 15, 1952. Appendix V, YaoTim Interview of November 21, 2016, para. 19, p. 5, and documents from YaoTim (passport and notations) attached to her interviews.

318 Both Miao Ying and YaoTim were extremely resourceful in raising funds. Miao Ying needed $200 to return to Shanghai and repay Mrs. Lueck's sister; she received that in the form of a loan – which Clifford later repaid – from an American doctor who had traveled on the train from Shanghai with them. YaoTim's fare as a passenger on the freighter Tatania was a personal loan from a priest whom she had just met at Catholic Charities in Hong Kong, where she had gone for help. Not only did this priest, Fr. Des Laurius (spelled by the author as DeLoria in some interviews) loan the money from his own personal funds and trust that it would be repaid by the father of this young girl he had just met but he also made sure that she was put on a ship with seven priests and a woman missionary to accompany her. Appendix V, YaoTim Interview of November 21, 2016, paras. 20-21, pp. 7-9.

319 Appendix V, YaoTim Interview of November 21, 2016, para.20, pp. 8-9.

320 *Id.*

321 "After my father left for the United States, I grew more and more unmanageable." Edward Lumsdaine (2016), *Rotten Gambler Two Becomes a True American*, p. 34.

322 *Ibid.* at pp. 1-3, 35-36 and 41.

323 As for Ed's reasons, see p. 37; for Miao Ying's, see p. 45 in Edward Lumsdaine (2016), *Rotten Gambler Two Becomes a True American*.

324 As of the end of July 1952, the six children left in Shanghai were George, 11; Robert, 10; Philip, 9; Milly, 6; Dolly, 4; and Joseph Albert, 2.

325 See Dolly's version, "[a]s legend has it" – "Robert and Milly broke our tall closet mirror while trying to climb though a window to our home because they were locked out." *1995 Grandparent Book*, Appendix 2, Section 3, Dolly, at bottom of p. 3. Milly's "first person" account, narrated in the text above, is likely more accurate: that she and Robert woke up from a nap and were playing around. Appendix V, Milly's Interview of May 9, 2017, para. 13, p.

326 When Robert and Joyce visited the Shikumen Open House Museum in Shanghai in August 2005, Robert identified the armoire with a mirror that he and Milly broke as similar to the one displayed there, which is pictured on page 79. Appendix V, Joyce's Interview Exhibit Pictures with commentaries by Robert and Joyce, at 2005 Shanghai RAL, p. 2.

327 Appendix V, Joyce's Interview of July 7, 2018, p. 2.

328 Appendix V, Milly's Interview of May 9, 2017, para.13, p. 3.

329 Appendix V, Philip's Interview of June 20, 2017, para. 8, pp. 3-4.

330 *Id.* As for the family tradition of asking their mother for forgiveness by bringing her hot tea and kneeling in front of her, see Appendix V, Philip's Interview of June 20, 2017, para. 8, pp. 4, and Appendix V, Philip's Questionnaire Response #43, p. 7. The author recalls personally witnessing both Robert and Philip perform this family "forgiveness ceremony" at least once each when the family lived in Hong Kong. Appendix V, Joe's Interview of January 21-26, 2019, p. 4.

331 In about 1953 or 1954, Robert and Philip removed a copper pipe from the communal toilet in the house, and later also removed copper wiring and connectors, and sold them without the money going to Mom, but which she later found out about. Appendix V, Milly's Interview of May 9, 2017, para. 14, pp. 3-4; Appendix V, Joyce's Interview of July 7, 2018, para. 8, p. 2. Joyce also recalls Robert telling her of "naughty antics" such as putting the "family chamber pot" in front of neighbors' door, ringing the bell, and running away to then watch them trip over the filthy pot. *Id.*

332 It is unclear who took Joseph Albert to the park and snapped the picture on page 81. The author speculates that it may have been his uncle, Choi Yuk Chuen – husband of Miao Ying's sister, Ng Yee – who often took some of Miao Ying's children on outings, including to amusement parks, and frequently gave them small treats or gifts. Dolly recalled that Yuk Chuen took her, Milly, and possibly Joseph Albert to "Su Chow" (aka Suzhou), a major tourist area with restaurants and gardens, on an outing, and it is possible this picture was taken there. Appendix V, Dolly's Interview of October 16, 2017, para. 7, p. 3.

333 "I did not actually see Mom cry, but I knew that she had by observing her afterwards. Many times, when Mom came home from trying to get visas to leave Shanghai, I could tell that she had been crying because her eyes were red." Appendix V, Philip's Interview of June 20, 2017, para. 10, p. 4.

334 Clifford was sending Miao Ying $100 per month in U.S. currency, which was the maximum amount allowed. *1995 Grandparent Book*, Appendix 2, Section 4, 1987 Interview of Dad, p. 9. *Cf.*; Appendix V, George's Interview of March1, 2017, para. 2, p. 1; and Appendix V, Philip's Interview of June 28, 2017, para. 11, p. 1.

335 Appendix V, George's Interview of March 1, 2017, para. 2, p. 1; Milly's Interview of May 9, 2017, para. 8, p. 1.

336 *Id.* Appendix V, Philip's Interview of June 28, 2017, para. 11, p. 1.

337 Appendix V, Dolly's Interview of October 16, 2017, para. 8, p. 3.

338 Appendix V, Dolly's Interview of November 1, 2017, para.10, p. 1.

339 Two types of visas were required: exit visas issued by the Communist Chinese government to leave China and entry visas issued by the then-British Hong Kong government to enter and reside in Hong Kong. Appendix V, Philip's Interview of June 28, 2017, para. 11, p. 1.

340 Appendix V, George's Interview of March 1, 2017, para. 2, p.3. Appendix V, Philip's Interview of June 28, 2017, para. 11, p.1

341 The family only had seats facing each other on the train, with no room to sleep. Appendix V, Dolly's Interview of November 1, 2017, para. 10, p. 1. "Most of our belongings were in a small wooden basket, the same one that hung in the loft in Shanghai." Appendix V, Philip's Interview of June 28, 2017, para. 12, at p. 2. Aside from the constraints of train travel, at the only crossing from China to Hong Kong at that time, "people had to carry their belongings across the wooden bridge." *Ibid.*

342 As to the few possessions that were carried out, see Appendix V, Philip's Interview of June 28, 2017, para. 12, p. 2. As to an example of things left behind, including Robert's sports trophies, see Appendix V, Joyce's Interview of July 18, 2018, p. 1.

343 Appendix V, Dolly's Interview of November 1, 2017, para. 11, p. 1.

344 *Id.* and Appendix V, George's Interview of March 1, 2017, para. 4, p.1.

345 Philip's recollection of this incident is so vivid that he recalls seeing "the bullets in the guns" that the two officers were holding (so most likely they were revolvers). Appendix V, Philip's Interview of June 28, 2017, para. 11, at p. 1.

346 *Id.* Appendix V, George's Interview of March 1, 2017, para. 4, at p. 1. The author, only 5 years old at the time, still could recall clearly – 64 years later – that he was standing next to and being held by his mother, who was seated in one of the chairs, as the charges were read. Appendix V, Joseph Albert's Interview of January 21-26, at p. 1.

347 Appendix V, Philip's Interview of June 28, 2017, para. 11, p. 1.

348 Appendix V, George's Interview of March 1, 2017, para. 4, p. 1. Miao Ying kept her children close and confined at the hotel because the place seemed "seedy" and unclean. Appendix V, Dolly's Interview of November 1, 2017, para. 12, at p. 2. The stay there was brief. Appendix V, Philip's Interview of June 28, 2017, para. 11, p. 1.

349 Appendix V, Milly's Interview of May 9, 2017, para. 15, p. 4.

350 When the Kowloon-Canton Railway Corporation (KCRC) first went into service, trains did not stop at Lo Wu, as there was no border patrol at the time. However, shortly after the People's Republic of China was created in October 1949, the KCR announced that trains would terminate at Lo Wu, and passengers would have to cross the border on foot. See, generally, https://en.wikipedia.org/wiki/Kowloon%E2%80%93Canton_Railway#History (November 27, 2019). Such was the case in the summer of 1955 when the Lumsdaine family went through.

351 Appendix V, Philip's Interview of June 28, 2017, para. 12, at p. 2.

352 Appendix V, Milly's Interview of May 9, 2017, para. 15, p. 4. One can only speculate as to why Miao Ying would take such risks as to sew jewelry and gold chains into her children's garments before attempting the border crossing. At a minimum, the items could have been confiscated. Beyond that, one can presume that the soldiers would have had authority to arrest Miao Ying and charge her with smuggling. Presumably, consequences would not be so negative for her children. Taken out of context, her actions would seem unwise or even foolhardy, yet Miao Ying was anything but foolhardy. Given the circumstances, including her knowledge that she would need the wherewithal to pay for food and shelter for herself and six children in Hong Kong without a bank account or her husband waiting for her there, smuggling out jewelry may have been the only option for continued survival for her family. It should also be kept in mind, at that time and place, that there was no social "safety net" for food, shelter, and health services in Hong Kong such as one might encounter today in the U.S.

353 Appendix V, Philip's Interview of June 28, 2017, para. 12, at p. 2. According to George: "Unknown to us, a maid at the hotel had put a bamboo brush in our luggage. The guards used a screwdriver to pry open the brush to see if there was any contraband hidden in the handle. This was very scary for the whole family because none of us had known anything about the brush." Appendix V, George's Interview of March 1, 2017, para. 5, p.at 2.

354 Appendix V, Philip's Interview of June 28, 2017, para. 13, p. 2.

355 *Id.*

356 The children had nothing to eat on the train despite the presence of "vendors that would run up to the train with pastries, eggs, etc." Appendix V, Dolly's Interview of November 1, 2017, para. 13, at p. 2. This may have been because Miao Ying had run out of money leaving Canton and purchasing train tickets. *Id.*

357 Appendix V, Philip's Interview of June 28, 2017, para. 13, p. 2; Appendix V, Milly's Interview of May 9, 2017, para. 16, pp. 4-5; Appendix V, Dolly's Interview of November 1, 2017, para. 13, p. 2. Miao Ying was "very upset" by Bieu Tse not offering anything for her children to eat. Appendix V, George's Interview of March 1, 2017, para. 6, p. 2. While the author was too young to remember specifically the discussions at that time, years later, he was told by Miao Ying that she considered it very unkind of her niece not to offer to give the children anything to eat or some idea of a place to stay. This incident seems to have left a lasting impression as well on George, Philip, Milly and Dolly; each of them vividly recalled it as shown in their interviews cited above in this footnote. This event was also recounted many years later by Miao Ying to her daughter-in-law Elaine. Appendix V, Elaine's Interview of August 13, 2018, p. 3. As to Bieu Tse having been orphaned and taken into the Lumsdaine home, see Chapter 4, *supra*.

358 None of the Lumsdaine children recalled the name of their mother's friend in Kowloon. This friend was married to a man who worked in a motorcycle shop in the "New Territories" of Kowloon. (The author wonders whether this man had any relation to Miao Ying's former boyfriend before Clifford, who owned a motorcycle shop in Shanghai; See pp. 14-15 *supra*.) Appendix V, Philip's Interview of June 28, 2017, para. 13, p. 3. Both the man's workplace and the apartment where the family stayed were in the New Territories. *Id.*, and see New Territories, britannica.com/place/New-Territories (November 28, 2019).

359 Appendix V, Milly's Interview of May 9, 2017, para. 16, at p. 5. Similar accounts were given by Philip, Dolly and Joseph Albert. Appendix V, Philip's Interview of June 28, 2017, para. 13, p. 3; Appendix V, Dolly's Interview of November 1, 2017, para. 13, p. 2: Appendix V, Joseph Albert's Interview of January 21-26, 2019, p. 1.

360 Appendix V, George's Interview of March 1, 2017, para. 6, p. 2; Appendix V, Philip's Interview of June 28, 2017, para. 13, p. 3.

361 Miao Ying told Ed, "I don't have any money. We had to leave everything behind in Shanghai." Edward Lumsdaine (2016), *Rotten Gambler Two Becomes a True American*, at p. 137; Appendix V, Ed's Interview of December 3, 2017, para. 17, at p. 7.

362 *Id.*

363 "The Mixed Fortunes of Eurasians: How Hong Kong, China and US Viewed Intermarriage," South China Morning Post, January 31, 2017, scmp.com/culture/article/2066738/mixed-fortunes-eurasians-how-hong-kong-china-and-us-viewed-intermarriage (November 30, 2019). "Teng" refers to Massachusetts Institute of Technology professor Emma J. Teng, author of many works on Asian studies, including *Eurasian: Mixed Identities in the United States, China and Hong Kong, 1842-1943* (2013), University of California Press, ISBN 978-0-520-27627-7. "Chinese nationalism...led to mounting hostility against Eurasians (especially those with European fathers) .... and many Hong Kong Chinese to form 'the idea that the Eurasian Chinese should no longer be classed as Chinese....'" *Ibid.* at pp. 239-240.

364 "When Mom looked for the new residence, she did not bring us kids because she did not want the landlord to know we had that many." Appendix V, Philip's Interview of June 28, 2017, para. 13, p. 3.

365 See "New Territories," britannica.com/place/New-Territories (November 28, 2019). For a historical review of Boundary Street, see "Boundary Street," September 21, 2016, zolimacitymag.com/boundary-street-hong-kongs-invisible-frontier/ (November 29, 2019).

366 Appendix V, George's Interview of March 1, 2017, para. 7, p. 2.

367 Appendix V, Philip's Questionnaire Response #13, p. 3. Mr. Ho stayed briefly at the family home at 396 Wall Street, Ventura, Calif., in 1963. Appendix V, Milly's Interview of May 17, 2017, para. 20, p. 1.

368 Appendix V, Milly's Interview of May 9, 2017, para. 17, at p. 5.

369 "There were usually four or five men – bus drivers – who slept in another room." Appendix V, George's Interview of March 1, 2017, para. 7, p. 2. "For part of the time we were there, there was a little room that may have had different tenants, namely a couple with no children, another couple with a small girl, etc." *Id.* "Then followed another room rented out with four bunk beds, with men living there; then there was a bathroom and another little room where the landlord's maid and the niece of the landlord lived. There was also an attic space where the landlord, Mr. Ho, slept. Then there was the kitchen area which led to a courtyard before a door leading to the street." Appendix V, Milly's Interview of May 9, 2017, para. 17, at p. 5.

370 Appendix V, Milly's Interview of May 9, 2017, para. 17, p. 5; Dolly's Interview of November 1, 2017, para. 14, p. 2; and George's Interview of March 1, 2017, para. 7, p. 2.

371 Appendix V, Milly's Interview of May 9, 2017, para. 17, p. 5, and telephone conversation between Joseph Albert and Milly on December 3, 2019. Underneath was used for storage. *Id.*

372 Appendix V, Joyce's Interview of July 18, 2018, p. 2.

373 Appendix V, Milly's Interview of May 9, 2017, para. 17, p. 5.

374 Appendix V, Philip's Interview of June 28, 2017, para. 15, p. 4.

375 For example, "none of the kids bathed alone." Appendix V, Milly's Interview of May 9, 2017, para. 17, at p. 6. Milly would bathe with Dolly. *Ibid.* Joseph Albert recalls bathing with both Robert and Philip. It is not clear if this was to conserve bathroom usage times or due to the water rationing that the city occasionally imposed during drought conditions.

376 Appendix V, Dolly's Interview of November 1, 2017, para. 14, p. 2.

377 *Id.*

378 Appendix V, Philip's Interview of June 28, 2017, para. 13, p. 4. For information on Nathan Road, see en.wikipedia.org/wiki/Nathan_Road (December 3, 2019)

379 Appendix V, Philip's Interview of June 28, 2017, para. 13, p. 4. As for what they spent the money on, see *Ibid.*"

380 As vividly recalled by the author: "Robert, with Philip, told me Mom wanted to see me and that I was going to get spanked. Either they suggested or I figured out to put a schoolbook in my pants (shorts). I went to see Mom, and she used a feather duster stick, heard the book with the first smack, then hit me on the bare legs. Don't remember how many times, but it was more than two or three, and it really hurt. I remember thinking it was dumb to put the book there."

381 Appendix V, Dolly's Interview of November 1, 2017, para. 14, p. 2.

382 Appendix V, Milly's Interview of May 17, 2017, para. 19, p. 1; Dolly's Interview of November 16, 2017, para. 16, p. 1; Appendix V, Philip's Interview of June 28, 2017, para. 15, pp. 3-4. Universal public education was not available in Hong Kong until the 1970s. See Chak Chung and Ming-yang Ngan (October 15, 2002), "The Development of Primary Schools in Hong Kong Since 1945," hkta1934.org.hk/NewHorizon/abstract/2002n/page24.pdf (November 23, 2020).

383 See en.wikipedia.org/wiki/St._Francis_Xavier%27s_College (December 4, 2019)

384 Appendix V, Philip's Interview of July 5, 2017, para. 15, pp. 3-4. George says he was one grade ahead of Robert and Philip at the school. When he got to the United States

and wanted to enter Ventura High School, they told him based on his transcript that he only needed a couple of history courses and would be given his high school diploma at Ventura College, which he enrolled in shortly after.

385 In the biography *Bruce Lee: A Life*, by Matthew Polly, ISBN 978-1-5011-8762-9 (2018), St. Francis Xavier College was referred to as "more like a reform school." Appendix V, Joyce's Interview of September 13, 2018, p. 3.

386 Appendix V, Philip's Interview of June 28, 2017, para. 15, pp. 3-4. Also, per Google Maps (December 13, 2019) both schools were about ½ mile from the family's home at 229 Sai Yeung Choi Street.

387 There was no free schooling, and Miao Ying had to scramble each month for the money to pay for all six kids' education. Appendix V, Philip's Interview of June 28, 2017, para. 16, p. 5. Tuition was reduced to half price for the three older boys at Xavier and likely the same for the three younger children at Assisi. Appendix V, Philip's Interview of June 28, 2017, para. 16, p. 5.

388 Appendix V, Philip's Interview of June 28, 2017, para. 16, p. 5.

389 Appendix V, Dolly's Interview of November 16, 2017, paras. 16, p. 1 and 19, p. 2.

390 Unlike present-day America, Hong Kong did not have any kind of public-assistance program at all until 1958 and even then "stressed the role of family in social welfare." en.wikipedia.org/wiki/Comprehensive_Social_Security_Assistance#Historical_overview (December 16, 2019). St. Francis Xavier did have occasional giveaways, usually "cornmeal or food and toy packages that we would usually receive because we were 'scholarship kids.'" Appendix V, Philip's Interview of July 5, 2017, para. 76, p. 2. "I believe that Mom was only allowed about $700 a month. She would take us to the U.S. Embassy, where we would get some used clothes, food, and sometimes attend a Christmas party." Appendix V, Dolly's Interview of November 16, 2017, at para. 19, p. 2

391 Appendix V, Dolly's Interview of November 16, 2017, paras. 16, p. 1 and 19, p. 2; George's Interview of March 1, 2017, para. 6, p. 2; George's Questionnaire Response #30, p. 4. Compare this time period for Miao Ying to when she only had two children – Dolly and Joseph Albert – at home to take care of in Ventura in the 1960s, when she would take on even menial work like cleaning tables and washing dishes at restaurants to make ends meet. Appendix V, Dolly's Interview of November 27, 2017, para. 29, p. 3.

392 *Cf.* Dolly's perspective in *1995 Grandparent Book*, Appendix 2, Section 3, Dolly at p. 1: "Another thing about Mom and Dad I think of is the kind of love they must have had for their many kids....What was it like for a woman alone, already in her 40s and early 50s, to have the energy to drag a bunch of unruly brats over thousands of miles, through several countries and borders?"

393 "McCarthyism" has been defined as "a vociferous campaign against alleged communists in the U.S. government and other institutions carried out under Senator Joseph McCarthy in the period 1950-1954. Many of the accused were blacklisted or lost their jobs, although most did not in fact belong to the Communist Party." *Oxford Dictionary* lexico.com/en/definition/mccarthyism (December 17, 2019).

394 Charlotte Brooks, *Between Mao and McCarthy: Chinese American Politics in the Cold War Years,* Univ. of Chicago Press (2015) ISBN 978-0-226-19373, at p. 105.

395 Appendix V, Cory's Interview of July 7, 2019, para. 11, p. 2.

396 *1995 Grandparent Book*, Appendix 2, Interview of Dad, Section 4, p. 11.

397 Appendix V, Dolly's Interview of November 16, 2017, para. 23, at p. 3.

398 *1995 Grandparent Book*, Appendix 2, Interview of Dad, Section 4, p. 11.

399 *Ibid.* at p. 13.

400 "Red Scare," the History Channel, history.com/topics/cold-war/red-scare (December 17, 2019). Aside from popular hysteria, all three branches of the government were impacted, with the Executive branch routinely investigating common citizens; the Supreme Court denying First Amendment rights to "accused Communists," and the infamous interrogations by the House Un-American Activities Committee. FBI Director J. Edgar Hoover even labeled Martin Luther King Jr. a communist and all civil rights demonstrations as communist subversion. *Id.* See also "Anti-Communism in the 1950s," Gilder Lehrman Institute of American History, ap.gilderlehrman.org/history-by-era/fifties/essays/anti-communism-1950s (December 17, 2019).

401 These statements are contained in heavily redacted government files that Dolly obtained in April 1999 and August 2002 through Freedom of Information Act (5 USC section 552) requests and subsequent appeal. See Appendix I, Dad, tab 2, "Communist Sympathizer's Report on Conditions in Shanghai" dated August 27, 1951, at pp. 34 and 36. Despite missing pages and other redactions, it is evident that this document was from a CIA agent who interviewed Clifford either at the port or shortly after his arrival in San Francisco.

402 Appendix I, Dad, tab 2, Memorandum to "Director, FBI" dated November 30, 1951, at p. 32.

403 Quoted remarks at Appendix I, Dad, tab 1, Memorandum to "Director, FBI" dated November 30, 1951 at p. 32. One stated reason for the CIA's suspicions of Clifford and the referral to the FBI was the mistaken belief that he had not been interned during the Japanese occupation of Shanghai. *Id.* Contrary to those quoted statements, however, birth and Japanese internment records clearly show that Clifford was born in Seattle and that he was interned by the Japanese for 30 months, from February 1943 to August 1945.

404 All these events are listed, with redactions, in Appendix I, Dad, tab 1, pp. 5-28, starting with an FBI cover sheet for file "San Francisco 105-1433." As stated therein, four pages were removed and not provided in addition to the text redactions, despite the passage of 48 years since the events.

405 See letters from Clifford to FBI in Washington, DC on April 9 and May 6, 1952, Appendix I, Dad, tab 1, pp. 12-14 & 18-19.

406 Appendix V, Dolly's Interview of November 16, 2017, para. 23, p.3.

407 *Id.* These events haunted Clifford so much that he had difficulty recounting them to Dolly even 20 years later. Appendix V, Dolly's Interview of November 16, 2017, para. 23, p. 4. The harassment fed Clifford's concern that his Chinese wife and biracial kids would not be treated well in the United States, leading to his eventual reluctance to have the rest of the family join him in the U.S. *Id.*

408 "Dad would get into arguments with coworkers in the lunch room." Appendix V, Dolly's Interview of November 16, 2017, para. 23, at p. 3. The FBI noted that "other employees of the company would 'needle' the subject [Clifford], and such action would cause LUMSDAINE to become emotionally upset." Appendix I, Dad, tab 1, FBI Memorandum dated June 26, 1952 at p. 24. This memorandum stated that when asked by an employee if he were a communist, Clifford "replied, 'Yes, and I am proud of it'" but also noted that "when the subject made this remark, the other employees had been antagonizing LUMSDAINE and the latter was emotionally upset." *Id.* Even this obviously angry and sarcastic retort was used against Clifford in that someone with the company went so far as to file a complaint with the FBI claiming that he had professed that he was indeed a communist, that he was trying to go back to China, and that he was "going by way of MOSCOW." Appendix I, Dad, tab 1, FBI Complaint Form dated April 14, 1952 at p. 24.

Given everything else that's known about Clifford, the allegation was absurd, which may have been why the FBI closed his file four days after the June 26, 1952, memorandum. Appendix I, Dad, tab 1, FBI Memorandum dated June 30, 1952, at p. 28.

409 Clifford worked for the Southern Pacific Railroad for four days, from September 17-21, 1951; Western Union for eight weeks, from October 19 to December 13, 1951; and Sharp and Dohme, a pharmaceutical firm, for five months, from December 17, 1951, to May 6, 1952. He was fired from Sharp and Dohme allegedly for multiple stated reasons: a) not doing his job; b) they wanted a woman in that position; c) he thought that wages should be enough for someone to support his family; and d) he was probably communist. Appendix I, Dad, tab 1, FBI Memorandum dated June 26, 1952, at p. 21. It appears to have been a classic case of pretextual termination, where multiple reasons are given – none of them true – to hide a more likely reason: The company did not want further visits from FBI.

410 When asked why the entire family didn't leave when he and Chuck did in 1951, Clifford answered simply, "We didn't have the money." 1995 Grandparent Book, Appendix 2, Section 4, 1987 Interview of Dad, at p. 12. When asked if the Chinese government would have allowed the whole family to leave, Clifford answered, "I don't know, I don't know whether they could have...." Id. He then went on to explain that there was a lot of confusion as to some of the children's nationality, including several who were considered "stateless." Ibid. pp. 12-13.

411 See, e.g., 1995 Grandparent Book, Appendix 2, Section 4, 1987 Interview of Dad, at p. 12.

412 As for YaoTim, see text accompanying footnote 243, supra. As for Ed, see Edward Lumsdaine (2016), Rotten Gambler Two Becomes a True American, pp. 38-100.

413 Appendix V, George's Interview of March 1, 2017, at para. 8, p. 3.

414 See, e.g., George's letter to YaoTim dated December 8, 1957, wherein George states that, "...mother has been to the American Consulate yesterday in connection with Millie's [sic] petition."

415 In his letter to YaoTim dated December 8, 1957, George acknowledges that YaoTim advised that Clifford finally signed the non-quota petition. Appendix V, George's Interview of April 4, 2017, letter attached thereto.

416 A September 1957 letter from George to YaoTim stated, in relevant part: "Sorry I didn't reply earlier...but mother told me to wait until the copy of Milly's birth certificate is accomplished, which she was able to do so only today afternoon. You will find the copy of Milly's birth certificate enclosed in this letter. I understand very well from your last letter that things will be much easier for you if you had dad's co-operation. ...I've already written to him yesterday and done my best to get him to co-operate with you...no matter what he might say, it shouldn't discourage you from doing your best to obtain Milly's visa as soon as possible, so that I and Milly will be able to come to [the United] States in the near future." See letter attached to Appendix V, George's Interview of April 4, 2017, and para. 10, p. 1 of that interview.

417 The term was coined by one-time NBC Nightly News anchor Tom Brokaw, who wrote a book of the same name. The generation is marked by those born between 1910 and 1924 who lived through the Great Depression and either fought or were otherwise severely impacted by World War II. Investopedia, "The Greatest Generation", investopedia.com/terms/t/the_greatest_generation.asp (January 11, 2020).

418 Appendix V, YaoTim's Interview January 13, 2020.

419 YaoTim was married and living with Bob's family in Kansas when the FBI visited the house and asked her to produce her passport later at their office in Missouri. The agents interrogated her about where her mother and siblings were and then advised her that

she should have Clifford sign a petition for the highest priority of four categories of entry visas, which was a non-quota visa for family members of a U.S. citizen, since Clifford was a U.S. citizen. Appendix V, YaoTim's Interview January 13, 2020.

420 *Ibid.*

421 Appendix V, Dolly's Interview November 16, 2017, at para. 23, p. 4. "Dad had a hard time talking about this." *Id.*

422 Appendix V, George's Interview of April 4, 2017, at para. 10, p. 1.

423 *Id.*

424 Appendix V, YaoTim's Interview of January 13, 2020.

425 Appendix V, Milly's Interview of May 17, 2017, at para. 21, p. 3.

426 *Id.*

427 Appendix V, Milly's Interview of May 17, 2017, para. 21, p. 3.

428 *Id.*

429 Appendix V, Milly's Interview of May 17, 2017, para. 22, pp. 2-3, at p. 3.

430 Appendix V, Ed's Interview of December 3, 2017, para. 19, p. 7.; Milly's Interview of May 17, 2017, paras. 22-23, pp. 2-3.

431 Appendix V, YaoTim's Interview of January 13, 2020. Truman Boyd American Gold Star Homes was an extensive housing project originally acquired by the federal government in 1953 for defense workers and their families. The buildings were replaced in 1973 and completely renovated in 2019. It is currently known as the American Gold Star Manor, located at 3021 Gold Star Drive off Santa Fe Avenue and Spring Street in Long Beach. Anna Todd, "A Sojourn in California," July 29, 2015, *Vita Brevis,* picture courtesy of Anna Todd https://vitabrevis.americanancestors.org/2015/07/sojourn-in-california/ (January 13, 2020); see also American Gold Star Mothers website at https://www.goldstarmoms.com/the-gold-star-manor.html (January 13, 2020).

432 Appendix V, YaoTim's Interview of January 13, 2020. As noted earlier (see text accompanying footnotes 340 to 354), Clifford had difficulty getting and keeping meaningful employment, largely because of having been blackballed as a result of spurious CIA and FBI investigations. As a consequence, he struggled to make enough money to support himself, even with taking on menial work like delivering newspapers, and could not afford to contribute to the fund for travel fares for those in Hong Kong. Appendix V, YaoTim's Interview of January 13, 2020.

433 Appendix V, Cory's Interview of July 7, 2019, paras. 10-11, p. 2.

434 See, e.g., Appendix V, Ed's Interview of December 3, 2017, para. 16, p. 7.

435 Appendix V, YaoTim's Interview of January 13, 2020.

436 *Ibid.*

437 *1995 Grandparent Book*, Appendix 2, Section 3, YaoTim's narrative, at p. 13.

438 Appendix V, Ed's Interview of December 3, 2017, at paras. 16-17, pp. 6-7.

439 *Ibid.*, para. 20, pp. 7-8.

440 Appendix V, George's Interview of March 1, 2017, at para. 9, p. 7. Point Mugu was a naval air station in Ventura County where most of the Navy's missiles were developed during the 1950s and 1960s. en.wikipedia.org/wiki/Naval_Air_Station_Point_Mugu (January 14, 2020)

441 Appendix V, George's Interview of March 1, 2017, at para. 9, p. 7.

442 Appendix V, Ed's Interview of December 3, 2017, at para. 20, p. 8.

443 Appendix V, Philip's Interview of July 20, 2017, para. 27, p. 1; Joyce's Interview of July 7, 2018, p. 4. The ship was originally commissioned as a troop transport but later cancelled and completed as a passenger ship in 1948. It was chartered to American President Lines under the name SS President Wilson. U.S. Maritime Commission type P2-SE2-R3 maritime.dot.gov/content/ss-president-wilson (January 14, 2020). Picture is of postcard in Appendix I, Original Documents.

444 Appendix V, Philip's Interview of July 20, 2017, para. 27, p. 1.

445 Appendix V, Dolly's Interview of November 16, 2017, para. 25, p. 1.

446 Appendix V, Joseph Albert's Interview of January 21-26, 2019, p. 5.

447 Appendix V, Dolly's Interview of November 16, 2017, para. 25, p. 4; Philip's Interview of July 20, 2017, para. 27, pp. 1-2; Joseph Albert's Interview of January 21-26, 2019, p. 5.

448 "Mom was going to leave me to watch Joseph Albert on the ship and take Philip and Robert on shore. I cried and then Mom said it was OK for me to go. But then I got stubborn and said, 'no.' Mom ended up taking only Robert, Philip and Joseph Albert, leaving me to stay on the ship by myself." Appendix V, Dolly's Interview of November 16, 2017, para. 25, at p. 1.

449 Appendix V, Joseph Albert's Interview of January 21-26, 2019, p. 6; Philip's Interview of July 20, 2017, para. 27, p. 1.

450 Appendix V, Joseph Albert's Interview of January 21-26, 2019, p. 6.

451 Appendix V, Joyce's Interview of July 7, 2018, p. 4; Philip's Interview of July 20, 2017, para. 27, p. 1;

452 "It was a long pier, like the ones that are still there." Appendix V, Joseph Albert's Interview of January 21-26, 2019, at p. 6.

453 "It was a Caucasian man, and I thought it was my father at first. But then I was told it was Mr. Schofield." Appendix V, Joseph Albert's Interview of January 21-26, 2019, at p. 6. "… we were met at the dock by Hayden Schofield. Robert and Philip at first thought that he was Dad." Appendix V, Philip's Interview of July 20, 2017, para. 28, at p. 2.

454 Id.; Appendix V, Dolly's Interview of November 27, 2017, para. 26, p. 1.

455 Airline travel in the 1950s was very expensive, costing about $3,000 in 2019 dollars to fly between Hong Kong and San Francisco, and was five times more dangerous. Cf. Huffington Post, "This Is What Your Flight Used To Look Like," June 15, 2014, huffpost.com/entry/air-travel-1950s_n_5461411 (January 20, 2020) and Fast Company, "What It Was Really Like To Fly During The Golden Age Of Travel," December 5, 2013, fastcompany.com/3022215/what-it-was-really-like-to-fly-during-the-golden-age-of-travel (January 20, 2020). A long-distance telephone call in 1955 cost the equivalent of $35 (in 2019 dollars) for the first 3 minutes, with additional charges for every 1-minute increment after that. Quora, "How Much Did A Long-Distance Call Cost In The 1950s?" quora.com/How-much-did-a-long-distance-call-cost-in-the-1950s-Per-minute-from-NYC-to-LA; Dollar Times, dollartimes.com/inflation/inflation.php?amount=3.7&year=1951 (both on January 20, 2020).

456 Appendix V, Milly's Interview of May 17, 2017, paras. 23-25, pp. 3-4; Philip's Interview of July 20, 2017, para. 29, p. 2; Dolly's Interview of November 27, 2017, para. 27, p. 1.

457 Appendix V, Philip's Interview of July 20, 2017, para. 29, p. 2.

458 Dolly and Joseph Albert first attended a public school. For Joseph Albert, it was Webster Elementary School; he still has the report card showing his attendance from April 25 to June 16, 1960, to finish third grade, and then summer school at Garfield Elementary School. Dolly believes she attended Garfield Elementary for fifth grade. In either case, she completed fifth grade while Joseph Albert completed third grade that year. (Joseph Albert had not started private school in Hong Kong until age 7, likely because there would be room for the extra tuition for him after Milly and George left in 1958.) Appendix V, Dolly's Interview of November 27, 2017, para. 27, p. 1; Joseph Albert's Interview of January 21-26, 2019, p. 6.

459 Appendix V, YaoTim's Questionnaire, Response 4, p. 2.

460 Conversely, none of the children had ever seen Miao Ying and Clifford hold hands or kiss or otherwise publicly display either affection or displeasure with each other.

461 Appendix V, Dolly's Interview of November 27, 2017, para. 28, at p. 2.

462 Appendix V, Joseph Albert's Interview of January 21-26, 2019, p. 7. Because Clifford left Shanghai in 1951, when Joseph Albert was barely 1 year old, Joseph Albert did not know the man that was his father until after meeting him again in 1960.

463 Appendix V, Dolly's Interview of November 27, 2017, para. 27, p. 1.

464 At the schools the Lumsdaine children attended, tuition for the second enrolled child from the same family half-price, and tuition for a third child was free. Appendix V, Joseph Albert's Interview of January 21-26, 2019, p. 11.

465 Joseph Albert recalled that store as McCoy's, but Dolly recalled it as Vons. *Cf.* Appendix V, Dolly's Interview of November 27, 2017, para. 28, at p. 2 with Joseph Albert's Interview of January 21-26, 2019, p. 6. The nearest supermarket to the family's Long Beach home in 1960-61 was in fact McCoy's, with the nearest Vons being many miles away. Groceteria. com, "Long Beach CA Chain Grocery/Supermarket Locations, 1923-1969," groceteria. com/place/california/los-angeles/chain-grocerssupermarkets-in-long-beach-1923-1969 (January 20, 2020).

466 Appendix V, Dolly's Interview of November 27, 2017, para. 28, at p. 2; Joseph Albert's Interview of January 21-26, 2019, p. 6.

467 From Ventura, Chuck moved to apartments closer to his work for Asbury Construction in Huntington Beach and other locations. Ed moved to New Mexico, where he attended the University of New Mexico at Las Cruces. George eventually moved to Lompoc, where he had gotten a job at Vandenberg Air Force Base. After living at the Ojai Valley Inn while they worked there, Robert went on to the University of California at Berkeley in 1963, and Philip first lived part-time in Orange County with either YaoTim or Chuck, until he was drafted into the U.S. Army in 1965. Appendix V, Phone Notes of Call with Philip on February 10, 2020; Joyce's Interview of July 7, 2018, p. 4.

468 The lengthy family mah jongg games were legendary, sometimes going into the middle of the night or even the next morning. Even after getting married, Robert, Philip and George continued with the practice of playing these long sessions of mah jongg, with their wives, Joyce and Elaine, acquiescing in such unusual aberrations of a somewhat common Chinese pastime. Appendix V, Linda's Interview of July 26, 2017, para. 7, pp. 2-3; Joyce's Interview of July 7, 2018, p. 8.

469 Appendix V, Philip's interview of July 26, 2017, para. 32, p. 1; Joyce's interview of July 7, 2018, p. 9; George paid the rent for the house on Wall Street for the years Miao Ying and Clifford lived there; George and Elaine Interview of March 2020.

470 Appendix V, Dolly's Interview of November 27, 2017, para. 29, at p. 2. Clifford would come back from work in the mornings and be asleep by the time Milly, Dolly, and Joseph Albert came home from school. *Id.*

471 Appendix V, Milly's Interview of May 24, 2017, para. 28, p. 1; Dolly's Interview of November 17, 2017, para. 29, p.2. "There was very little money in Ventura." Dolly's Interview of November 17, 2017, para. 30 at p.3.

472 Appendix V, Joyce's Interview of July 7, 2018, p.9; YaoTim's Questionnaire, Response 9, p. 28.

473 Clifford would wake Joseph Albert up about 5 a.m. for work before school in late seventh grade and the beginning of eighth grade. He introduced Joseph Albert to coffee as a way to wake up and also showed Joseph Albert the ledger where he kept track of Joseph Albert's hours worked and payment due him. Clifford was responsible for managing either one or two laundromats in Ventura, including keeping them clean, collecting the coins and depositing them in the bank, and giving an accounting to the owner. Appendix V, Joseph Albert's Interview of January 21-26, 2019, p. 6. Joseph Albert stopped working with Clifford sometime in eighth grade, when Clifford got him a Social Security card, and Miao Ying helped him get an evening job as a dishwasher, and later, as a busboy at the Hong Kong Inn, a Chinese restaurant owned by a family friend in Ventura. *Ibid.*, pp.7-9.

474 "I lived with our family in Ventura only while I was attending St. Catherine's Academy in Ventura. I did not fit in with the other girls there, mostly of whom were from upper class families, so I moved out to live with YaoTim and Bob in Orange County and finish high school there." App*endix V, Milly's Interview of May 17, 2017,* para. 26, p. 4.

475 Dolly graduated from Holy Cross School in 1963; Joseph Albert graduated in 1965. Dolly graduated from St. Bonaventure High School in 1967 and left the family home in Ventura to attend University of San Francisco in 1968. Joseph Albert graduated from St. Bonaventure in 1969 and went on to attend St. Mary's College in Moraga, Calif., the same year. Appendix V, Dolly's Interview of November 27, 2017, para. 31, p. 4; Joseph Albert's Interview of January 21-26, 2019, p. 10. Also see Joseph Albert's 1961 and 1965 report cards from Holy Cross School and 1965 graduation certificate from St. Bonaventure High School.

476 Appendix V, Dolly's Interview of November 27, 2017, para. 29, at p. 2.

477 YaoTim Interview of April 13, 2020. Miao Ying also took trips to Hong Kong in 1966 and 1971, both of which she financed herself. The 1971 trip also included tours of Taiwan and Japan, and Miao Ying took along her granddaughter, Monica, with Bob and YaoTim paying their daughter's way. *Id.*

478 See Appendix III, at Mom's passport and re-entry permits. On the 1966 trip, part of the length of Miao Ying's stay was owing to not only being there for George and Elaine's wedding but staying for months afterward waiting for Elaine to obtain her visa and then traveling with Elaine by ship to the U.S. Appendix V, Elaine's interview of August 31, 2018 at p. 2; George's Interview of February 10, 2020.

479 Appendix V, Dolly's Interview of November 27, 2017, para. 29, pp. 2-3. See Appendix III, at Mom's passport and re-entry permits.

480 "In Ventura, Milly recalls talking Miao Ying into getting an aluminum Christmas tree. Milly told her mother that they had to have it because everybody had it. Miao Ying went along with it. Appendix V, Milly's Interview of May 24, 2017, para. 28, at p. 1. "Dolly recalls

holidays with inflatable reindeers, aluminum Christmas trees with a rotating color wheel." Appendix V, Dolly's Interview of November 27, 2017, para. 30, at p. 3.

481 Miao Ying's favorite Western shows included "Bonanza," "Gunsmoke," and "The Rifleman," as well as some of John Wayne's Western movies. She also enjoyed game shows like "The Price is Right" and "Let's Make A Deal." She even sat through some shows that Clifford and Joseph Albert liked to watch, like the nightly news (Clifford) and "Star Trek" (Joseph Albert). Appendix V, Joseph Albert's Interview of January 21-26, 2019, p. 10; YaoTim's Questionnaire Responses 16 and 23, pp. 17 & 20; Philip's Questionnaire, Response 15, p. 3; Joseph Albert's Questionnaire, Responses 15 and 16, p. 3.

482 Appendix V, YaoTim's Questionnaire, Response 14, pp. 13-14; Philip's Questionnaire, Responses 15 and 24, pp. 3 and 4; Joseph Albert's Questionnaire, Response 25, p. 4.

483 The award was first prize in the American Legion Auxiliary's essay contest for an essay titled, "What I Can Do Today For My Country." *Ventura County Star Free Press* picture and article of March 25, 1965, Appendix I, Original Documents. "I had to go to one of their meetings to receive the award. It was on Ventura Avenue all the way past Main Street, a long way to walk at night from our house on Wall Street. Easily a mile. Dad walked with me to have dinner and receive the award. I was thrilled to have him with me and the fact that he took the time to go there with me. I was thrilled to think he was proud of me." Appendix V, Joseph Albert's Interview of January 21-26, 2019, at p. 8.

484 "When I got accepted into college, Mom was very upset. She told me that I should get married instead of going to college. Acceptance into college took a long time because Dad at first refused to sign scholarship papers because Mom did not want me to go to college." Appendix V, Dolly's Interview of November 27, 2017, para. 31, at p. 4.

485 Appendix V, Joseph Albert's Interview of January 21-26, 2019, at pp. 8-9.

486 "Clifford always did whatever Miao Ying told him to do. They were gentle with each other. I never saw them argue, although I also never saw any displays of affection between them...." Appendix V, Elaine's Interview of August 31, 2018, at p. 4.

487 Appendix V, Joseph Albert's Interview of January 21-26, 2019, at pp. 8-9; Dolly's Interview of November 27, 2017, para. 31, p. 4. Clifford would continue to provide help and support toward Joseph Albert's schooling even after his entry into college in 1969 by helping Joseph Albert complete and even mail scholarship and loan applications for St. Mary's College and later for UC Berkeley. See Appendix III, letters from Dad to Joseph Albert dated February 15, April 15, and May 5, 1970. Additionally, Clifford often would give fatherly advice, such as telling Joseph Albert not to work too many hours during school and not to get discouraged about an initial bad grade in college. Appendix III, letters from Dad to Joseph Albert dated August 21 and November 17, 1969.

488 Appendix V, Joseph Albert's Questionnaire, Response 52, p. 8. It was not until years later, in adulthood, that Joseph Albert learned that the accompaniment of all meals with white rice was something common to poorer Chinese families. Miao Ying's instruction to Joseph Albert – always take in a mouthful of white rice before taking any meat or vegetables – then made total sense because it would conserve the more costly meal items of meat and vegetables while filling one's stomach up first with the cheaper plain rice.

489 Appendix V, Linda's Interview of July 26 and August 16, 2017, para. 4, p. 2; Joseph Albert's Interview of January 21-26, 2019, p. 13. In Hong Kong, Miao Ying had raised chickens in the backyard and would slaughter them herself, first twisting the bird's neck for a quick and merciful death, then slitting its throat to drain out the blood (which was steamed to make a sort of savory pie) before butchering it into pieces for cooking. Appendix V, Dolly's Interview of November 16, 2017, para. 17, p. 1.

490 Appendix V, Philip's Questionnaire, Response 14, p. 3.

491 *Id.* Miao Ying's friendships with other Chinese families with whom she played mah jongg also provided some collateral benefits. For example, her friendships were instrumental in Miao Ying obtaining part-time work at a Chinese restaurant and Joseph Albert's full-time summer job as a stock clerk and box boy at Jue's Market in Ventura. Appendix V, Dolly's Interview of November 27, 2017, para. 29, p. 2; Joseph Albert's Interview of January 21-26, 2019, p. 9.

492 "Another hobby of Mom's was planting flowers in the garden, especially gladiolas and roses. Sometimes Mom seemed to enjoy just watering the grass around the house in the evenings, with the dog (Rocky) running around." Appendix V, Elaine's Interview of August 31, 2018, para. 15, at p. 6.

493 "Mom and I planted a whole bunch of roses. Mom instructed me to first dig a hole and put down chicken poop into it, stick a rose stem into the poop, and then cover it with dirt. Before we left Ventura, I remember counting 42 rose bushes thriving at the Wall Street home." Appendix V, Joseph Albert's Interview of January 21-26, 2019, at p. 8.

494 Appendix V, Joyce's Interview of July,7, 2018, pp. 4-5 and 8-9; Joyce's Interview of August 14, 2018, para. 14, p. 1 and para. 31, p.2.

495 Appendix V, Milly's Interview of May 24, 2017, paras. 29-30, pp. 1-2.

496 Appendix V, Milly's Interview of May 24, 2017, at para. 30, p. 2.

497 Elaine's grandfather, who had worked at the docks in Macau during World War II, had met Choi Yuk Chuen, Ng Yee's husband, during and after the war as Yuk Chuen had visited the port. When he and Ng Yee migrated to Hong Kong in the 1950s, Elaine's father had helped Yuk Chuen get a job on a ship there, so the families knew each other well and socialized often. Appendix V, Elaine's interview of August 31, 2018, p. 1.

498 "My initial impression of your mother was that she was a strong woman, very considerate, and … She was always trying to give me a good piece of meat at mealtime." Appendix V, Elaine's interview of August 31, 2018, at p. 1.

499 Appendix V, Phone Call Notes with George and with Elaine on February 10, 2020. They were married at Elaine's parish church, St. Theresa's. *Id.*

500 Appendix V, Philip's Interview of July 26, 2017, paras. 32-33.

501 Appendix V, YaoTim's Interview of February 21, 2020; Linda's Interview of July 26, 2017, para. 5, p. 2; Dolly's Interview of November 27, 2017, para. 33, p. 4.

502 *Id.*

503 Appendix V, Dolly's Interview of November 27, 2017, paras. 34, p. 4-5. According to Dolly, Miao Ying and Clifford refused all communications from her from 1969 until about February 1972. *Id.* But according to Clifford, in a series of letters he wrote to Joseph Albert between 1969 and 1970, he and Miao Ying did not have Dolly's address, and "if she does not wish Mom and I to know her address, there does not seem to be any point in anyone else in the family giving it to us, if she herself does not want us to know." Appendix III, letters from Clifford to Joseph Albert 1969-1970, at letter dated November 17, 1969. At one point in 1969-1970, it appears that both Dolly and her parents tried to communicate to each other through Joseph Albert as the go-between. *Cf.* Appendix III, letters dated November 10, 17 and 29, 1969, and January 15, 1970, from Clifford to Joseph Albert; and letter dated November 3, 1969, from Dolly to Joseph Albert.

504 Appendix V, YaoTim Questionnaire, Response 10, p. 28; Milly's Interview of May 24, 2017, para. 31, pp. 2-3. Miao Ying and Clifford chose to move from Ventura to Cypress mainly because they wanted to be closer to their daughters, YaoTim and Milly. The

house was purchased jointly by YaoTim, George, and Milly with an equally shared down payment of $19,500 on May 1, 1969, with a move-in date of May 15, 1969. Appendix III, email from YaoTim to Joseph Albert dated March 20, 2020. Clifford insisted on paying the utilities from his meager monthly Social Security payments. Appendix V, YaoTim's Interview of February 21, 2020.

505 For an example of hardships, such as night work at a restaurant, that were endured to get Miao Ying and Clifford into the La Homa house, see Appendix V, Milly's interview of May 24, 2017, para. 31, pp. 2-3. Chuck and Robert continued to give Miao Ying and Clifford money for expenses as well. Appendix V, YaoTim Questionnaire, Response 10, p. 2; Joyce Interview of July 7, 2017, p. 9.

506 Appendix V, Philip's Interview of August 16, 2017, para. 35, p. 1; Linda's Interviews of July 26 & August 16, 2017, pars. 1 & 8, pp. 1 & 3.

507 Appendix V, Milly's Interview of May 24, 2017, para. 32, p. 3. Milly lived close enough that she and Miao Ying would take Milly's sons in strollers and walk between their houses. Miao Ying also had time to garden and cook with Milly. *Id.*

508 Elaine's Interview of August 31, 2018, pp. 3 & 6; Milly's Interview of May 24, 2017, para. 32, p. 3; Linda's Interviews of July 26 & August 16, 2017, para. 6, p. 2. Even before Dianne was married to Joseph Albert, Miao Ying showed her how to make Chinese BBQ pork ("cha sieu") and stuffed pork bun ("char sieu bao"). Appendix V, Joseph Albert's Interview of January 21-26, 2019, p. 13.

509 The "golden years" have been defined as "...the leisure years in later life after one has retired from employment" or "the period during which someone or something flourishes." en.wiktionary.org/wiki/golden_years (February 21, 2020).

510 Appendix III, letters from Dad to Joseph Albert dated August 14 and 17, 1971, and to Dianne on June 24, 1971.

511 Andrew, Anne, Alfred, and Arnold are the children of Ed and Monika Lumsdaine. They lived in South Dakota but were visiting during the summer because Ed had a summer job at Caltech's Jet Propulsion Laboratory (JPL). Email from Monika dated April 18, 2020. Miao Ying and Clifford also spent a lot of time babysitting Philip and Linda's son Greg while his parents were at work.

512 For example, work that Clifford found distributing advertising flyers wasn't worthwhile after deducting taxes and the cost of gas for his car. Letter from Dad to Joseph Albert dated August 22, 1969.

513 YaoTim Interview of April 13, 2020. Miao Ying's work was for a sewing factory in El Segundo that was owned by the sister of her friends from Ventura, Mr. and Mrs. Bill Jue. She also was considering earning credit for potential Social Security benefits when she would turn age 62. Id. Appendix III, Letter from Dad to Joseph Albert dated August 22, 1969.

514 Appendix V, *Milly's Interview of May 24, 2017*, para. 35, p. 4. In a letter to Joseph Albert in 1970, Clifford detailed the monthly contribution from YaoTim, George and Milly ($65 each); and Robert and Ed ($50 each), as well as their monthly expenses in explaining why he needed Joseph Albert to reimburse him for car insurance and other advances Clifford had made for him. Appendix III, letter from Dad to Joseph Albert dated October 14, 1970. To put in perspective the amount of these contributions, in 2020 dollars, they would have been $430 a month from YaoTim, George, and Milly and $330 dollars each month from Robert and Ed. *CPI Inflation Calculator,* www.in2013dollars.com/us/inflation/1970?amount=1 (April 11, 2020)

515 Clifford acknowledged, and seemed grateful, for three money orders that Joseph Albert sent to Miao Ying and Clifford totaling $400 (equivalent of $2,600 in 2020 dollars) in the

summer of 1969, when Joseph Albert had a well-paying full-time job working for AMF Tuboscope, an oilfield servicing company. Clifford also cautioned Joseph Albert not to work so many hours when school started so he could attend to his studies. Appendix III, letters from Dad to Joseph Albert dated August 11 and 12, 1969.

516   Appendix V, Dianne's Interview of October 1, 2018; Joseph Albert's Interview of January 21-26, 2019.

517   *Id.* Joseph Albert did cut his hair about a year later, dedicating it to the memory of his Mom, who passed away less than six months after this incident.

518   Appendix V, Dianne's Interview of October 1, 2018; Joseph Albert's Interview of January 21-26, 2019.

519   *Id.*

520   Appendix V, Dianne's Interview of October 1, 2018; Joseph Albert's Interview of January 21-26, 2019.

521   Appendix V, Interview of YaoTim on March 11, 2020; Interview of Philip on August 16, 2017, para. 36, p. 1; Interview of Milly on May 24, 2017, para. 37, p. 4.

522   Milly never heard Miao Ying complain about her health. Appendix V, Milly Interview of May 24, 2017, para. 37, p. 4. Starting around Christmas 1971, Miao Ying sometimes complained of stomach pain from indigestion. Appendix V, YaoTim's Interview on March 11, 2020. They both took Miao Ying to the hospital. Appendix V, YaoTim's Interview on March 11, 2020; Milly's Interview of March 12, 2020. Miao Ying was admitted to the hospital at 7:55 p.m. on October 1, 1972. Appendix I, Documents, La Palma Intercommunity Hospital, Record of Admission; Dr. Robert C. Touchon's letter of November 2, 1972, p. 1. The distance between Miao Ying and Clifford's house and the hospital is 0.9 miles. It was a new, acute care hospital at the time. Wikipedia, La Palma Intercommunity Hospital, en.wikipedia.org/wiki/La_Palma_Intercommunity_Hospital (March 11, 2020).

523   Appendix I, Documents, La Palma Intercommunity Hospital, Record of Admission.

524   Appendix V, Interview of Joseph Albert, January 21-26, 2019, p. 13; Interview of Dolly, November 11, 2017, para. 35, p. 5.

525   Appendix V, YaoTim's Interview on March 11, 2020; Milly's Interview on March 12, 2020.

526   Dr. Robert C. Touchon, a cardiologist at La Palma Intercommunity Hospital who treated and diagnosed Miao Ying, recommended surgery at Santa Ana Hospital, which was later performed by Dr. Louis A. Taucher, a cardio-vascular surgeon. See Appendix I, Documents, La Palma Intercommunity Hospital, Medical Justification for Hospitalization dated October 4, 1969; and Santa Ana Community Hospital, Operation Record dated October 5, 1969.

527   See Appendix I, Documents, La Palma Intercommunity Hospital, Patient Transfer Report and Record of Admission. Appendix V, Dolly's Interview of November 11, 2017, para. 35, p. 5.

528   Santa Ana Community Hospital, Operation Record dated October 5, 1969.

529   See, e.g., Ed's Interview of March 14, 2020.

530   Appendix V, Interview of YaoTim, March 11, 2020; Interview of Ed, March 14, 2020; Interview of Milly, March 12, 2020; Interview of Joseph Albert, January 21-26, 2019, p. 14 Dianne and Joseph Albert went out to eat with others and also brought food back for those who stayed in the waiting room.

531 Appendix V, George's Interview of March 27, 2020.

532 Appendix V, Joseph Albert's Interview of January 21-26, 2019, p. 14.

533 Appendix V, Milly's Interviews of May 24, 2017, para. 37, p. 4, and March 12, 2020.

534 Appendix V, YaoTim's Interview of March 11, 2020.

535 Appendix I, Documents, Santa Ana Community Hospital, Operation Record dated October 5, 1969. The official cause of death was "cardiovascular collapse ... due to dissecting thoraco-abdominal aneurysm, with bilateral renal infarction." Appendix I, Documents, Certificate of Death dated October 5, 1972, at item number 29. A medical intake sheet signed by Dr. Tseu on October 1, 1972, listed "Past medical history" of "no severe illnesses except mild hypertension." Appendix I, Documents, La Palma Intercommunity Hospital. Yet a post-mortem report by the cardiologist who treated Miao Ying in the emergency room at La Palma Intercommunity Hospital, and later at Santa Ana Community Hospital, attributed her multiple aneurysms to "a long history of high blood pressure" and went on to mention in varying forms at least five more times in his two-page report that her "long-standing, devastating hypertensive disease" caused the problems that necessitated her surgery. Appendix I, Documents, Dr. Robert C. Touchon's letter of November 2, 1972.

After Miao Ying's death, YaoTim discovered that her mother's medicine cabinet was full of unused prescriptions for painkillers that her attending Chinese-speaking physician, Dr. Joseph Tseu, MD, had prescribed. Miao Ying had complained of stomach pain for years, and painkillers appeared to have been the only thing that Dr. Tseu prescribed. Surprisingly, there were no prescriptions for high blood pressure, which apparently had never been diagnosed despite the fact that Miao Ying had consulted with Dr. Tseu for more than three years. Appendix V, YaoTim Interview of March 11, 2020. As recently as May 1972, Dr. Tseu appeared to have been giving Miao Ying pain injections for "arthritis" pain. See Appendix I, Documents, letter from Dad to Joseph Albert dated May 1, 1972. It appears that Dr. Tseu never diagnosed or treated Miao Ying for years of high blood pressure, which was the primary contributing factor in her surgery and death.

536 Appendix V, George's Interview of March 27, 2020.

537 Appendix V, Interview of Dolly on November 27, 2017, para. 35, p. 6; Interview of *Joseph Albert, January 21-26, 2019*, pp. 13-14.

538 *Id.*

539 Appendix V, *Interview of Dolly on November 27, 2017*, para. 35, p. 6; *Interview of Joseph Albert, January 21-26, 2019*, pp. 13-14; and *Interview of Dianne, October 1, 2018*, p. 3.

540 Appendix V, *Milly's Interview of March 12, 2020.*

541 Those who were with Clifford during that period described him as depressed and unmoving, to the point of appearing catatonic. He was incapable of making any decisions and would simply respond to his children's questions with "I don't know" or "Whatever you think." Appendix V, Interview of YaoTim on March 11, 2020; Interview of Milly, March 12, 2020; and Interview of Dianne, October 1, 2018, p. 4.

542 As Dianne observed, it seemed an unusual reversal of traditional American roles, with the children taking care of their parents instead of the parents taking care of the children, when the Lumsdaine children banded together to help Clifford, who was in shock following Miao Ying's death. Appendix V, Dianne's Interview of October 1, 2018, p. 4.

543 Appendix I, Documents, Certificate of Death dated October 5, 1972, at item number 20.

544 Chuck consulted his brothers and sisters, but he would make final decisions and delegate or execute as needed. He paid for the funeral arrangements but likely had help from Robert, his business partner in Lumsdaine Construction, Inc. Appendix V, YaoTim Interview of March 17, 2020; Joseph Albert's Interview of January 21-26, 2019, p. 14. Forest Lawn in Cypress was chosen because Miao Ying had told YaoTim that she wanted to be buried there. They had driven by the site during construction, and without first knowing it was a cemetery, Miao Ying had commented on how beautiful the building (Ascension Mausoleum) was. When YaoTim told her it was a cemetery, Miao Ying said, "I want to be buried there." Appendix V, YaoTim Interview of March 11, 2020.

545 Appendix V, Interview of Milly on March 12, 2020 ("a daze"); Interview of Philip and Linda, March 31, 2020 ("a blur").

546 Appendix II, *1995 Grandparent Book*, section 2, p. 13. In responding to the question on the "saddest or most painful time" of his life, Clifford wrote, "Death of my wife, Mrs. Ho Miao Ying Lumsdaine" and referring also to his interment by the Japanese as not sad but painful. *Id.* As to Uncle Art Lumsdaine's presence, see Philip and Linda's Interview of March 31, 2020.

547 Appendix V, Milly's Interview of March 18, 2020. "Dad was in shock; he looked and acted lost. He just floated along." *Id.*

548 Clifford was prescribed Valium, a sedative, at the hospital immediately after Miao Ying's death on October 5, 1972. Appendix I, Documents, Santa Ana Community Hospital, at Physician's Orders. Clifford took a dose at the hospital with Robert's help, and it is believed he took additional dosages, the extent of which is unknown. Appendix V, YaoTim Interview of March 11, 2020.

549 Appendix V, Milly's Interview of March 18, 2020.

550 YaoTim and Milly cleared out Miao Ying's clothing and other personal items that Clifford would not need. Appendix V, YaoTim Interview of March 11, 2020; Milly Interview of March 18, 2020.

551 Appendix V, Dianne's Interview of February 6, 2019, p. 5; Milly's Interview of March 18, 2020.

552 YaoTim, Milly, and Clifford drove to San Francisco in January 1973, to have the jewelry appraised by a gemologist, who issued his report on February 18, 1973. Appendix III, YaoTim email of April 22, 2020.

553 Appendix V, Milly's Interview of March 18, 2020.

554 Guy Gardner, September 29, 2017, "Chinese Grieving Etiquette," classroom.synonym. com/chinese-grieving-etiquette-12085228.html (April 17, 2020).

555 At the wake (reception) at Milly and Marcel's house after Miao Ying's funeral on October 7, 1972, that Joseph Albert's siblings first suggested that his wedding to Dianne should be postponed. The compromise was reached in the interests of continuing family harmony. Appendix V, Dianne's Interview of February 6, 2019, pp. 5-6.

556 At least three of Clifford's daughters-in law volunteered, in their interviews, their personal observations of Clifford's gentlemanly demeanor throughout his life and his consistently kind consideration of others. Appendix V, Interview of Elaine on August 31, 2018 at p. 3; Interview of Joyce on August 14, 2018 at p. 1; Interview of Dianne on October 1, 2018, at pp. 2, 3, and 9.

557 *Cf.* Appendix III, YaoTim's email of April 22, 2020; Appendix I, Documents, letter from Dad to Joseph Albert and Dianne dated March 20, 1973; and Appendix III, Monika's email of April 19, 2020; showing early trips to San Francisco with YaoTim and Milly, visit with George and Elaine at Lompoc and visit with Ed and Monika in Tennessee.

558 Appendix I, Documents, letter from Dad to Joseph Albert and Dianne dated September 4, 1973.

559 Appendix V, George's Interview of March 27, 2020.

560 *Cf.* Appendix I, Documents, letter from Dad to Joseph Albert and Dianne dated May 19, 1974 and Appendix III YaoTim's email of April 22, 2020, where Clifford states that his furniture was being brought up to Lompoc from Bekins storage and YaoTim states that the La Homa house was leased from August 31, 1973, to February 27, 1976.

561 Appendix I, Documents, letter from Dad to Joseph Albert and Dianne dated September 4, 1973.

562 Clifford wrote about some of his outings with Ed and Monika's family, including shopping, the Knoxville Fair, and Cedar Springs Presbyterian Church; and trips to Big Ridge State Park, Norris Dam, and Goldrush Junction. On the first anniversary of Miao Ying's death, Clifford presented flowers at the Presbyterian Church. Clifford also listed in his letters to Joseph Albert and Dianne at least 18 books that he read; some were given to him by Monika and some were checked out from the local library. Appendix I, Documents, letters and postcards from Dad to Joseph Albert and Dianne dated September 12, October 5 and 24, November 9 and December 5, 1973; and January 4 and 30, 1974.

563 Appendix V, Interview of YaoTim on March 29, 2020; Interview of Milly on March 18, 2020; Appendix III, Documents, Dad's letter to Joseph Albert and Dianne dated October 24, 1973.

564 Appendix I, Documents, letters from Dad to Joseph Albert and Dianne dated April 24 (portion quoted), May 19 and June 21, 1974. His apartment was approved for rental assistance on August 24, which was likely what is commonly known as "Section 8 Housing." Appendix I, Documents, letter from Dad to Joseph Albert and Dianne on August 27, 1974. See John Barrymore, "History of Section 8 Housing," home. howstuffworks.com/real-estate/buying-home/section-8-housing1.htm (April 24, 2020).

565 Appendix I, Documents, Dad's letters to Joseph Albert and Dianne dated November 1, 1974, and March 31, 1975.

566 Appendix V, Interview of YaoTim on March 29, 2020; Interview of Milly, March 18, 2020; and Interview of Dianne, October 1, 2016.

567 Appendix V, Interview of YaoTim on March 29, 2020; Interview of Philip and Linda, March 31, 2020; Interview of Milly, March 18, 2020; and Interview of Dianne, October 1, 2016. Robert and Joyce would visit, stay overnight in nearby Solvang, and take Clifford there for lunch. Appendix V, George's Interview of March 27, 2020.

568 See Appendix V, Interview of Dianne on October 1, 2016, p. 6; Interview of Milly, on March 18, 2020. Appendix III, Dad's letters to Joseph Albert and Dianne dated August 27, 1974; March 31, June 30 and August 24, 1975; and October 27, 1975.

569 Appendix III, Documents, Dad's letters to Joseph Albert and Dianne dated March 31 and August 4, 1975 (Solvang, Santa Barbara County Fair, Busch Gardens); September 5 (LA Chinatown) and October 17, 1975 (St. Helena, Vallejo and Lake Tahoe).

570 Appendix I, Documents, Dad's letters to Joseph Albert and Dianne dated February 4, 1976 (Hong Kong and Macau); September 14, 1976 (Honolulu). Appendix III, YaoTim's email of April 26, 2020.

571 Appendix V, George's Interview of March 27, 2020. Appendix III, Documents, Dad's letters to Joseph Albert and Dianne dated August 4 and September 10, 1975. Clifford even got into the Halloween spirit by passing out candy from his apartment. *Ibid.* Letter dated November 1, 1974.

572 Clifford was particularly fond of this neighbor, "Miss Ann," who invited him over for his first Christmas dinner in Lompoc. Appendix I, Documents, Letter from Dad to Joseph Albert and Dianne dated December 21, 1975. Their relationship, as he told Milly, was "platonic." Appendix V, YaoTim's Interview of March 29, 2020. Clifford made a point of mentioning in a postcard to Joseph Albert that he and Miss Ann had separate rooms when they travelled to Honolulu in 1976. Appendix I, Documents, Postcard from Dad to Joseph Albert dated September 14, 1976.

573 Appendix I, Documents, Dad's Perpetual Calendar, entries at January 3, January 7 and October 7; Certificate of Ordination date January 2, 1977.

574 Appendix V, George's Interview of March 27, 2020; Dianne's Interview of October 1, 2018, p. 7.

575 Appendix V, George's Interview of March 27, 2020; YaoTim's Interview of March 17, 2020; Milly's Interview of March 18, 2020; Alert, January 21-26, p. 15-16; Philip and Linda's interview of March 31, 2020. Even George and Elaine, who lived in Lompoc, never met Helen before the wedding announcement. Still, none of Clifford's children objected to the marriage, even though – in Clifford's own words to George – it was "abrupt." All of them except Ed attended the wedding, but both the wedding and the marriage seemed very strange and almost surreal. Some noticed how odd Clifford and Helen looked and acted together. She was much bigger than him (by at least 3 inches in height) and talked and wrote using crude language that Clifford, ever the gentleman, neither used nor condoned. Id.

576 Appendix I, Documents, Nick Harris Detectives, Inc., Investigation Report dated May 6, 1983; Undated Note handwritten by Dianne Lumsdaine in 1983 from conversation with Helen Hinnrichs between April and November 1983. The Investigation Report suggested that three of Helen's previous husbands died in auto accidents while the fourth died of "blood clots caused by a faulty pacemaker." In conversation with Dianne, however, Helen stated that the first husband "beat her" and "killed himself drinking"; the second died in a car accident; the third she divorced because he impregnated his mistress; and the fourth died of stroke, heart failure, emphysema, and asthma. Id.

577 Appendix V, Interviews of George on March 27, 2020; YaoTim, March 17, 2020; Milly, March 18, 2020; Joseph Albert, January 21-26, p. 15-16; Philip and Linda, March 31, 2020. Helen began answering phone calls for Clifford and speaking and writing letters for him. She told YaoTim that Clifford did not want to visit or talk to her and wrote letters saying that Clifford did not want to travel to visit his children anymore, even to attend a family gathering in November 1983 to celebrate Chuck and Bob's 50th birthdays and Clifford's 74th birthday. Id. See also, Appendix I, Documents, Memorandum to Helen Hinnrichs File, dated November 15, 1983. Although Helen told family members that Clifford was developing a serious heart problem, that he could not safely travel anymore and that she was giving him her own heart medication (Id. and Appendix V, Dianne's Interview of October 1, 2018, pp. 6-7), Joseph Albert subsequently called Clifford's treating physician, Dr. Nesbitt, who denied that Clifford had any heart problem at all and said he absolutely could travel to Los Angeles. See Joseph Albert's handwritten note attached to Appendix I, Documents, Memorandum to Helen Hinnrichs File, dated November 15, 1983.

578 Several of Clifford's children observed that Helen appeared to completely control and intimidate Clifford. Appendix V, Interview of YaoTim on March 29, 2020; Interview of George on March 27, 2020. In addition, when both Milly and Linda asked Clifford why he couldn't refuse Helen anything, he told them that she kept a big knife under the bed. Appendix V, Interview of Philip and Linda on March 31, 2020; Interview of Milly on March 18, 2020. Helen told Joseph Albert and Dianne that she had once beaten a man to almost to death with a bag full of nickels. Appendix I, Documents, Memorandum to Helen Hinnrichs File, dated November 15, 1983. Additionally, there were concerns about Clifford's increasing isolation and deteriorating health. Finally, there were concerns arising from Helen's repeated requests to Clifford's children for money and what would happen to Clifford if some of them refused. Id.

579 Appendix V, Joseph Albert's Interview of January 21-26, 2019, at p. 16. When Chuck asked Clifford if he wanted to leave with him, YaoTim, and Joseph Albert and go down to Joseph Albert's house, Clifford agreed. *Id.* See also YaoTim's Interview of March 17, 2020. It was observed at that time that Clifford's overall demeanor seemed similar to how he acted just after his release from the Japanese concentration camp at the end of World War II. Appendix V, Philip and Linda's Interview of March 31, 2020. Helping Clifford out of a situation where he felt trapped was totally a collaborative effort by his children. Even those who didn't go up to Lompoc to bring him back provided significant psychological support for the endeavor; for example, when Joseph Albert was doubting whether he was doing the right thing in planning the Lompoc intervention, Robert told him, "Nobody will fault you for doing what you think is right for Dad." Appendix I, Documents, Joseph Albert's handwritten note dated November 11, 1983, attached to Memorandum to Helen Hinnrichs File, dated November 15, 1983.

580 Appendix V, *Dianne's Interview of October 1, 2018*, p.7.

581 Pictures of this Ryon Avenue development are as of August 2016 in Google Maps, google.com/maps/place/15748+Ryon+Ave,+Bellflower,+CA+90706/@33.890156,-118.1285882,3a,75y,88.48h,90t/data=!3m6!1e1!3m4!1sUz1fFxz5woziRS2ItyIKBw!2e0!7i16384!8i8192!4m5!3m4!1s0x80c2cd4ceb54ca37:0x83a075970aa74666!8m2!3d33.890072!4d-118.1280961?hl=en&authuser=0 (April 29, 2020).

582 Appendix V, Interviews of Dianne on October 1, 2018, at pp.7-8; Joseph Albert, January 21-26, 2019, pp. 16-17.

583 See Appendix I, Documents, Clifford's 1984 Daily Reminder, January 4, 22, and 29, 1984. Starting in January 1984, perhaps as part of his efforts to get his life back on track, Clifford started to keep a daily journal of each day's events. He wrote in his journal faithfully, every day and without significant lapses, for more than 10 years, from January 1, 1984, until March 24, 1995, when his diminishing health forced him to discontinue. For Summaries of these annual journals, see Appendix V, Interview of Joseph Albert on January 21-26, 2019, Notes on Dad's Journals 1984-1995.

584 Appendix I, Documents ,Clifford's 1984 "Daily Reminder", January 1-31, 1984. Similarly, for February, Clifford noted 19 visits and 23 telephone calls. *Ibid.*, February 1-29, 1984.

585 Clifford's favorite restaurants were Curly Jones (American food) and Ming's (Chinese Food) in Bellflower. Almost every one of his children, and sons-in-law or daughters-in-law, had taken Clifford to one of these two restaurants, while occasionally taking him to other eateries as well. As for home meals, Clifford would eat at Philip and Linda's or Joseph Albert and Dianne's mostly because of their geographic proximity to him. See Appendix I, Documents, Dad's Journals of 1984 through 1995 or summaries thereof at Appendix V, Joseph Albert's Interview of January 21-26, 2019, at Notes on Dad's Journals 1984-1995.

586 The term "English gentleman" today generally refers to one who is well-mannered, puts people at ease and exhibits appropriate values. wikihow.com/Be-an-English-Gentleman (April 30, 2020). An excellent example of Clifford's gentlemanliness was the occasion when Clifford was to be picked up by Dianne for the funeral of Jean Franco, the mother-in-law of David Niethamer (Dianne's brother). While Clifford waited patiently in front of the Manor on a hot day in August, Dianne went to the funeral, having totally forgotten to pick up Clifford. "When Dianne apologized, Clifford just told her that he was relieved that nothing bad had happened to her." Appendix V, Dianne's Interview of October 1, 2018, at p. 10. In his journal entry, Clifford made note of Jean Franco's funeral, but did not mention Dianne forgetting to pick him up. Appendix I, Documents, Dad's 1984 Daily Reminder, August 28, 1984.

587 Clifford's visits, celebrations and other events attended often included extended family or in-laws, such as Harry and Clara Niethamer, who often gave him rides to or from the

events, and whose birthday celebrations he was always a part of, as they were of his birthdays, from 1984 to 1995. He sometimes also attended celebrations of the families of Dianne's brothers, David and Gary, and their families. Clifford frequently noted in his journal visits with Johnny Dees, Linda's nephew, at Philip and Linda's house; as well as close friends of Bob and YaoTim, such as Larry and Carol Hiatt. See Appendix I, Documents, Dad's Journals of 1984 through 1995; Appendix V, Joseph Albert's Interview of January 21-26, 2019, at Notes on Dad's Journals 1984-1995 and at pp.17-18.

588 Clifford was not confined by geographic proximity when it came to participation in major celebrations of family members, travelling to San Diego for confirmations and gradua-tions of Ratermann grandchildren or to Placerville for marriages and baptisms of Allen grandchildren and great-grandchildren. *Id.*

589 See Chapters 4 and 6, *supra.*

590 After Clifford moved into the senior living center in 1986, he proudly and frequently spoke of how, at age 77, he was no longer the oldest because many of his new friends there were octogenarians – people 80 years of age or older. Appendix V, Joseph Albert's Interview of January 21-26, 2019, p. 17.

591 Being his frugal self, Clifford would only play one nickel at a time, which made his cache of nickels last longer but also made for a very long night for Milly, who faithfully sat with him until he was ready to call it quits. Appendix V, Milly's Interview of March 18, 2020.

592 For a listing of Clifford's birthday celebrations, see entries in early November of each year in Appendix I, Documents, Dad's Journals of 1984 through 1995, or summaries thereof at Appendix V, Joseph Albert's Interview of January 21-26, 2019, at Notes on Dad's Journals 1984-1995. See also, Appendix V, Interview of Joseph Albert on January 21-26, 2019, at pp. 17-18; Interview of Dianne on October 1, 2018, pp. 12-13.

593 See Appendix I, Documents, Dad's 1984 and 1986 "Daily Reminder," May 7, 1984, and May 31, 1986.

594 Bellflower Friendship Manor was built in 1973 by Bellflower Friendship Church and purchased and renovated by Community Preservation Partners in 2016. cpp-housing. com/bellflower-friendship-manor/ (May 1, 2020). The distance from the Manor to the Nutrition Center was .3 miles and to the Presbyterian church was .2 miles, compared to over 1 mile and over .7 miles, respectively, from his Ryon Avenue bungalow.

595 See Appendix I, Documents, Dad's Journals of 1984 through 1995 or summaries thereof at Appendix V, Joseph Albert's Interview of January 21-26, 2019, at Notes on Dad's Journals 1984-1995.

596 See, e.g., group bus tour to Tehachapi Mountains on October 14, 1986, as noted in Appendix I, Documents, Dad's 1984 Daily Reminder.

597 While he made many new friends at the Manor, Clifford also kept in regular contact with his friends from prior years with frequent letters, cards, and telephone calls. These included friends he had made while living on Ryon Avenue, those from the Bellflower Presbyterian Church, people from the eight years he lived in Lompoc, members of the Lompoc Presbyterian Church community, those he met at the 1976 House of Lumsden Gathering, and even a neighbor from the years he was raising his family in Shanghai, Mr. Chuc Chin Liang. See Appendix I, Documents, Dad's Journals of 1984 through 1995 or summaries thereof at Appendix V, Joseph Albert's Interview of January 21-26, 2019, at Notes on Dad's Journals 1984-1995.

598 *Id.*

599 Appendix I, Documents, Dad's 1984 Daily Reminder. Appendix V, Dianne's Interview of October 1, 2018, p. 9.

600 See Appendix I, Documents, Dad's Journals of 1984 through 1995 or summaries thereof at Appendix V, Joseph Albert's Interview of January 21-26, 2019, at Notes on Dad's Journals 1984-1995.

601 Clifford was in Juneau, Alaska, from 1913-1918, from about age 4 to age 9. He lived there with his stepmother, Gerry; his half-brother, Arthur Allan; and his father, Arthur Henry, who was working in Juneau at the time. See Chapter 1, p. 2, *supra*.

602 Appendix V, YaoTim's interview of April 26, 2020. In Seattle, they visited the house where Clifford spent his first few years and the cemetery where his mother, half-brother, and step-mother were buried. In Juneau, they visited where his father worked and where Clifford attended elementary school. Bob and YaoTim drove with Clifford to and from Seattle, with Chuck meeting them in Seattle and later departing from there, both times by flights. *Id.*

603 Appendix V, YaoTim's interview of April 26, 2020.

604 While in Placerville, Clifford underwent a medical procedure to widen his esophagus to allow him to swallow better. *Id.* While he was apparently not well enough to make many entries in his daily journal during that time, Clifford did note the specific days he was in Placerville, in Downey, and back at the Manor. Appendix I, Documents, Dad's 1993 Diary, entries January 16 through May 17, 1993.

605 Appendix II, *1995 Grandparent Book*, compiled by YaoTim (Lumsdaine) Allen.

606 See Appendix I, Documents, Dad's 1993 Diary from January 16 through April 23, 1993.

607 *Ibid.* from April 24 through July 1993. On June 24, 1993, Clifford had a heart pacemaker implanted. Appendix I, Documents, Dad's 1993 Diary at June 24, 1993.

608 Clifford was told repeatedly by his physician, Dr. Yoon, that he needed to walk for circulation despite the sharp pains he would get due to the curvature of his spine, which was caused by osteoporosis. One of the rare times that Dianne recalled Clifford raising his voice in anger at her was when she questioned him as to why he had not walked yet that day, and Clifford yelled back, "It just hurts." Appendix V, Dianne's Interview of October 1, 2018, p. 10. Clifford would often note in his diary in 1994 the number of times he walked across his apartment at the Manor; when he was at YaoTim's, he noted the number of times he walked around Bob's pool table. See Appendix I, Documents, Dad's 1993 Diary.

609 See Appendix I, Documents, Dad's 1993 Diary and 1994 Calendar and Planner; and Appendix V, Dianne's Interview of October 1, 2018, p. 11, and Joseph Albert's Interview of January 21-26, 2018, p. 18. Dianne and YaoTim visited a number of facilities in Bell-flower to see if a place could be found close to Clifford's church and doctors, but nothing suitable was available. *Id.*; Appendix V, YaoTim's Interview of March 29, 2020.

610 Appendix V, Joseph Albert's Interview of January 21-26, 2018, p. 18. See also Appendix I, Documents, Dad's 1994 Calendar and Planner.

611 "There was a woman who complained about everything and did not like him. Dad hated it there." Milly's Interview of March 18, 2020.

612 See Appendix I, Documents, Dad's 1994 Calendar and Planner and 1995 Diary.

613 Appendix V, Interview of Joseph Albert on January 21-26, 2019, p. 18; Interview of Dianne on October 1, 2018, p. 11; Interview of YaoTim on March 29, 2020.

614 The collaboration by Miao Ying and Clifford's children began as soon as each approached age 18: Chuck, YaoTim, and Ed helping Clifford financially support the rest of the family in Hong Kong; George contributing to help bring the rest of the family to the United States; Robert and Philip contributing to family finances in Ventura; YaoTim, George, and

Milly putting up the downpayment for Clifford and Miao Ying's house in Cypress and then paying the mortgage. But it wasn't only about money. After Miao Ying died, everyone rallied to provide Clifford with the emotional support he needed, including Dolly; Clifford opened up to her about his life under McCarthyism, which he had not done to any of his other children. When Clifford needed rescuing from an abusive marriage, everyone contributed in their own way so Clifford could eventually get a final dissolution with the help of Joseph Albert, his youngest son, who also was his lawyer. Thus, when Clifford, during his final illness and treatment in 1995, had to move in with Joseph Albert and Dianne, it was not a surprise to Clifford, or any of his children, that all of them would collaborate in giving their time, talents, and treasures toward making sure that Clifford's last days would be spent without worries. "The siblings never squabbled about money for care of Mom and Dad." Appendix V, YaoTim's Interview on March 29, 2020.

615 Appendix V, Interviews of Dianne on October 1, 2018, p. 9; Joseph Albert on January 21-26, 2019, p. 19; YaoTim on March 29, 2020.

616 Appendix V, Dianne's Interview of October 1, 2018, at p. 13.

617 *Ibid.*, p. 12.

618 Appendix V, Milly's Interview of March 18, 2020. Clifford did not want to be admitted to Sharp Memorial Hospital in San Diego, which was nearby. Instead, he asked Milly to transport him back to Downey, to his own doctor and hospital. However, the urgent care doctor indicated that, in his condition, Clifford would not survive the trip. *Id.*

619 Even without words, final moments with Clifford were meaningful for many of his children. See Appendix V, Interviews of YaoTim on March 29, 2020; George, March 27, 2020; Philip, March 31, 2020; Milly, March 18, 2020; Joseph Albert, January 21-26, 2019. Ed held Clifford's hand and Clifford held Ed's, something Ed could not recall ever happening before. Appendix V, Ed's Interview of March 14, 2020.

620 Appendix V, YaoTim Interview on March 29, 2020.

621 Appendix V, George's Interview on March 27, 2020.

622 Appendix V, YaoTim's Interview of March 29, 2020. "During the time that Dad was very sick, I started reading lots of books on cancer, dying process, etc., to be prepared, but still it didn't help with the grief of Dad dying." *Id.*

623 Appendix I, Documents, Clifford's death certificate. Immediate cause of death was listed as pneumonia, with "significant conditions contributing to death" including "carcinoma of lung." *Id.*

About the Author

Joseph Albert Lumsdaine, JD, MA, lives with his wife, Dianne, in Downey, Calif., near their four children and four grandchildren. He is a retired trial and probate attorney with the law firm of Tredway Lumsdaine & Doyle, LLC. This is his first published work.

Made in the USA
Middletown, DE
01 February 2021